Lewis Hough

For Fortune and Glory

Fourth Edition

Lewis Hough

For Fortune and Glory
Fourth Edition

ISBN/EAN: 9783337267025

Printed in Europe, USA, Canada, Australia, Japan

Cover: Foto ©ninafisch / pixelio.de

More available books at **www.hansebooks.com**

FOR FORTUNE AND GLORY

A STORY OF THE SOUDAN WAR

FOR FORTUNE AND GLORY

A Story of the Soudan War

LEWIS HOUGH

Author of "Doctor Jolliffe's Boys," "Jack Hamilton's Luck," &c. &c.

WITH EIGHT ORIGINAL ILLUSTRATIONS BY WALTER PAGET

Fourth Edition

CASSELL AND COMPANY, LIMITED
LONDON, PARIS & MELBOURNE
1895

CONTENTS.

CHAPTER I.
A Mysterious Relative 9

CHAPTER II.
Mr. Richard Burke visits his Lawyer 25

CHAPTER III.
From Gay to Grave 32

CHAPTER IV.
"Ways that are Dark and Tricks that are Vain" . 46

CHAPTER V.
In passing 55

CHAPTER VI.
In Farnham Park 64

CHAPTER VII.
A very long Paper-Chase 77

CHAPTER VIII.
Kavanagh's Choice 94

CHAPTER IX.
The Army of Hicks Pasha . . 109

CHAPTER X.
Sent out Scouting . 123

CHAPTER XI.
A Glimpse at a Tragedy . . 138

CHAPTER XII.
Abdul Achmet . . . 151

CHAPTER XIII.
An Unexpected Meeting 166

CHAPTER XIV
Trinkitat 186

CHAPTER XV.
El Teb 210

CHAPTER XVI.
Touch and Go' . . . 233

Contents

CHAPTER XVII
A Search 262

CHAPTER XVIII
Against the Stream . . . 275

CHAPTER XIX
Across the Loop . . . 294

CHAPTER XX
Bir Hump . . . 310

CHAPTER XXI
The Convoy . . . 340

CHAPTER XXII
Sword *versus* Bayonet . . . 356

CHAPTER XXIII
In the Ranks of the Enemy . . . 369

CHAPTER XXIV.
At Sheen . . . 381

LIST OF ILLUSTRATIONS.

"His Uncle passed him in a state of great Enthusiasm" . . . . . *Frontispiece* 371

"'I wish we could go like this all the way, Hassib,' he said" . . . . *To face page* 56

"The Arab passed on like a lion through a crowd of wolves" . . . . . . *To face page* 89

"Hicks Pasha looked up . . . *To face page* 113

"He turned Harry Forsyth over to give him a drink of water" . . . . . . *To face page* 153

"Green . . . managed to clutch his revolver"
. . . . *To face page* 269

"He . . . put aside the spear of the other"
. . . . *To face page* 327

"He saw a figure . . . literally bounding towards him" . . . . *To face page* 362

"HIS UNCLE FOUND HIM IN A STATE OF GREAT DEJECTION"

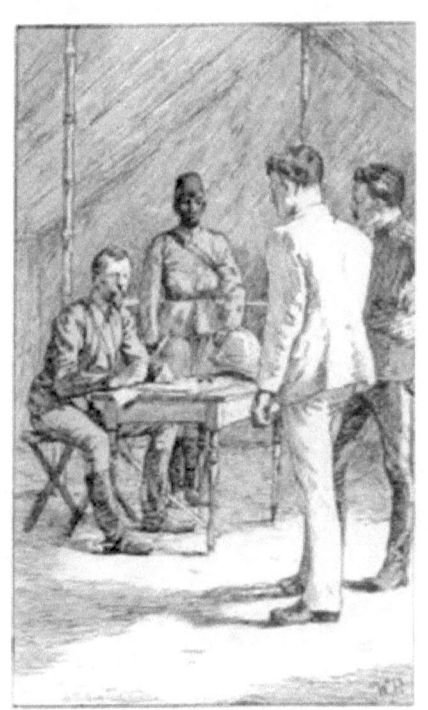

"HE TURNED GAILY FORWTH OVER TO GIVE HIM A DRINK OF WATER" (p. 111).

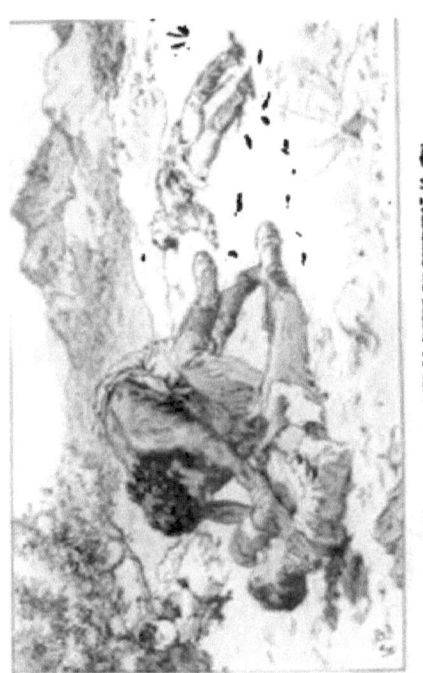

"HE . . . FELL AMONG THE SPEAR OF THE OTHER." (p. 217).

"HE... SAW A FIGURE... LITERALLY BOUNDING TOWARDS HIM" (p. 262).

FOR FORTUNE AND GLORY.

A STORY OF THE SOUDAN WAR.

CHAPTER I.

A MYSTERIOUS RELATIVE.

IT is nice to go home, even from Harton, though we may be leaving all our sports behind us. It used to be specially nice in winter; but you young fellows are made so comfortable at school nowadays that you miss one great luxury of return to the domestic hearth. Why, they tell me that the school-rooms at Harton are *warmed!* And I know that the Senate House at Cambridge is when men are in for their winter examinations, so it is probable that the younger race is equally pampered; and if the present Hartonians' teeth chatter at six o'clock lesson, consciousness of unprepared lessons is the cause, not cold.

But you have harder head-work and fewer holidays than we had, so you are welcome to your warm school-rooms. I am not sure that you have the best of it: at any rate, we will cry quits.

But the superior material comforts of home are but a small matter in the pleasure of going there after all. It is the affections centred in it which cause it to fill the first place in our hearts, "be it never so humble."

Harry Forsyth was fond of Harton; fond of football, which was in full swing; fond of his two chums, Strachan and Kavanagh. He rather liked his studies than otherwise, and, indeed, took a real pleasure in some classical authors—Homer and Horace, for example—as any lad who has turned sixteen who has brains, and is not absolutely idle, is likely to do. He was strong, active, popular; he had passed from the purgatorial state of fag to the elysium of fagger. But still his blood seemed turned to champagne, and his muscles to watch-springs, when the cab, which carried him and his portmanteau, passed through the gate into the drive which curved up to the door of Holly Lodge. For Holly Lodge contained his mother and Trix, and the thought of meeting either of them after an absence of a school-term set his heart bounding, and his pulse throbbing, in a way he would not have owned to his best friends for the choice of bats in the best maker's shop. He loved his father also, but he did not know so much of him. He was a merchant, and his business had necessitated his living very much abroad, while Cairo did not suit his wife's health. His visits to England were for some years but occasional, and did not always coincide with Harry's holidays. Two years previously, indeed, he had wound up his affairs, and settled permanently at home; but he was still a busy man—a director of the Great Transit Bank, and interested in other things, which took him up to London every day. He was also fond of club-life and public dinners; and, though he was affectionate with his wife and children, too much of their society rather bored him.

When she heard the cab-wheels crunching the gravel, Beatrice Forsyth ran out without a hat, and Harry seeing her, opened the door and "quitted the vehicle while yet in motion," as the railway notices have it, whereby he nearly came a cropper, but recovered his balance, and was immediately fitted with a live necklace. Beatrice was a slight, fair, blue-eyed, curly-haired girl of fifteen; so light and springy that her brother carried her, without an effort, to the hall steps, where, being set down, she sprang into the cab and began collecting the smaller packages, rug, umbrella, and other articles, inside it, while Harry hugged his mother in the hall.

"Your father will be home by four," said Mrs. Forsyth, when the first greetings and inquiries as to health were over.

"And Haroun Alraschid has taken possession of his study," added Trix, with a sort of awe.

"Haroun, how much?" asked Harry.

"Don't be absurd, Trix!" said Mrs. Forsyth. "It is only your uncle, Ralph Burke."

"Burke, that was your name, mother; this uncle was your brother then?"

"Of course, Harry. Have you never heard me speak of your uncle Ralph?"

"Now you mention it, yes, mother. But I had a sort of idea that he was dead."

"So we thought him for some time," said Mrs Forsyth, "for he left the Indian Civil Service, in which he had a good appointment, and disappeared for years. He met with disappointments, and had a sunstroke, and went to live with wild men in the desert, and, I believe, has taken up with some strange religious notions. In fact, I fear that he is not quite right in his head. But he talks sensibly about things too, and seems to wish to be kind. We were very fond of one another when we were children, and he seems to remember it in spite of all he has gone through."

"I am frightened to death at him," said Trix. "I know he has a large cupboard at home with the heads of all the wives he has decapitated hanging up in a row by the back hair!"

"I wonder at your talking so foolishly, Beatrice. You must not be prejudiced by what she says, Harry. Except your uncle in Ireland, he has no other relatives, and he may be very well off; and he is quite harmless."

"You know that you were afraid of him yourself, mamma, when he first came."

"A little, perhaps, because I did not recognise him, and thought him dead. And then, you know, I fear he is not quite orthodox. But go and see him, Harry, and never mind what any one says."

"All right, mother; you have made me a bit curious, I confess," said Harry, leaving the room.

The garden in front of Holly Lodge was formal—just a carriage-drive, and a bit of shrubbery, and a grass-plat with prim beds on it, which had various flower eruptions at different periods of the year. First snowdrops, aconites, and crocuses, then tulips, then geraniums. The real garden was at the back, and the study looked out upon it. Not upon the lawn, where bowls, or lawn-tennis, or other disturbing proceedings might be going on; no, from the oriel window, which alone lighted the room, one saw a fountain, a statue, rose-bushes, and a catalpa tree, enclosed in a fringe of foliage, syringa, lilac, laurel, chestnut, high and thick enough to make it as private and quiet as any man with a speech to prepare, or sums to do, might require. Harry went along a passage, turned to the left up five steps, passed through a green-baize swing door, and knocked at that of the study.

A deep musical voice, which seemed, however, to come from a strange distance, told him to "come in," and on opening the door, he found that he had to push aside a curtain hanging over it, and which had dulled the sound of the voice. Smoke wreaths floated about the apartment, bearing an aromatic odour quite different from ordinary tobacco, and a curious gurgling sound, like that of water on the boil, only intermittent, came from the direction of the broad low sofa, which had been brought from the drawing-room, and was placed between the fire and the window. Close to this was a small table with writing materials, a note-book, and a pile of letters ready for the post, upon it.

On the sofa reclined a man dressed in a black frock-coat, buttoned, and dark trousers, the only Oriental thing about him being the red cap with a silk tassel which he wore on his head. But smokers often have a fancy for wearing the fez, so there was nothing peculiar in that. And yet there was something different from other people about him. Most men lounging on a sofa are ungainly and awkward-looking, while the attitude of this one was easy and graceful, and the motion of his hand, with which he indicated the chair on which he wished his nephew to be seated, was courteous and yet commanding.

His complexion was sallow, and appeared the darker from the contrast afforded by the silvery whiteness of his long beard, moustache, and thick bushy eyebrows, from the deep cavities beneath which his dark eyes seemed literally to flash. His nose was aquiline, his cheek-bones prominent. His hands were small, but strong and nervous, with little flesh upon them, and the fingers were long and shapely.

When Harry was seated he resettled himself on the sofa, and, keeping his eyes fixed on the lad, placed the amber mouth-piece of a long spiral tube connected with a narghile which was smouldering on the floor to his lips, and the gurgling sound was once more produced. But to Harry's astonishment, no cloud issued from his uncle's mouth; like a law-abiding factory chimney, he appeared to consume his own smoke. Then, deliberately removing the amber tube which he held in his hand, he said—

"And you are my sister's son? I like your looks, and my heart yearns towards you. Pity that she did not wed with one of her own land, so that you might not have had the blood of the accursed race in your veins. But it was the will of the All Powerful, and what can we avail against fate?"

What these words meant Harry could not imagine Were not his parents of the same land and race? His mother was Irish and his father English, and he had no more idea of Irish, Scotch, Welsh, or English being of different races than of the inhabitants of Surrey and Essex being so. They were all Englishmen he had always thought. His bewilderment was by no means diminished when, after this speech, and without again putting the stem of his narghile near his mouth, his uncle raised his head and poured out a volume of smoke, which it would have taken the united efforts of a couple of Germans about five minutes to produce. He was quite veiled by the cloud, through which the gleam of his eyes seemed to Harry to have an almost supernatural effect.

"You are nearly seventeen years of age, and will soon be leaving school," he resumed. "What are they going to do with you then?"

"I have not quite made up my mind what profession I should like," said Harry, somewhat hesitatingly. "I am fond of drawing, and like being out of doors, and so I have thought at times of getting articled to a civil engineer."

"Ay, ay; to aid the march of civilisation, as the cant phrase goes; to bring nations closer together, that they may cut one another's throats when they meet. To make machines do the work by which men earn their living, and so first drive them into cities, and then starve them. Or, perhaps, you will be a lawyer, and learn how to darken language into obscure terms, by which a simple, honest man may be made to sell his birthright without knowing what he is doing. Or a doctor, fighting madly against the decree of the Omnipotent, daring to try to stem the flowing tide of death. If your eyes were but opened, how gladly would you cast off the trammels of an effete society, and follow me to a land where a man can breathe freely. I will give you a horse fleet as the wind, and a sword that would split a hair or sever an iron bar, boy!"

"I have thought I should like the army, too, sir," said bewildered Harry, trying vainly to understand, and catching at the sword and horse as something tangible.

"The army! To be a European soldier! A living machine—the slave of slaves! To fight without a cause, even without an object! To waste your blood in the conquest of a country and the ruin and slaughter of its inhabitants, and then to leave it! Madmen! ye kill and are killed for nothing; not even plunder."

He drew several long inhalations, repeating the conjuring trick of swallowing the smoke and emitting it several seconds afterwards, for quite ten minutes before he spoke again.

"But the ties of home and kindred are strong," he continued in a calmer tone. "Your mother, your sister, will draw you back from the nobler lot. I know what the love of family is; I, who have returned to this seething cauldron of misery, vice, disease, and degradation which fools call civilisation, and take a pride in, in order to see my sister once more. Partly for that at least. And you are her son, and you have the stamp of the Burke upon your face. Hark you, boy! In the time of Cromwell, not two hundred and fifty years ago, your direct ancestor was a powerful Irish chief, with large domains and many brave men to follow him to battle. When the English came with the cold-blooded, preconceived scheme of pacifying Ireland once and for all by the wholesale massacre of the inhabitants, our grandsire was overpowered by numbers, betrayed, surprised, and driven to his last refuge, a castle but little capable of defence. He was surrounded; his wife and children were with him, all young, one an infant at the breast; and there were other women, helpless and homeless, who had sought shelter within the walls. Therefore, resistance being quite hopeless, our chief offered to surrender. But the English leader replied, 'Give no quarter; they are wild beasts, not men. Burn up the wasps' nest, maggots and all!' They did it; faggots were piled round the building and set on fire, and those who attempted to escape were received on the English spears and tossed back into the flames. The eldest son was away with a detachment at the time, and so escaped the fate which would otherwise have annihilated our race. But his estates were stolen from him and conferred on the murderers, whose descendants hold them to the present day. Have the Burkes best reason to love the English or to hate them?"

Harry Forsyth was a practical youth, who took things as he found them, and he could not even understand how anybody's feelings, much less their actions, should be affected by anything which happened in the days of Oliver Cromwell. He might just as well refuse a penny to an Italian organ-grinder, because Julius Cæsar ill-treated the ancient Britons. Besides, he was half a Forsyth, and the Forsyths were probably all English. For all he knew, some old Forsyth might have had a hand in burning up the Burkes. He did not offer any such suggestion, however, but sat somewhat awe-stricken, wondering what this strange uncle would say or do next.

He relapsed into thought, and for some time the silence was only broken by the bubbling of the water in the narghile. When at last he spoke again, it was in a calmer tone of voice, and with eyes withdrawn from his nephew's face.

"Serve not the English Government, civil or military," he said. "Or, if you do, confine yourself to your allotted task. That which is exactly due for the pay you receive, do for honour and honesty's sake. But do no more; show no zeal: above all, trust not to any sense of justice for reward of any work done in excess of the bargain. Incur no responsibility, or you will be made a cat's-paw of.

"Listen. At the time of the Crimean War a young man in the Indian service had a severe illness which obliged him to return to England on furlough. At one of the stations where his ship touched a number of women and children and invalids belonging to a regiment which had gone on to the seat of war were taken on board, and he, according to previous arrangement, was placed in charge of them.

"It came on to blow hard in the Gulf of Lyons, and the old transport strained so that she sprang a leak, which put her fires out. Later on her masts went, and after beating about for several wretched days, she went ashore on a desolate part of the coast of Spain. The officers and crew of the ship behaved well enough, and though many of them, including the captain and chief mate, were lost, nearly all the passengers were safely landed. But though rescued from the sea, there seemed to be every prospect of their perishing from exposure and famine. With great difficulty the officer in charge managed to find some rude shelter and insufficient food for immediate succour, and then, making his way to the nearest town, he applied to the authorities, and being a linguist who included something of the language in which Don Quixote was written amongst his acquisitions, he obtained clothes, food, and a sum of money for present necessities, with the promise of a vessel to transfer the unfortunates to Gibraltar.

"Of course he had lost everything when the ship went to pieces, and he could only get this aid by signing bills and making himself personally responsible. True, he was engaging himself for more than he could perform, but he could neither desert these people who were entrusted to his care, nor stand idly by to see them perish. And he never doubted but that the authorities at home would take the responsibility off his hands. They refused to do so, or rather, worse than that, they drove him about from pillar to post, one official directing him to a second, the second to a third, the third to the first again. And they made him fill up forms, and returned them as incorrect, and broke his heart with subterfuges.

"In the meantime he had to meet the claims, and was impoverished. Then, excited by this infamous treatment, he forced his way into a great man's presence, and was violent, and the consequence of his violence was that he lost his Indian appointment. It was well for him that he did so; but his story will none the less show you what a country England is to serve."

Again there was a long period of stillness, broken only by the hubble-bubble. Gradually the smoker raised his eyes in the direction of his nephew, but Harry saw that he was looking *beyond* him, not at him. And this gaze became so steadfast and eager that he turned his head to see what attracted it, almost expecting to see a face on the other side of the window.

There was nothing, but still the intense look remained, and it made Harry feel as if cold water was running down his back. His uncle spoke at length, low and slowly at first, more energetically as he went on.

"I see it; the crescent rises; the sordid hordes of the West fall in ruin around. The squalid denizens of cities find the fiendish devices of destruction to which they trust for putting the weak over the strong fail them. Man to man they have to stand, and they fall like corn before the scythe."

He dropped his pipe tube, and slowly rose to his feet, still gazing fixedly at nothing in particular in the same uncanny manner, and bringing his right hand round towards his left hip, as if ready to grasp a sword-hilt.

"One prophet," he continued, "was raised up for the destruction of idolatry, and wherever he appeared the false gods vanished. There were those who worshipped the True God, but received not his Prophet, and with them Islam has for centuries waged equal war, for their time was not yet come, and the mission of Mohammed was not for them. But the years of probation have expired, and the nations of the West remain in wilful darkness. They receive not the commandments of the Prophet; they drink fermented liquor, they eat the unclean beast, their worship of gold and science has become a real idolatry. Another prophet has arisen for their destruction, and Asia and Africa shall, ere another generation has come and gone, be swept clean of the Infidel. Swept clean! swept clean! with the scimitar for a besom!"

He remained with his eyes fixed and his lips parted, and Harry did not quite know what to do next. But he summoned courage to rise and say that he hoped his father would have come home by now and as he had not seen him yet, he thought he would go.

Filial affection might surely be taken as a valid excuse for withdrawal. And yet, having had no experience of the etiquette due to prophets when the orgy of vaticination is upon them, he was not quite comfortable on the question of being scathed. There was no need for fear; Sheikh Burrachee was too rapt to heed his presence or absence. He heard not his voice, and knew not when he crossed the room and closed the door softly behind him. He found Trix in the hall looking out for him.

"Well?" she cried.

"Oh, my prophetic uncle!" ejaculated Harry.

"That is a mis-quotation."

"It is not a quotation at all; it is an exclamation, and a very natural one under the circumstances."

"Has he been telling your fortune?" asked Beatrice, her large eyes expanding with the interest which is begotten of mystery.

"Not exactly," replied Harry; "except that he hinted something about the propriety of my choosing the profession of a Bedouin, and, I suppose, making a fortune by robbing caravans. But he told the misfortunes of other people with a vengeance. The Mohammedans are going to turn the Christians out of Asia and Africa everywhere."

"Good gracious, Harry! Why, papa's a director of the Great Transit Bank, and all our money is in it, and it does all its business in the East."

"By Jove! Let us hope the prophet *doesn't know*, then. But, upon my word, he looked like seeing into futurity. At least, I could not make out what else he was looking at."

"Poor man, he had a sunstroke when he was quite young in India, and has led a queer life amongst savages ever since. But papa has come home and been asking for you. You will find him in the drawing-room."

Harry thought his father thinner and older than when he had last seen him, and asked how he was in a more earnest and meaning manner than is customary in the conventional "How do you do?"

"Do I look altered?" asked Mr. Forsyth, quickly.

"Oh, no, father, only a little pale; tired-looking, you know," said Harry, rather hesitatingly, in spite of the effort made to speak carelessly.

"I have not been quite the thing, and have seen a physician about it. Only a little weakness about the heart, which affects the circulation. But do not mention it to your mother or sister; women are so easily frightened, and their serious faces would make me imagine myself seriously ill. Well, how did you get on with your uncle? You see he has turned me out of my private den."

"Is he at all—a little—that is, a trifle cracked, father?"

"A good deal, I should say. And yet he is a very clever man, and sensible enough at times, and upon some subjects. He was most useful to me out in Egypt on several occasions when we happened to meet. A great traveller and a wonderful linguist."

"Was he badly treated by Government? He told me a story in the third person, but I expect that he referred to himself all the time," said Harry.

"Well," replied Mr. Forsyth, "it is difficult to tell all the rights of the story. Ever since he had an illness in India, as a very young man, he has been subject to delusions. No doubt he behaved well on the occasion of a certain shipwreck—if that is what you allude to—and incurred heavy expense, which ought to have been made up to him. But I doubt if he went the right way to work, and suspect that his failure was due very much to impatience and wrongheadedness, and the mixing up of political questions with his personal claims. He wrote a book, which made some noise, and caused him to lose his appointment. Then he came to me in Egypt, and was very useful.

"I should have liked him for a partner, but he went off to discover the source of the Nile. He thought he had succeeded, and after a disappearance of some years came back triumphant. But he had followed the Blue Nile instead of the real branch, and the discoveries of Speke, Grant, Livingstone, and Stanley were terribly bitter to him—drove him quite mad, I think. Since then he has identified himself with the Arab race, and seems to hate all Europeans, except his sister and her family. With me he has never quarrelled, and I think remembers that I offered him a home and employment when his career was cut short. What he is in England for now I do not know. Perhaps only to see your mother once more, but I suspect there is something else.

"He writes many letters, and makes a point of posting them himself. I fear that he takes opium, or some drug of that kind, and altogether, though it is inhospitable perhaps to say so, it will be a relief when he is gone, and that will not be many days now."

After leaving his uncle in such a rapt state, it was curious to Harry to see him walk into the drawing-room before dinner in correct evening costume, and not wearing his fez. He was somewhat taciturn, ate very little, and drank nothing but water, but his manners were those of a perfect gentleman. After dinner he retired, and they saw no more of him that evening.

Harry Forsyth had several other interviews with his uncle, who showed more fondness for his company than he had for that of any other member of the family, but who kept a greater guard over himself, and was more reticent than he had been on the occasion of his first interview. He spoke of Eastern climes, war, sport, and scenery, with enthusiasm indeed, but rationally, and Harry grew interested, and liked to hear him, though he never got over the feeling that there was something uncanny about him.

One night, after dinner, when a fortnight of Harry's holidays had elapsed, the uncle, on retiring, asked his nephew to come and see him in the study at eleven on the following morning, and Harry, punctually complying, found him seated on a chair before the large table with three packets before him.

"Sit down, my lad," he said, and the deep musical tones of his voice had an affectionate sadness in them.

"I am going back to my own land to-morrow, and shall never leave it again. But we shall meet, for such is the will of the All-Powerful, unless the inward voice deceives me, as it has never hitherto done. You will, or let us say you *may*, need my aid. You will learn where and how to find the Sheikh Burrachee—which is my real name—from Yusuff, the sword dealer, in the armourers' bazaar, at Cairo. But you will more certainly do so by applying to the head Dervish at the mosques of Suakim, Berber, or Khartoum. At the last town, indeed, you will have no difficulty in learning where I am, and being conducted to me; and, indeed, in any considerable place above the second cataract of the Nile, you will probably learn at the mosque how and where to obtain the required direction, even if they cannot give it you themselves. If there is hesitation, show the holy man this ring, and it will be removed at once. Should you meet with hindrance in your journey from any desert tribe, ask to be led to the chief, and give him this parchment.

He may not be an ally to help you, but he may, and if not, he will probably not hinder you. Lastly, take these three stones, and see that you keep them securely in a safe place, and that no one knows that you possess them. They are sapphires of some value I exact no promise, but I bid you not to part with these for any purpose but that of coming to me. For that, sell them. Should you hear of my death, or should ten years elapse without your coming to me, they are yours to do what you like with. Lest you should forget any part of my directions, I have written them on a paper which is at the bottom of the box containing the sapphires. Come."

Harry rose and stood by his side. His uncle fitted the ring on his fore-finger, put the morocco box containing the sapphires, and the thin silver case, like a lady's large-sized card-case, that protected the written document, into his breast pocket, and then rising himself, rested his two hands on the lad's shoulders, and gazed long and earnestly into his face.

Then turning his eyes upwards, he muttered a prayer in Arabic, after which he gently drew him to the door, and, releasing him, opened it, and said, "Farewell."

CHAPTER II.

MR. RICHARD BURKE VISITS HIS LAWYER.

MRS. FORSYTH had another brother, named Richard, living in Ireland. When Ralph Burke—the Sheikh Burrachee of to-day—was in trouble, and lost his Indian appointment, he went to his brother, whom he had not met since boyhood, and who welcomed him at first cordially. But Ralph, possessed by the one idea of injury received from the Government, engaged in seditious plots, and nearly involved his host in serious trouble. The brothers quarrelled about it, and Ralph left in anger, and never afterwards mentioned his brother's name.

Probably he did not know at present whether he was dead or alive. But alive he was, though in failing health. He was the eldest of the family, ten years senior to Ralph, and seventeen to his sister, Mrs. Forsyth. In spite of Ralph's story about Oliver Cromwell, the elder brother had some land, though whether it was part of the original estates, or had been acquired since, I know not. He had no tenants, but farmed himself, and was therefore not shot at. The farming consisted principally, however, in breeding horses, in which he was very successful.

It was not that he realised such large profits, or grew rich rapidly, but he always made more than he spent in the course of the year, and invested the balance judiciously. And in twenty years hundreds grow to thousands in that way.

Rather late in life Mr. Burke had married a widow

with a son, an only child. He lost her early, and, having no children of his own, attached himself to her boy for her sake, and made a will leaving him sole heir to his property, after a legacy had been paid to his sister, Mrs. Forsyth, and a provision of £200 a year made for Reginald Kavanagh, an orphan cousin for whom Richard Burke had stood godfather, and was now educating at his own expense, the boy spending all his holidays with him in Ireland, and becoming a greater favourite with him as time went on.

For his step-son, Stephen Philipson, had disappointed him grievously, developing idle, dissipated, and extravagant habits as he grew into manhood. Mr. Burke bore with him for some years, hoping that he would sow his wild oats and reform. But instead of this, he became worse and worse, till at last it was evident that he would make the worst possible use of any money which came to him.

And then Mr. Burke had an accident in the hunting field, and, while he lay between life and death, his step-son behaved and spoke in a heartless and ungrateful manner, which was reported to him on his unexpected recovery; and in his indignation he determined to take a step which he had for some time contemplated. For, though he was able to get about again, he felt that he had received injuries which would bring him to the grave before very long, and that he would never be the man he had been. And, indeed, when pressed, his doctor did not deny that he had reason for his conclusion.

So as soon as he was strong enough to get about, he wrote to secure a room at the hotel he used in Dublin, and took the train to that city. And the next day called upon his solicitor, Mr. Burrows, of the firm of Burrows and Fagan.

Mr. Burrows, a sleek little man, particular about his dress, and as proud of his small hands and feet as a cat is of her fur, was waiting for him in his private room.

"I am going to alter my will," said Mr. Burke.

"Exactly," said the lawyer, with a slight shrug of the shoulders, which intimated that he was not at all surprised.

"I have drawn up a rough copy of what I want put into legal terms; it is very short and simple; we can get it done to-day, can we not?"

"Certainly, I expect so. Let me see what you wish," replied Mr. Burrows, taking the sheet of note-paper.

Now, do not skip, reader, if you please. If you do you will either have to turn back again from a more interesting chapter, or you will fail to follow the thread of my story. I promise not to bore you with legal terms; only read straight on, as Mr. Burrows did.

"I revoke my former will. I now leave to two trustees as much money as will yield £240 a year to be paid monthly to Stephen Philipson, the son of my late wife by a former husband. My land to be sold, and that, with the rest of my property, to be equally divided between my sister, Mary Forsyth, or her heirs, and Reginald Kavanagh."

"Not long, certainly, as you have put it," said Mr. Burrows, with a smile. "But here is land to be sold, and other descriptions of property to be entered correctly. Can you not give us till the day after to-morrow? If not, I will send the will to you, and you can sign it, and get it witnessed at home."

"No, no; I had sooner remain in Dublin, and get the thing off my mind at once. The day after to-morrow, then, at this time."

"It will be all ready by then."

As he passed through the outer office, the head clerk came from his desk, smiling and bowing obsequiously. He was a young man of dark complexion, and black hair, worn rather long.

"Ah, Daireh, how do you do?" said Mr. Burke with a nod, but not offering to shake hands, as the other evidently expected.

Daireh was an Egyptian *protégé* of Mr. Forsyth, who had employed him as a boy clerk, brought him to England with him, and placed him in a lawyer's office. He was clever, sharp, and a most useful servant; and, entering the employ of Messrs. Burrows and Fagan, had ingratiated himself with both of them, so that he was trusted to an extraordinary degree. He professed great gratitude to Mr. Burke, as the brother-in-law of his benefactor, and as having spoken for him when he was seeking his present engagement. But Mr. Burke did not like the look of him. He was prejudiced, however, against all foreigners, especially Greeks and Egyptians, so that his dislike did not go for much. But certainly an acute physiognomist would have said that Daireh looked sly.

Mr. Burke had friends to call on, and business to transact, so the delay did not really matter to him; and he called at the lawyer's office again at the appointed time, Daireh, bowing obsequiously as usual, ushering him into Mr. Burrows' private room.

"Well, we have put your good English into what you profanely call legal jargon," said that gentleman.

"Just listen, and try to understand your own directions while I read them over."

It was all plain enough, and short enough, in spite of Mr. Burrows' little joke, and then Mr. Burke put his mouth to a speaking-tube, and called Daireh to come and witness the document. Then there was some signing, and the new will was consigned to the tin box bearing the name of Richard Burke, Esq., upon it.

"Better destroy the old one," said he.

"Certainly," replied Mr. Burrows. "Throw it behind the fire, Daireh."

Then Daireh did a curious thing. He took another parchment, exactly like the old will, out of his breast coat pocket, and managed, unperceived, to exchange it for the document; so that the object which Mr. Burke and the lawyer watched curling, blazing, sputtering, till it was consumed, was not the old will at all, but a spoilt skin of some other matter, and the old will was lying snugly in Daireh's pocket.

What motive could he have? What earthly use could this old will be, when one of more recent date lay in that tin box? Daireh could not have answered the question. He kept it on the off-chance of being able to make something out of it. He was a thorough rogue, though not found out yet, and he knew that Stephen Philipson, who had just been disinherited, was both rogue and fool.

So he carried off the now valueless document, which would not eat or drink, he reckoned, and might be put to some purpose some day.

Mr. Burke returned home and wrote to his sister, and to Stephen Philipson, telling them what he had done. He did not write about it to Reginald Kavanagh, not thinking it necessary to take from him any inducement to exert himself, for though he was a good-enough lad in most respects, he certainly was not studious. He was also accused by his schoolfellows of what they called "putting on a good deal of swagger," a weakness not likely to be improved by the knowledge of his godfather's kind intentions towards him.

So that altogether Mr. Richard Burke was, perhaps, judicious.

CHAPTER III.

FROM GAY TO GRAVE.

TEA was a comfortable meal at Harton in the winter half of the year, when the boys had fires in their rooms, at least, for social fellows who clubbed together. Not but what it is cosy to linger over the meal with a book in your hand, or propped up, as you sit alone at the corner of the table, half turned to the hearth.

But Forsyth, Strachan, and Kavanagh liked to mess together, and Strachan's room being the largest of the three, they selected that to have their breakfast and tea in. All their cups, saucers, and so on, were kept in a cupboard in that room, but toasting or such other light cookery as their fags performed for them was done in their respective apartments, for the avoidance of overcrowding and dispute amongst the operators. Also, when bloaters, sprats, or sausages were in question, it was well not to feed in the room in which the smell of preparation was most powerful.

Though the half was drawing to its close, the evening board was bountifully spread; for Forsyth's birthday had come off two days before, and brought with it a token from home—a wicker token which the Lord Mayor himself would not have despised. There was a ham, succulent and tender; a tongue, fresh, not tinned, boiled, not stewed, of most eloquent silence; a packet of sausages, a jar of marmalade, and, most delicious of all, some potted shrimps. Harry knew, but did not tell, that every one of those shrimps had been stripped of its shell by the hands of Trix, who plumed herself, with unquestionable justice, upon her shrimp-potting. Unfathomable is the depth of female devotion; fancy any one being able to skin a shrimp, prawn, or walnut, and not eat it! The shrimps, the sausages, were gone, the tongue was silent for ever, but the ham and the marmalade remained.

The three friends were the oldest boys in the house, and almost in the school. Two of them, Strachan and Kavanagh, were to leave at the end of the half, and Forsyth was to do so after the next.

"Where's Kavanagh?" said the latter, coming into the room and sitting down by the fire.

"At his tutor's," said Strachan; "he is bound to be in directly. Let the tea brew a bit longer."

"It's uncommonly cold this evening; going to snow, I think. I hate snow in February; there is no chance of real frost for skating, and it spoils the football. Oh, here's Kavanagh."

The youth named strolled deliberately in at the moment, sat down at the table, and began to shave off a slice of ham.

"Has the cold wind made you hungry, or has the effort to understand that chorus in Euripides exhausted you?"

"I never try to understand what I firmly believe to have no meaning whatever," drawled Kavanagh; "and I am never hungry. I consider it bad form to be hungry; it shows that a fellow does not eat often enough. Now the distinguishing mark of a gentleman is that he has too many meals a day ever to feel hungry."

"I see; then you are only carving the ham for us."

"That does not exactly follow. Never jump to conclusions. A fire may not actually require coals, yet you may put some on to keep it going; so it is with a gentleman's stomach. You may take ham to appease hunger, or you may take it to prevent the obtrusion of that vulgar sensation. Not that I object to helping you fellows. The carving of ham is an art, a fourpenny piece representing the maximum of thickness which the lean should obtain. With a carving-knife and fork this ideal is not too easy of attainment, but with these small blunt tools it requires a first-rate workman to approach it. Now this slice, which I sacrifice on the altar of friendship, is, I regret to say, fully as thick as a shilling."

At this moment a little boy, Kavanagh's fag, came into the room bearing a muffin on a toasting-fork.

"Devereux!" said Kavanagh, severely, "do you know what Louis the Fourteenth of France said when his carriage drew up, as he stepped outside his front door?"

"No."

"He said, 'I almost had to wait!' Now I, too, say to you that my tea is poured out, my ham cut, and I almost had to wait. Not quite, happily not quite, or the consequences to you would have been— terrible!"

The little boy did not look very frightened, in spite of the tone in which the last word was uttered. Kavanagh had never been known wilfully to hurt anything weaker than himself in his life. As he was tall and strong, this is saying a great deal.

The two other fags grinned; one of them filled up the tea-pot, and then Strachan said "Go!" and all three lower boys vanished in a twinkling to prepare their own teas.

"We shall not have many more teas together," said Forsyth.

"No, but we may dinners," replied Strachan.

"Suppose we all get into the same regiment."

"The job is to get into any regiment at all," said Kavanagh. "There is that abominable examination to be got over. Awfully clever and hard reading fellows get beaten in it every time, I can tell you."

"Well, but I believe it is easier through the Militia than direct into Sandhurst, is it not? and that is the way you and I are going to try. At any rate, then we can go into the same Militia regiment, and that will give us two trainings, besides preliminary drills, and so forth, to have some fun together. And Forsyth must come in too."

"I have not quite made up my mind to go into the army, or rather to try for it, at all yet," said Forsyth. "It seems such a waste of time to sap for it, and then be sold after all. I can never do half so well as I fairly ought in an examination, because I take so long to remember things I know quite well, even if I have plenty of time to think them out. I can learn, but I can't cram, so I fear I should never be in it."

"Oh, have a shy, man; it is only going in for something else if you fail. And there is no life like the army if you succeed."

"If we fail, we fail. 'But screw your courage to the sticking-place, and we'll not fail,'" quoted Kavanagh.

"Well, it is very tempting; perhaps I shall try," said Forsyth.

"Look here, then," said Strachan, "there are two vacancies amongst the sub-lieutenants in the fourth battalion of the Blankshire, and my father is a friend of the Colonel. I am to have one, and I have no doubt you, Kavanagh, will get the other. There is almost sure to be another vacancy before the next training, and if there is, don't you think your friends would let you leave Harton at once, and take it? Then you could serve one training this year, and another next year, and be ready to go in for the Competitive at the same time that we do."

"Thanks, old fellow," said Forsyth. "I will talk it over with my people when I go home at Easter, and will let you know as quickly as I can."

"That is settled then. Oh, we won't say good-bye yet awhile."

"It is a strange thing," said Kavanagh, who, having finished his tea, had tilted his chair so that his back leaned against the wall, while his feet rested on another chair, less for the comfort of the position, than to afford him an opportunity of admiring his well-cut trousers, his striped socks, and his dandy shoes; "it is a strange thing that there should only be one career fit for a fellow to follow, and that it should be impossible for a fellow to get into it."

"It sounds rather like a sweeping assertion that, doesn't it?" observed Strachan, who was helping himself to marmalade.

"That is because you do not grasp the meaning which I attach to the word *fellow*. I do not allude to the ordinary mortal, who might be a lawyer, or a parson, or a painter, or fiddler, or anything, and who might get any number of marks in an examination. I mean by fellows, the higher order of beings, who are only worth consideration; I do not define them, because that is impossible; you must know, or you mustn't know, according to your belonging to them or not. Anyhow, there they are, and everything and everybody else is only of value so far as he, she, or it is conducive to their comfort and well-being. For them the army is the only fit profession, and only a few of them can get enough marks to enter it.'

"Am I one of these extra superfines?" asked Strachan.

"You may be, perhaps, if you don't eat too much marmalade."

"Come, you are pretty fond of jam yourself, Kavanagh," cried Forsyth.

"Well, yes; we all have our little weaknesses."

"That reminds me," said Strachan, turning round and poking the fire. "Our school career is drawing to a close, and I have never made my confession. I committed a crime last November which I have never owned, which no one suspects, but which weighs, whenever I think of it, on my conscience."

"Unburden," said Kavanagh.

"Well, then, you may remember that the weather was very mild up to the seventh of the month."

"Don't; but grant it. Go ahead."

"On the eighth of November it grew suddenly colder, and I got out my winter things, and in the afternoon I changed. Having done so, I put my pencil in the right-hand waistcoat pocket. There was something round and hard there—a lozenge? No, a shilling, which had remained there ever since I changed my winter clothes in the spring. Now at that time we were reduced to anchovy paste for breakfast, and our bare rations for tea. Money was spent, tick was scarce, stores were exhausted. Faithful to a friendship which has all things in common, I went out to Dell's and bought a pot of apricot jam for tea, the time for which had arrived. As ill-luck would have it, both you fellows were detained at something or another—French, I rather think. I had to go to my tutor myself at seven, so I could not wait, and began my tea alone. Well, the jam was good, very good, hanged good; I never ate such jam! Had I had quite a third of it? Not quite, perhaps; I gave myself the benefit of the doubt. But, then, the gap looked awful. Happy thought! I would turn it out into a saucer, and you might take it for a sixpenny pot. After all, not expecting any, you would be pleased with that. But it looked rather more than a sixpenny pot, so I had a bit more to reduce. And then—you would not come, and you knew nothing about it. Why make two bites of a cherry? I finished it, threw the pot out of window, and held my tongue. But oh! next day, when Kavanagh received his weekly allowance, and laid it out in treacle and sprats for the public good, I did indeed feel guilty."

"But you ate the sprats and treacle all the same, I expect."

"I did. I would not shirk my punishment, and flinch from the coals of fire which were heaped on my head. I even enjoyed them. But my conscience has been very sore, and feels better now than it has done for a long time."

"You have not got absolution yet," said Forsyth.

"Not by long chalks," cried Kavanagh. "Jam! and apricot of all jams. If you really want to wipe out the crime you must make restitution."

"Gladly; but would not that be difficult?"

"Not at all; you can do it in kind. At compound interest three pots will clear you. I should say; or, if it don't run to that, say two."

"Two will do," echoed Forsyth. "Who's that at the door?"

"It's me," said a youth—dressed in a chocolate coat with brass buttons—entering the room.

"Oh, happy Josiah!" exclaimed Kavanagh; "careless of rules, and allowing your nominative and accusative cases to wander about at their own sweet will; what pangs would be yours at mid-day to-morrow if you were a scholar instead of a page, and said '*Hominem sum*,' or uttered any other equivalent to your late remark! Shades of Valpy and Arnold—'It's me!'"

"Mr. Wheeler wants to see you at once," said Josiah, not listening to the criticism on his grammar, and addressing Forsyth.

"My tutor wants to see me? What on earth about, I wonder?"

Obviously, the best way to satisfy his curiosity on this head was to go at once, and this he did.

Mr. Wheeler sat at the paper-laden desk in his private study, under the brilliant light of a lamp with a green glass shade over it. There was no other light in the room, which was consequently in shadow, while the tutor was in a flood of illumination.

"Sit down, Forsyth," he said. "I am sorry to say I have bad news for you from home."

"My mother!"

"No, no, my boy; bad enough, but not so bad as that. There are money losses. Your father was connected with a bank, and it has been unfortunate. It seems that it was a great shock to him, and he was not in very good health. You may have known that?"

"Yes, sir, yes. I noticed that he looked ill when I went home at Christmas."

"To be sure—yes. Then you will not be surprised at this sudden blow having affected him very seriously?"

Harry could not take it all in at once; he had to sit silent awhile, and let the meaning of his tutor's words sink in. At length he asked—"Is he dead?" And the sound of his own voice uttering the word made him give a sob.

"No," said Mr. Wheeler; "he is very ill, and insensible, but living, and while there is life there is hope, you know. People often recover from fits, and this seems to be an attack of that nature. But it is as well that you should go home at once. Put a few things together, and you will catch the 8.30 train. A fly and your travelling money shall be ready by the time you are."

"Thank you, sir," said Harry, and went back to his Dame's House in a dazed state. Strachan and Kavanagh heard him come upstairs, and as he went straight to his own room they followed him.

"Well, have you got the medal for alcaics?" asked Strachan, for they had concluded that that was the news his tutor had for him. But seeing his friend's face he stopped short.

"Something the matter, old fellow, I am afraid," he said. "Bad news from home?"

"Yes," said Harry, in a voice he just kept from faltering. "I must go home to-night; my father is ill."

"I am awfully sorry," said Strachan, uncomfortably, wanting to do something to aid or cheer his friend, and unable to think what. Kavanagh made no remark, but, seeing at a glance how the land lay, took a candle to the box-room, caught up a travelling bag belonging to Forsyth, and brought it down to him just as he was going to call Josiah to find it for him.

It was not long before he got some things into it, and was ready to start. A grip of the hand from each of his friends and he was gone.

What a bad time he had during that short journey; feverishly impatient, and yet dreading to get to the end of it. It was an express train, and he got to London in an hour, and was just in time for another on the short line to his home. So he reached Holly Lodge by eleven. Before he could ring the door opened. Trix was listening for the wheels, and ran to let him in. She had been crying, but was very quiet.

"He is alive, but cannot see or hear," she said. "Come."

His mother was there, and two doctors, who looked very grave. One soon left, but the other, who was the regular medical attendant and a friend, remained, not, as he plainly said, that he could do anything for the sick man, who was dying. And in the course of the night he passed away without regaining consciousness.

But there is no good in dwelling upon that, or on the gloom of the next few weeks. Poor Mr. Forsyth had a heart disease, and when the Great Transit Bank came to final smash, the agitation killed him then and there.

For he was quite ruined. It was not only the money he had invested in the bank which was gone, but, as a large shareholder, he was responsible for the enormous sums due to those who had dealt with the bank.

Harry thought at first that they were penniless, and wondered almost in despair how he should be able to support his mother and sister. For he had learned no trade, he was not a skilled artisan, and mere manual labour and clerk-work are, he knew, very poorly paid.

But when Mrs. Forsyth had recovered sufficiently from the first shock of her grief to grapple with the cares of every-day life, she showed him that it was not so bad as he had feared.

"There is my five thousand pounds," she said— "my very own, which I had before marriage, and which is secured to me. Two hundred and fifty pounds a year I get from it, and it has always been a little pocket-money which I had, without going to your dear father for every penny. And now we must manage to live upon it."

Of course they had to go into a very small house, and could not take the whole of that. And Harry did not go back to Harton, but began to try at once for immediate employment which might bring some little grist to the mill. And he was more fortunate than young fellows generally are when starting on that heart-breaking search, for he had something to go upon. He went straight to the London representative of the Egyptian house of business with which his father had been connected, told his story, and asked for employment.

"But your father was bought out fully, and you have no claim on us, you know," said the merchant.

"I make no claim, sir," replied Harry; "I ask a favour. I don't know why you should employ me more than anybody else, but still I thought the connection might interest you. My father had a hand in establishing the business, and I had a hope that that might weigh with you, if you have found it a good one."

"Well, you have had a hard trial, and it is to your credit that you want to go to work at once instead of sitting down in despair. The worst of it is that you have been educated at Harton, and can know nothing of what is useful in an office. What sort of hand do you write?"

"A shocking bad one, I fear, but any one can read it. And I am not so very bad at figures. And I am ready to learn. Won't you give me a chance, and pay me nothing till I am useful?"

"There is one thing, at any rate, you have learned at Harton," said the other, with a smile, "and that is to speak up boldly, and to speak out plainly. I was a friend of your poor father's, and shall be glad to help you, since you are reasonable and see matters in their right light. But you must not expect much."

So Harry was taken into the office as a clerk just for a month on trial. And he showed so much zeal and intelligence that he was taken into regular employment at the end of it, and received a five-pound note for his work during the time of probation. And the joy and triumph with which he brought home this, the first money he had ever earned, to his mother and sister in the evening, cheered them all up in a manner to which they had been strangers since ruin and death had fallen upon the household.

Many castles did they build in the air that evening, but they were not extravagant, their highest present ambition being to have the whole cottage, which was but eight-roomed, to themselves, and to keep two maids instead of one. And this, if Harry's salary rose to a hundred and fifty, they thought they might manage. Of course it was a dreary life for him after what he had been accustomed to, but he made the best of it, and really interested himself in Egyptian trade, till he became a connoisseur in gum. His principal recreation was shooting at the Wimbledon butts on Saturday afternoons, he having joined a volunteer corps for that purpose. He had done so at Harton, and was the best shot there. He now had to compete with the best in the world, but he had a marvellous eye, and up to three hundred yards could hold his own with anybody. At any rate he won enough in prizes to pay all his expenses, and a little over.

Even when their resources looked lowest, he never thought of selling the sapphires his mysterious uncle had given him. He did not look upon them as his own till the ten years were up, or to be used for any purpose but that of going to find him. They, together with the silver case containing the parchment and the ring, were locked up in his old-fashioned, brass-bound desk which he kept in his bedroom. Nobody, not even Trix, knew anything about them.

That was the one secret the brother and sister did not share. Beatrice was disrespectful to her Mohammedan relative, and always called him Uncle Renegade till Harry read Byron's "Siege of Corinth" aloud one evening. After that she called him Uncle Alp.

But Harry Forsyth was destined to go to Egypt without needing his uncle. He became more and more trusted by the firm which employed him, and at last it was determined to send him out to the house at Cairo on important business. His absence was a desolation for Mrs. Forsyth and Beatrice; but it meant money for one thing, and, what was far more important in the mother's estimation, it was a change for Harry from the gloomy monotony of a London office. As for the future she was under no concern. She knew of Richard Burke's will, and that her children at all events would be comfortably provided for by it, though she herself might not outlive her elder brother.

Harry, as he was actually going to the country to which his uncle had prophesied he would, took to wearing his ring, and carried the silver case in an inner waistcoat pocket. The sapphires he left in his desk.

CHAPTER IV.

"WAYS THAT ARE DARK AND TRICKS THAT ARE VAIN."

WHILE the Forsyth family was passing through its time of trial there had been other chops and changes going on in the lives of those with whom their fortunes were more or less connected. Mr. Richard Burke had still further declined in health, and could not be expected to last long; but what was unexpected by those who knew them both was that he outlived his legal adviser, Mr. Burrows, who was attacked with pleurisy, which carried him off soon after he had made Mr. Richard Burke's last will.

His son came into his place, but he was a mild and not very intelligent young man, not long out of his articles, and very dependent upon Daireh, who knew all the details of his father's clients' business, and was so deferential and obsequious, that he made him think very often that he had originated the course of conduct which the wily Egyptian had suggested. As for the other partner, Fagan, he confined himself entirely, as he always had done, to the criminal and political part of the business.

Daireh was a bachelor, living in lodgings, and might have saved money to a reasonable extent in a modest way. But he was anything but modest in his desire for wealth, and the law would have given a very ugly name to some of the transactions by which he sought to acquire it if they had but come to light.

One February afternoon he left the office rather

earlier than usual, and after a hurried dinner repaired to his lodgings, where he mixed himself a strong glass of whisky. Then he took a flask of glass and leather with a metal cup fitting to the bottom, and, unlocking a bureau, took out of a drawer a small phial.

He listened ; went to the door—opened it, and looked out on the staircase ; shut it again, locked it, and returned to the bureau. His hand shook so that he took another pull at his grog, and then uncorking the phial he poured the contents into the flask, filled it up with whisky, screwed the top on, and put it into his pocket.

Then he went out once more, and bent his steps to a railway station, where he took a ticket to a small country place about an hour's ride from Dublin. It was growing dark when he arrived, but there was a moon, and the sky was fairly clear from clouds.

He walked for a mile along the road, and then turned off by a path which crossed a moor, and pursued this until he came within sight of a small disused quarry, from which all the valuable stone had been long ago carried.

As Daireh approached the place he clapped his hands three times, and a man came out of the shadow into the moonlight.

"Stebbings, is that you ? " said Daireh.

"Yes, it is," replied the other, sulkily. "No thanks to you for having to skulk like a fox. As I told you in my letter, the police are after me, and if I cannot get out of the country I'm done."

"What made you come to Ireland, then? It would have been just as easy to have shipped abroad."

"Because I wanted to see you, for I couldn't trust you to send me a farthing."

"How was it? You must have managed very badly."

"The numbers of those bonds were known, though you were so sure they could not be, and they are advertised, and traced to having passed through my hands. That is certain to bring it out that I passed the forged cheque, too. Bad management yourself! However, there's no good in blaming one another. Have you got the two hundred?"

"It is a large sum; but still, if it will get you out of your scrape, I will make the sacrifice. Only——."

"Get *me* out of *my* scrape! If I am taken, my fine fellow, you will be taken too."

"Why, what good would it do you to pull me in with you?" asked Daireh.

"You know precious well. If all the facts came out I should get about two years, and you fourteen at least. You actually took the bonds; you forged the cheque. I was only your tool, employed to cash the things."

"And am I to have you sucking me like a leech all my life?" cried Daireh in a shrill voice, stamping his foot.

"That is as it may be; you must take your chance of that. Perhaps you had sooner I gave myself up and told the whole story. I am not sure that it would not be the best thing for me to do."

"That is nonsense. Here is the money. You know how to get to South America, you said."

"Ay, I know. If the police have not tracked me here; and I think I have given them the slip," said Stebbings, counting the notes before putting them away. "Now the sooner you are off the better."

"It is a chilly night," said Daireh, producing his

flask, "and I am going to have a sup of whisky. Will you have a drop?"

"Don't mind if I do," replied Stebbings.

And the Egyptian filled the metal cup and handed it to him.

"Here's better luck," he said, taking a mouthful.

Then suddenly he spat it out again.

"No, hang me, if I will trust you!" he cried. "And there is a queer taste about it, too!"

"What nonsense!" said Daireh, forcing a laugh. "It is good whisky, very good; I had a glass just before I left. Well, good-night, for all your bad suspicions."

And Daireh walked quickly away in the direction of the road which led to the station. When he was well hidden from the quarry he poured away the rest of what was in the flask.

"If he had but swallowed it," he muttered fiercely between his teeth, "I should have been two hundred pounds richer, and safe!"

When he went to the office in the morning, one of the under clerks told him that Mr. Burke was dead, and Mr. Burrows was wanted to go over as soon as he could.

"All right," said Daireh, "I will tell him when he comes. Where are those papers about the Ballyhoonish Estates? In his private room, I think."

He passed in, and without hesitation took out a pass key which unlocked a drawer where all the keys of the deed boxes were. Selecting that belonging to the Burke box, he opened it; took out the will, put it in his pocket; locked, and replaced the box; put the keys back in the drawer, and locked *that*, and walked out with the documents he had spoken of under his arm. It had not taken him more than three minutes to do the whole thing.

His plan was this. He had now both wills in his possession. He did not exactly know where Stephen Philipson was to be found, but he was sure to turn up now, and he would make terms with him for destroying the second will and producing the first, which was in his favour. But he would not destroy the second will, but keep it to extort more money out of him with it. Also, if Philipson were to die—and his habits were such that he was not likely to be long lived—he would find out Mary Forsyth or Reginald Kavanagh, the persons interested, and see what they would give for the document, the loss of which had disinherited them.

When Mr. Burrows came in and received the news of Mr. Burke's death, his first idea was to open the deed box bearing his name, to see if there was a will there. Finding none, he called Daireh, and asked him if he knew of any such document. Yes, Daireh said, he did; he had witnessed one not so many months ago. He fancied Mr. Burke had taken it away with him, but he was not sure. It might be well to look in the deed box. Mr. Burrows had already done that? Ah, then, no doubt Mr. Burke *had* taken it. Had made another since, very likely; he believed Mr. Burke was constantly altering his mind about the disposal of his property. But no doubt Mr. Burrows would find a will among the papers at the house.

But Mr. Burrows didn't, and Daireh, as he went home that evening, bought a large piece of oil silk, in which he afterwards wrapped each of the two wills separately. Then he spent a considerable portion of the evening in making two large pockets inside a new waistcoat, one on each side, between the lining and the cloth, and each of these was to contain a will.

Stephen Philipson heard of his step-father's death, and soon appeared at the office to know if the old man had really been as good, or bad, as his word, and cut him off with a mere allowance. He asked to see Daireh, with whom he had had a good many transactions.

"That was a real will, was it?" he asked.

"Real enough. I witnessed it."

"But it cannot be found, I hear."

"Oh, it will turn up at the funeral, never fear."

"I wish it might not."

"Why?"

"Because then, by the old will, I should come in for the lot."

"But if the old will is not forthcoming, or the new one, or any other, the property devolves to the heir-at-law, Ralph Burke, and you will not even get your allowance."

Philipson, whose nervous system was considerably shattered, was so affected by this consideration, that Daireh thought it better to revive him with a dram of hope.

"If I can see you privately, without fear of interruption, I may be able to give you a useful hint," he said. "The funeral takes place on Saturday, and if nothing is heard of a will then I will meet you next day. Where are you staying?"

Philipson gave his present address and left, thinking to himself as he walked up the street—

"I wonder what bit of roguery that scoundrel is up to now? If he has got anything good for me I shall have to pay rarely for it. Well, I am in too bad a way to care much for that; but he shall not bring me within the reach of the law. I have no fancy for going to jail, where there's no liquor to be got—not likely. None of that, Mr. Nigger. If he will take the risk I will pay the piper, and that is a fair enough division, I think. But I wonder what his little game is!"

But Daireh never made that Sunday call on Philipson. For on Saturday evening he heard a cry in the streets—" Important Arrest! Great Bond Robbery! Scandalous Disclosures!"

He invested a penny in the evening paper, and carried it up to his room.

His fears were verified. It was Stebbings who had been arrested. He had thought much about what he would do in such a case, and kept his wits about him. Of course, the "Scandalous Disclosures" heading was premature—inserted, indeed, to give a filip to the sale of the paper. But the disclosures would certainly come very soon, and there was no time to be lost.

He destroyed a good many letters and papers; stowed all his money, and documents which meant money, about his person; packed a small valise which he could carry in his hand, and started for the station. He crossed the Channel that night, and got to Liverpool early on the following morning. He knew—so carefully had he laid his plans—that there was a trading vessel, with accommodation for two or three passengers, which was advertised to start from the port of Liverpool for Trieste that afternoon, and he would be unusually unlucky if he could not get a passage in her. He found, indeed, no difficulty about that, and might go on board at once if he liked.

Before he did so, however, he had a good meal on shore, and wrote a letter to Mr. Burrows regretting that he was forced to absent himself, without leave, from the office. And then, his imagination warming as he sat pen in hand, he told how his poor father, a stranger, speaking little English, had arrived in London, and been there seized with a serious illness; that he had not received the news till the night before, and had started at once to see that his aged parent received proper attention.

When the letter was finished, he went to the railway station and found a guard, whom he asked whether he was going to London that night. The guard said he was.

"Then I wish you would do me a favour," said Daireh. "A lady—a friend of mine—wants to send a valentine to a man in Ireland, and is anxious to mystify him. She has got me to direct it, and would like it to have the London post-mark. Will you drop it in for her?"

He tendered the letter and a shilling, which the guard took with a grin and an "All right, sir," and the foxy Egyptian walked back to the quay, having done his best to put the police on a wrong scent when the revelations of Stebbings should set them trying to track him. At the same time he felt that he was taking needless trouble, making assurance doubly sure; for, once at home in Alexandria, for which place he was bound, he would be safe enough. Or, if there were any fear, he had only to go up the Nile to Berber, where he had relatives, and what detective dare follow him there, or dare touch him even if he did?

A more anxious consideration was—how to make

any profit out of the wills which he had stolen. To treat for their restitution, or even for that of the last and true one, would be a very ticklish operation indeed. I think it is really the worst part about rogues that they are so utterly selfish, and regardless of the misery they inflict upon other people, even when they cannot benefit themselves by it. If Daireh had had an ounce of good nature in his composition, he would have torn up the old will and sent back the new one, now there was so poor a chance of his making money out of his scheme.

But that idea never even occurred to him. I am glad to say, however, that he had a bad voyage, and suffered much from sea-sickness.

CHAPTER V.

IN PASSING.

THE fierce sun was declining towards the west, and it was becoming possible to breathe and move about with a little more comfort on board the somewhat cumbrous vessel, fitted with huge lateen sails, which went swinging down the Nile between the lofty black rocks near Samneh. I say *fitted* with the sails, not borne along by them, for the stream just there took all the carrying power upon itself, rushing along its narrowed channel like a mill race.

High above rose a hill, on the top of which was a temple, entire, with a balcony round it, heedless of the lapse of ages. There is some little difference between the ancient and modern ideas of substantial building.

They had no ninety-nine year leases in the time of the Pharaohs; if there were such things at all, nine thousand would probably be nearer the mark.

Harry Forsyth sat on the deck admiring the different points as they went by, and delighting in the glorious pace at which they were going; a great contrast to their sluggish progress earlier in the day, when the river was broad, placid, and leisurely, and there was hardly a breath of wind stirring to urge them on.

He had been entrusted with a trading expedition as far as Dongola, carrying merchandise and exchanging it for gum, and ostrich and marabout feathers. He had been allowed a little venture on his own account, and had embarked it all in the latter article of commerce—marabout feathers—and had been rather lucky in his bargain. On returning to Cairo he expected to go back to England, and that made him none the less glad to be spinning along so quickly.

"I wish we could go like this all the way, Hassib," he said to the Nubian sitting by him; "we should soon get home then, eh?"

"We shall go faster than this when we come to the cataract," said Hassib, with a grin; for there was a joke here. Harry on the way up had not shown any liking for the cataracts. In fact, had preferred, under pretence of shooting doves, to walk round while the operation of towing the vessel up took place.

He and Hassib conversed in a queer lingo, for Harry was trying his hardest to learn Arabic, but had to eke it out at present with a good many English and French words. Hassib had a smattering of both those languages, and after a little practice they got on glibly enough.

But I am sure you will pardon my translating the palaver between this supercargo and the reis or captain of the boat. The reis was the proper companion for Harry, being a respectable fellow, and wearing some clothes. Harry himself was dressed in a linen suit of European cut, with a tarboosh or red cap on his head, with a turban twisted round it. Not elegant, but sovereign against sunstroke they told him.

"I wish I could get a crocodile," he said. "Every day we get lower down the river there is less chance."

"Plenty of them yet. There is an island near where we stop to-night where there are always many crocodiles."

"And do you think that I shall get one?"

Hassib thought a bit over this, and then replied gravely—

"If it is the will of Allah that you should get a crocodile, you will get a crocodile. If it is not the will of Allah that you should get a crocodile, you will not get a crocodile."

There was no gainsaying this. Mohammedan races are fond of propounding truisms with an air of having evolved a new idea out of their unassisted brains, and that is why people often think them so very wise.

"You see," said Harry, after bowing his head in assent to the last proposition, "I promised my mother a crocodile, and it seems so absurd to go up the Nile and not be able to get one. Then they are all white, and I expected them to be black."

"White men call the devil and crocodiles black; black men call them white," replied Hassib, who was a wag. "You now see which is right."

"Good again; that is one for me!" laughed Harry. "But I should really like to get one if I could."

"And the English think the crocodile such a pretty ornament!" said Hassib. "It is a strange taste."

And then Harry thought for the first time where on earth would they put the crocodile if they got it. But that was a future consideration.

"Shall we shoot the cataract to-night?" he asked, presently.

"No," said Hassib, "there will not be light enough. We shall anchor for the night soon, and start at daybreak."

The river soon grew broader and calmer, and in half an hour they came to the place where they were to remain, and cast anchor.

Harry went ashore with his rifle, in hopes of a

shot at the amphibious creatures, and his fishing tackle to keep him in patience while he was waiting for it. Hassib accompanied him to point out the place he had mentioned where the monsters were wont to lie.

For some time he got neither a shot nor a bite; but presently there came a tremendous tug at his line. The fish tugged, and Harry tugged, and the line being strong enough to hold a whale nearly, it seemed to be a question whether Harry pulled the fish out, or the fish pulled Harry in. In fact it was a regular tug of war.

Harry was the victor, and his opponent came to bank with a bound and flop.

"By jove! I have got a crocodile after all!" cried Harry, jumping back, as a hideous thing four feet long, and having the same number of legs, and a tail, seemed making towards him. The reis, laughing in a manner most contrary to our notions of the staid impassive Arab, began hammering the creature with a stick, until it lay quiet enough.

"What is it?" asked the captor, approaching cautiously.

"A big lizard," replied Hassib, "so your learned white men say; 'alligator lizard' I heard one call it. But it is really a thing that comes out of an addled crocodile's egg."

Harry looked up quickly, but the reis was perfectly grave. And on such occasions he always pretended to believe, whether he did or no. Hassib was quite confident of the correctness of his information, and how could it be disproved, or, for that matter, why should it be?

The sun was now very low on the horizon, and would soon take its sand-bath. Hassib laid his hand on Forsyth's arm and ducked behind a mound on the edge of the bank. Harry did the same.

"One, two, five, seven," counted Hassib. Harry peeped, and saw that mystic number of grey crocodiles lying on the island where he had been looking for them.

The nearest was about two hundred yards off. By stalking him along the bank, as he was not quite opposite, he got perhaps thirty yards nearer. As has been said, he was a really first-rate rifle shot, and the prospects of that crocodile could not be considered rosy.

Scales are hard, but so are conical bullets. Harry took a steady aim at what he had been taught to consider the most vulnerable part get-at-able, and pulled. Crack! smack! He heard the ball tell as plainly as if it were on an iron target. But the absurd crocodile acted as all the others he had shot at had done: he rolled over into the water and disappeared, and the other six kept him company.

"He is killed! Oh, he is killed!" cried the reis, much excited. "He will float soon, you will see. When they are shot dead their bodies soon float."

Whether this creature was an exception, or was not shot dead, or was carried down to the cataract before he got to the floating stage, and so came up where no one wanted him, cannot be said. But they saw him no more, and he was numbered among the partridges who have gone away to die, and the rabbits that were hit so hard, but crept away into holes!

Going back to where the boat lay they found another lying near her, which had been dragged up the last bit of the cataract and brought up so far since their arrival, while the crew had gone ashore and lit a fire, round which they were gathered.

Forsyth and Hassib went up to them for news, but there was not much. Alexandria was being rebuilt after the bombardment; Arabi's insurrection was quite over, and Mohammed Tewfik Pasha firmly established. The English soldiers were leaving, and the country would soon be quit of them entirely.

"Not it," said one of the new comers, who seemed to be a passenger. Certainly not a sailor, for his hands were delicate, and he lacked manliness when compared with the others of the party. "The English will not be so easy to get rid of, make sure of that."

And one of the others said to Hassib, alluding to the speaker—

"You knew his father; this is Daireh."

"And I knew him as a boy," said Hassib.

"It is years since I left," said Daireh.

Here Reouf the pilot joined the group, and he, too, was a friend of the family, and was made known.

Harry Forsyth, seeing that old acquaintances had met after an absence, kept in the background, and lit his pipe. He listened indeed, but simply to try what words of Arabic, in which the conversation was being held, he could pick up, not from any interest or curiosity which he felt in the subject of their talk.

"Quite a boy when you went to England," said Reouf; "and yet I think I can recognise you. Do you remember you went in my diabeheeh from Berber home to Alexandria?"

"Have you been to Berber lately? Are my people there well?"

"I was there less than a year ago, and all was well with them. You are journeying there now?" said Reouf.

"I am," replied Daireh. "I returned from the

land of exile to visit my home, hoping to share my hard-earned gains with my own people, when what did I find? Ruins in the place of my home, my family dispersed, my father slain by the English."

"Not so," said Hassib. "I heard of the misfortune; but it was by the hand of Arabi's soldiers that he fell; not that of the English. Arabi's soldiers, or plunderers who called themselves such. The English sailors caught them red-handed, and hung them up for it then and there."

"May their graves be defiled, whoever they were," said Daireh. "I have no friends now except at Berber."

Harry made out a good deal of this, and his heart bled for the Egyptian, coming back as he thought to a home, to find nothing but desolation, and to be driven out again from his native land. For there is nothing in common between the Egyptian and the Nubian but religion. The former race affects to despise the latter, and the latter really despises the former. And with reason.

So when he rose to go back to his diabeheeh (Nile boat), he bade him good-night in English, and expressed regret for the grievous disappointment and sorrow he had experienced. And Daireh said of course it was a great affliction, but he hoped to make a new home in the Soudan. And so they parted, courteously enough.

The diabeheeh Daireh was travelling by had sustained some injury from a sharp rock during the process of being hauled up the cataract, and the crew were going to remain where they were for the purpose of repairs. So when a sudden red flush burst on the eastern horizon, and spread and deepened till it seemed as if a large city was on fire, and Hassib, recognising this as the dawn, began kicking his lazy sailors into wakefulness, the down-stream boat was the only one which made preparations for a start.

By the time the anchor was up and the sails hoisted, however, there was some movement on board the other diabeheeh, and parting greetings were exchanged. Harry Forsyth, seeing the man who had excited his compassion the night before on deck, waved his hand to him and shouted good-bye! And the other returned the salutation. And the local pilot for the second cataract took the helm, and the vessel entered the boiling waters, and was whirled in apparent helplessness, though really guided with great skill amidst innumerable rocks, any one of which would have crushed her like an egg-shell.

And Harry, in the excitement and anxiety of the passage, forgot all about the casual traveller from whom he had just parted. Little did he dream that that man carried in his breast the document upon which his fortune depended, and the obtaining of which would establish his mother and sister in comfort, besides changing all the future prospects of his old friend Kavanagh. And Daireh, had he but known that the Englishman he had just parted from was Harry Forsyth, what a lucky opportunity he would have esteemed it for making a bargain, and securing at least some profit out of what threatened to be the barren crime he had committed.

For though it was not to be expected that the poor clerk and agent should have command of sufficient funds to pay even the more moderate ransom which he was now prepared to accept, he had formed all his plans for eventually securing it. Something of course would have to be trusted to the pledged word of the man with whom he treated, but though he had no scruples about breaking his word, or his oath, indeed, for that matter, himself, he knew well that other people had, and had before traded, not without success, on what he considered a foolish weakness.

But the chance was gone both for the robber and the robbed. They had met, and not known it, and now their paths diverged more widely every minute.

Is there any truth in the notion of people having presentiments? Whether or no, certainly Forsyth had none, for he was only too eager to get back to Cairo. And the boat went well, though not fast enough for his impatience, making a quick trip of it.

His employers were well satisfied with the result of their venture, and Harry himself made as much as he expected out of his marabout feathers.

Shortly afterwards, as had been arranged, he sailed for England, and had a warm greeting from his mother and Trix, though he did not bring the promised crocodile.

And then he learned that his uncle, Richard Burke, was dead, and that his will had mysteriously disappeared, as well as the confidential clerk of the Dublin solicitors who had charge of it, who was therefore supposed to have taken it.

"We would not write to you about it," said Mrs. Forsyth, "because you were on your way home, and the will might have been found in the interim. But it hasn't."

CHAPTER VI.

IN FARNHAM PARK.

CHURCH parade was over, and quiet reigned in the camp of the Fourth Battalion Blankshire Regiment, which was undergoing its annual training at Aldershot.

A young man in civilian clothes sat at breakfast in the officers' mess-tent. He was a visitor and guest, who had no obligation to early rising, so he lay snug till the band, marching the Church of Englanders off at nine o'clock, roused him and then performed a leisurely toilet.

And now he, the subaltern of the day, and the officer who was to take the Roman Catholics, had the tent to themselves. The former was some distance off, the latter sat next to him.

"I came only just in time for mess yesterday, so we had no opportunity for a private chat," said the one in plain clothes. "But I have a lot to say to you."

"Well, look here," replied the other, "my parade is at eleven; the dress bugle has just gone for it. I shall be back by half-past twelve. Then we will have lunch and go for a walk, you, I, and Strachan, if you like."

"I should like it very much, though how you can expect me to eat lunch after such a breakfast as this, at such a late hour, I cannot imagine."

"Oh, the air here is wonderful for the appetite. Not like London and Egypt, which seem to be your haunts."

"And the unaccountable disappearance of this will of uncle Richard's, Kavanagh, has it put you in a very big hole?"

"Not just yet. The dear old man felt himself failing, and thought he might forget me as weeks went on. So, instead of sending a quarterly cheque, he paid my allowance for the whole year into the agent's hands. So kind and thoughtful of him, was it not? But for the future, of course, it will be rather awkward for me if the will does not turn up. I go in directly after the training for the Competitive Examination, and so does Strachan. We have both passed the Preliminary, and shall have served our two trainings. Well, if I pass, it will be hard enough to live on my pay, but I must get into the Indian or Gold Coast Services, and try it that way. If I don't succeed, why then I have no idea what to do next. At least, I have an idea, but there is no need to think it out till the necessity comes."

"What do you think of your chance?"

"Well, my coach thinks it doubtful. He has known fellows get their commissions who were worse up than I am, and he has known fellows fail who were better up than I am. It depends on the lot of competitors, and also on their quality, and a little bit on luck. There is a good bit of luck in having the questions you have crammed set, you know."

"I can imagine there must be. And how about Strachan?"

"Well, if he has not got a good bit in hand, I am not in it, that's all. He could give me a hundred marks and a beating. However, I fancy that he must be safe. But there is the Fall-in; I must be off."

As Kavanagh left the tent Strachan came into it

"Well, old fellow, and how did you sleep?" he asked.

"Not badly," said Forsyth. "I fancy I should have been still at it but for that big drum of yours."

"Hush! It is lucky the Colonel is not here. Never speak of the big drum in that irreverent tone to him, I pray. It would well nigh give him a fit. The big drum is his fetish, though he nearly smashed it himself last year."

"How was that?"

"We were out on the Queen's Birthday, and had to fire a *feu de joie*. Rattle up the front rank, rattle down the rear rank, three times, you know. The horses hate it, and the chief had a young one who did not like ordinary firing very well, though he had got him in hand for that. But the roll was too much for the gee's nerves; he went wild with terror, bolted slap through the band, and finally reared up till he rolled over. It looked as if the Colonel was under him, and those who went to help thought him smashed. But he got up, and said, with a face of intense anxiety—

"'Is the big drum safe?' But, I say, how jolly it is to meet you again, old fellow. Don't you remember that last evening at Harton, we said we were sure to meet, we three; and here we are, you see. But, I say, this is a bad story for Kavanagh about this will being missing, is it not? Bad for you, too, though. Your mother was in it, was she not?"

"Yes; but as the testator's sister she will come in for something, probably, anyhow. True, it is mostly land, and I believe an uncle abroad will inherit that. But I don't know the legal rights of the matter yet quite. Anyhow, she has something of her own, and I have learned how to get work and earn my bread by it. So all round it is worse for Kavanagh. What is his chance of passing?"

"Not very good, I fear," said Strachan. "I don't feel safe, and I have read more than he has. And he is such a good fellow! He was awfully sorry about Mr. Burke's death, but made no trouble whatever of the missing will. That is, of course, he thought the prospect of being penniless a great bore, but he never got into low spirits, or worried others about it. And with his tastes and ideas, too!"

"Yes," said Harry; "fellows at Harton used to think him a tremendous swell. And those who did not know him were apt to take a prejudice against him. 'Lady Kavanagh' some called him, you remember. But we must have a long talk, we three, for my time is short; I must go back to-morrow. Kavanagh proposed a walk after lunch."

"Certainly, if you like. We generally walk over to Farnham on a fine Sunday afternoon: where the bishop's palace is."

"I know. I have often heard of Farnham, and should like to see it," said Harry. And others coming in, the conversation became general.

Then lunch time arrived, and was on the table very punctually, though Harry did not want anything. But with the majority, who had breakfasted before eight, it was different. Kavanagh came in ready dressed for the walk, and expressed impatience at Strachan being still in uniform.

"I have got to pay my company," explained Strachan; "but I shall do it directly the dinners are over, and then it won't take me five minutes to change." And he was as good as his word, for by a quarter to two he was ready to start.

It was a fine afternoon and a pretty walk; round the end of the Long Valley by Cocked Hat Wood, skirting the steeple-chase course; through shady lanes to the wild furze-clad common land; up the sides of the hill range, where the old Roman encampments can still be clearly traced.

"This one looks precious modern," said Harry, doubtfully.

"Oh, the engineers may have been digging about a bit. And this certainly is a modern shelter trench. There are battles fought here, you know, whenever the generals are too lazy to go as far as the Fox Hills," said Strachan, irreverently.

"But look at the view. Over there to the left, where you see the queer-shaped black wood, is Sir Walter Scott's novel—what's his name: the first one and the least interesting; at least, I could never get through it."

"Waverley," said Kavanagh. "Don't expose your ignorance and want of taste, Strachan. You could not see the abbey if we went there, Forsyth, or else I should have proposed it. But the grass is not cut yet, and till it is no one may go to the ruins. That is Farnham Park below us. Yonder is the Hog's Back."

A pretty road led them down to the park paling, which they skirted till they came to a ladder stile, which they crossed into the park, close to the solid old-world walls and towers of the bishop's castle.

"What splendid trees!" cried Harry, as the three old friends settled themselves comfortably under one of them. "I don't know when I have seen such beeches."

"Very condescending of you to admire anything

in England, such a traveller as you have been," said Strachan. "And you have been to Egypt? I envy you; I have always longed to see Egypt."

"There are more unlikely things than that when you are in the Line. Things are not settled there yet."

"Why, Arabi's insurrection is completely quelled, and he is a prisoner. And the Government will have nothing to do with the Soudan business, they say."

"Who is *they?* One set of *theys* say so, and another set of *theys* say we can't help having to do with it, let the Quakers say what they will. For my part, I hope all will be quiet," said Forsyth.

"Quiet!" cried Strachan. "Why, if there is no war there will be fewer vacancies, and I am less likely to get my commission in the Line!"

"Modest youth! So you want some tens of thousands of fellow-creatures to be slaughtered, palms and fruit-trees to be destroyed, and a whole country made desolate and miserable for years, and millions upon millions of pounds drained from the British tax-payer, in order that you may get your commission with a little less trouble! You remind me of the reasonable prayer in the poem—

> 'Oh, gods! annihilate both Time and Space
> To make two lovers happy.'"

"Oh, bother! I don't look so deep into things as that," said Strachan; "I can't declare a war, and I would not take the responsibility if I could; but if it comes and does me good, I can't help liking it. It is like winning a wager—I am sorry the other chap should lose, but I am consoled by the reflection that I win."

"Exactly," said Harry; "and I strongly expect that I should lose by any disturbance in the Soudan, and that Kavanagh would too. It is a long story; but you are such an old friend that it won't bore you, Strachan, though it does not concern you personally. You both know all about the will and its mysterious disappearance, so I need not recapitulate that. Well, I have been to Ireland and seen the lawyers—Burrows and Fagan. I could not make much of Burrows, who is a duffer; but Fagan has his wits about. He had never had to do with that branch of the business, but now the credit of the firm was at stake he busied himself in making searching and pertinent inquiry. A sharpish boy-clerk was certain that the will was left at the office, and kept in the Burke deed box in the late Mr. Burrows' time; and, when closely pressed and questioned, the present Burrows recalled having seen it there since he came into the partnership. Then the question arose—Who could profit by its disappearance? The answer was, if a former will were in existence, Philipson—my uncle's son-in-law, who was his original heir—would. But the old will is not forthcoming either, and Philipson is done both ways, for he neither gets the property left him by the first will, nor the allowance secured to him by the second. Indeed, he is barely existing on small sums advanced him by a speculative solicitor on the chance of one of the wills turning up. I saw a lot of Philipson: such a jolly nose—like a big red truffle. He said he was certain the late head clerk—a chap of Egyptian or Arab extraction, named Daireh—had got the will, or wills, having abstracted them after my uncle's death, because he had hinted at being able to tell him how to find them, and had appointed the Sunday to meet him, but had failed to keep tryst, and had disappeared. All this had to be wormed out of Philipson, who spoke very reluctantly at first. And I suspect he is as big a rascal as the other, and was in a plot with him to destroy will No. 2, and prove will No. 1, only the other would not trust him, but wanted money down. The reason he did not keep his appointment is evident, for the police wanted him for forgery about a fortnight later, and of course he had found out that he was discovered, and made tracks at once without waiting to come to terms with Philipson. The police have tried to track him everywhere without hitting on a ghost of a clue beyond London, from which place a letter was sent to his employers. But I know the direction in which to look for him."

"You do?" cried Kavanagh, much interested.

"Yes. The ugly beggar was vain, and liked being photographed, so there were lots of his likenesses extant. I was certain I knew the face from the first, and I soon was able to associate it with that of a fellow I passed on the Nile just above the Second Cataract. He was going up, and I was coming down, and I did not see very much of him; but I would swear to his ugly face anywhere."

"And you heard where he was going?" asked Strachan.

"Yes, to Berber. And I know natives who know him, so I have a good chance of tracking him; and if he don't produce the will he shall eat stick."

"Let him eat a little stick, as you poetically call it, even if he *does* produce the will. I think a hundred on his feet, or any suitable portion of his person, might have a good moral influence upon him," said Kavanagh. "Oh, to have the handling of the bamboo!"

"We have got to catch the beggar first," said Harry.

"And are you going after him really?" said Kavanagh.

"Or are you only chaffing? It seems a wild goose chase."

"Yes, I am going," said Harry; "and I think better of our chances than you seem to do. In the first place, I have picked up a smattering of Arabic, and that is a help; and then I have friends who can give me recommendations to the Egyptian authorities in any town which is held for the Khedive on the Upper Nile, and I am pretty confident I can make them help me."

"But suppose this fellow has not got the will, or has destroyed it, or has hidden it somewhere, and won't tell?"

"That would be hard lines for you, Kavanagh, and I hope better things. But even in that case it would not follow that my journey would be useless to myself. I have got a crazy uncle, a brother of uncle Richard, who is heir-at-law if a will is not forthcoming. He has turned Mohammedan, and lives like an Arab, and I believe has considerable authority amongst them. He was in England the last Christmas we were at Harton, and I saw him in the holidays, and he gave me directions how to find him if ever I wanted, for he took a fancy to me, and wanted me to go and live as he does. With all his eccentricity, he has a strong love for his sister—that is my mother, you know—and if he could be told that his brother was dead, and that he had made a will in his sister's favour which had been stolen, by which means he had become heir to the Irish property, I am convinced he would try to do something to set matters straight. Anyhow, it is worth trying."

"Rather!" said Kavanagh. "And if the country is in insurrection, and barred against Egyptians and European travellers, your relative's pass may enable you to get at Master Cream — Butter — what's his name?"

"Dairch."

"Ah, yes; I knew it had something to do with a dairy — to get at him, after all."

"By Jove, what an enterprising chap you are, Forsyth!" cried Strachan. "You deserve to succeed, I am sure."

"He does; and I heartily hope he will, for if he does not find the will, I shall have to forego all the comforts of life, at least, all I know of, for I daresay I shall find others. Now periwinkles may be a comfort, but what I shudder at is the idea of dirty linen. Not to have a clean shirt every day! it is quite too awful to think of. I am sure I wish you speedy and complete success, and that you may eat salt with the Arabs, and put some on Dairch's tail. That is how the Nubians catch their prisoners, Strachan."

"And when do you start?" asked Strachan, a great deal too much interested to listen to Kavanagh's nonsense.

"On Wednesday," replied Harry, "that is why I cannot stop to-morrow to benefit by your hospitality. I must go in the morning pretty early."

"I'm off to Berber early in the morning,
I'm off to Berber, a little while to stay,"

chanted the incorrigible Kavanagh, getting on to his

feet. "Catchee Dairy, or no catchee Dairy, Forsyth has got to see the old town of Farnham, and walk home by road, and get there comfortably for dinner. So come on. I am sure Forsyth must want to rest his tongue a bit and give his eyes a turn."

They left the park, and went down into the town by the steps beneath the palace; and so through the broad street with the restored houses, the bank and others, the inhabitants of which ought to wear coifs and pinners, knickerbockers and doublets, and where tall black hats should be unknown; then into the main street, past the Workhouse, which has a letter-box soliciting books and newspapers for the amusement of the paupers, and so back to camp.

Each of the three recalled that Sunday walk often and often in after years, with a pleasure which those who have formed school friendships, and met those they had "conned" with after several, yet not too many, years' absence, will understand. They talked no more of Forsyth's adventurous journey, or the imminent examination lowering over Strachan and Kavanagh. No, the future was banished from their thoughts, which were full of the past. Their talk, indeed, on the way home, would have been a terrible infliction upon an outsider, had one been of the company. "I say, do you remember Baum major?" "Rather." "Don't you remember when he thought he was sent up for good, and he wasn't, and his face when he found out that old Williams had smelt his jacket of tobacco smoke?" "I remember!"

And then a roar of laughter, the joke being only known to the three, but needing no further elucidation for them. For every period of every public school has its jokes, which are no jokes to any human being unconnected with that time and place, but to those who are so connected are a subject of life-long enjoyment.

When they got back to camp each felt that one of the happiest days of his life was drawing to a close. At mess that evening the Adjutant announced that the Commander-in-Chief was coming down next morning, and there would be a Field Day on the Fox Hills. They were to be brigaded at half-past five, so the "Fall-in" would be at five.

"We are sure to be back about one," said Strachan to Harry later in the evening. "You can wait till then, and have lunch."

"No, thank you," said Harry; "I have a lot to do before I start, and cannot spare another day. Besides, it would not be fair to my mother. I should have gone off early in the morning anyhow; not so early, indeed, as you march, but by nine; so it makes no difference in my plans, you see."

"Well, we shall breakfast at four; there is no need for you to disturb yourself then. Get up at your own time, and order what you like, you know."

"Thanks, you may trust me," said Harry. "But I shall see you off." Those overnight resolutions do not always find fulfilment in the morning. But when the companies were told off and equalised, and only waiting for the Adjutant to call out the markers and form the parade, Harry Forsyth emerged from the spare tent kept for guests, and went to the reverse flank to give his two old chums a final hand-grip. Then the Colonel appeared and mounted his horse, and they had to fall in. And the band struck up, and the battalion trickled away, till the rear company was clear of the ground, and Harry found himself alone.

"Poor old Kavanagh!" he murmured. "Strachan does not matter half so much. If he gets spun he has two more chances; and if he fails to get into the Line, then his friends have money and interest to start him in something else. But Kavanagh can't stop on in the Militia, or pay a tutor another six months, and it is neck or nothing with him. If I find the will it will put him square; but what is he to do till then?"

Ruminating in this way, Harry returned to his tent and lay down again for a couple of hours. Then he tubbed and dressed, and had a comfortable breakfast all by himself; for he was too experienced a traveller by this to let melancholy partings spoil his appetite.

He was in town by eleven, getting what was wanted to complete his modest outfit, and at the Sheen cottage with his mother and sister in time for their early dinner.

They were a thoroughly happy trio, for whatever interested one of them became at once equally interesting to the others, and so Harry could have his talk out about the friends he had just parted from without fear of boring any one.

It was a great sorrow to Mrs. Forsyth that her son should be going back to Egypt so soon. She had hoped that the anxiety she had suffered during his former absence was at an end, at least, for some considerable time.

"If his constitution were but settled," she said, "I should not so much mind; but he is not quite nineteen yet."

And Beatrice tried to be cheerful, and make light of it, but she was sorely disappointed also.

CHAPTER VII.

A VERY LONG PAPER-CHASE.

IT was not without very careful consideration that Harry Forsyth had determined to sacrifice his immediate salary, if not his prospects of success in the commercial line for ever, in order to track Dairch, and obtain the abstracted will.

On learning the whole story on his return to England, he had indeed at once thought that that was the best thing to be done, but had not been hasty in settling to do it.

His first act was to go to Dublin; his next to tell the whole story to Mr. Williams, the head of the house which employed him in London, and he somewhat reluctantly fell in with his views, his hesitation arising principally from Harry's youth.

"You are very young," he said, "but you have proved that you have a head on your shoulders; and if your mother and sister have enough to support them, and you possess funds for the journey, I cannot dissuade you from the attempt. If you fail, come back to us, and we will see if we cannot give you employment again. And even if you succeed you had better not lead an idle life, and need not sever all connection with us. At any rate, I will do what I can by letters of introduction to aid you."

Harry thanked Mr. Williams heartily, and that gentleman was better than his word, for, besides the letters, he gave him charge of some goods which had to be sent out to Cairo, by which he not only got a free passage, but salary up to the date of his arrival out.

Under the circumstances, and considering the object of his present visit to Egypt, Harry had no hesitation in selling the amethysts given to him by his uncle Ralph, or the Sheikh Burrachee. For he fully intended to seek him, if he could not find Daireh, a matter which he felt to be extremely problematical. Without the sale of these jewels he could not attempt the rescue of the will at all. He was surprised at their value, for he got more for them than he expected, and it seemed a great risk to have left them in the secret drawer of his desk all this time. You may be sure he did not forget the signet ring and the thin silver case, these being taken with him as before.

The trip to Cairo was uneventful, and he passed the time in improving his Arabic, by the aid of a grammar, dictionary, and Koran. As soon as he had delivered his cargo, and called upon the member of the firm who resided out there, who was as kind and cordial as Mr. Williams, he started up the Nile.

The traveller who does that, proposing to do more than visit a pyramid or two, requires a good deal of patience; and so would a reader if the ordinary routine of travel were to be recorded. Suffice it then to say that Harry voyaged up the Nile to Korosko, and there joined a caravan across the desert to Abu Hamed, from which place he got passage again on board a diabeheeh, which carried him to Berber.

With what excitement he beheld the white houses, the minarets, the palm trees, grow nearer and nearer! Within those walls, as he hoped, Daireh was living. If so, and he could find him, and get the will, the object of his journey would be accomplished.

For he had laid his plans. Armed with a letter he had got for the Governor, he would find no difficulty in having his man seized unexpectedly before he would have time to make away with the document, and there was little doubt means would be found to make him give it up.

Confidence, which had fluctuated, revived at the sight of the place, and when at length he was landed, Harry walked through the bazaars, expecting every man he met to be the one he was in search of. After many disappointments he recognised himself for an idiot, and calmed down.

How should he set to work in a methodical manner?—that was the point. The letter to the Pasha denounced Daireh as a criminal, and therefore if he employed his officers to make search for him the fact might get about, and Daireh, hearing of it, might hide, escape, or at any rate get rid of all incriminatory documents. It was more prudent, perhaps, to pretend to have business with him, and make inquiry in the bazaars.

The one advantage of the tedium of his journey was that Harry had acquired much more fluency by constant practice in speaking the language. The dress he had selected was not one to attract attention; he had modelled it on that of a Greek merchant who was continually trading with the interior. He wore full pantaloons, a loose sort of jacket, with a shawl bound round the waist, and his head was protected by a tarboosh, with a turban wrapped round it.

But though his clothes did not look European, the pistol stuck in his shawl belt was of the best, strongest, and most hard-hitting type. Old-fashioned, indeed, so far that it was not breech-loading; for he had considered that if he lost his cartridges, or spent them, his weapon would become a useless lump of iron, whereas percussion caps, powder, and lead, are procurable almost everywhere.

He went to the stall of a man who sold filigree work, and at his invitation squatted down and had a pipe and a cup of coffee, while he asked the price of several things. That was very well, but when he began to inquire about the object of his search, the shopkeeper lost all interest in the conversation.

He tried a money-changer with better success; he knew Daireh, but had not seen him for months. More he could not say. After many more failures Harry turned into a coffee-house, to sit down and rest, and have a glass of sherbet and enjoy a smoke.

While resting in the comparative cool portico where he was served, a barber came and offered his services, and Harry, suddenly remembering how the barber in the "Arabian Nights' Entertainments" always knew everybody, thought he would try his luck with him.

"I have come all the way from Cairo," he said, in reply to a bit of characteristic curiosity, "and my business is with one Daireh, who should reside here; for the last time our house transacted business with him he was here."

"He was here but six moons back. And he came from the land of the English to his cousin, who lived here. If you have dealings with Daireh, I know your business"—and here the barber looked inexpressibly cunning—"Gordon Pasha spoilt that trade; but since he has gone there is good profit to be made. And what are the pagans fit for but slaves, sons of pigs that they are? But they tell me there will be fine times when the Mahdi rules. Not that I know, but while I shave heads the tongues wag and I listen. It is nothing to me. Mahdi or Khedive, what do I care! All want to be shaved."

"To be sure," said Harry; "the wise man has the same opinion as his customer. And where has the family moved to?"

"They moved to Khartoum when trade grew better, and you will find them there if Allah wills."

How long he would have gone on talking it is impossible to conjecture, had it not been that a customer entered his stall, which was on the opposite side of the street, and he shuffled off to attend to him, for which Harry, who had got all the information he required, was by no means sorry.

His one great desire now was to get away. To be so close, to find the form of the hare almost warm, and yet to be just too late, was very trying to his patience. It was all very well to say to himself that he had only two hundred miles farther to go; and after travelling more than a thousand from Cairo, let alone the journey out from England, what were two hundred miles? But the answer he made himself was that two hundred miles was a great distance, and there was the sixth cataract. He had forced himself to be cool—mentally, of course, bodily coolness was quite out of the question—all the way along, with looking upon Berber as the end of his voyage. And here he had to go on another two hundred miles, and up another tedious cataract. It was very disheartening.

However, there was no help for it; so he went at once down to the quay, and began inquiries about boats going up. Luck here turned in his favour, for there was one starting next day, and he engaged a passage by it. And what was still more fortunate, the next day was Friday, and so there was not any likelihood of the delay which is so charming to the Nubian sailor mind. For Friday is their lucky day, and they would not miss the chance of commencing any undertaking upon it on any account. Now we account Friday an unlucky day (or used to do so). So either we or the Soudanese must be utterly wrong —radically wrong. Which is it, I wonder?

The dreary business commenced again on the morrow. A fair breeze, and sailing; a foul one or a calm, and rowing; running on banks, and pushing off; getting nearly wrecked half a dozen times in the rapids, and escaping. And so they progressed until at length the mighty river divided into two streams, that to the left the Blue Nile, that to the right the White, and the real Nile, and they found at the junction the city of Khartoum, dazzling in the glare of the sunshine, with the governor's house and the mosque rising above the flat roofs.

Opposite the city, and on the west side of the Nile, there were a number of tents visible, and Harry asked the reis what place that was.

"That is Um Durma, where the camp is," he replied.

"And what is the camp for? It seems a very large one."

"Yes, O traveller, it is large! seven thousand foot soldiers, a thousand of them that fight on horseback; many cannon, many camels to carry powder, shot, provisions, water; thousands of those who fight not themselves, but load and lead the baggage camels, sell things to the soldiers, and live upon the camp. In all a large encampment, and must cost the Khedive much money."

"Who commands the force, and what is it collected for?" asked Harry.

"Hicks Pasha commands it; he is an Englishman, and his principal officers are also English; the men are Egyptians and Bashi-Bazooks."

The reis paused. He was a Soudanese; and a smile played over his face as he added, "They are going to do wonderful things; to take El Obeid back again, to destroy the Soudan army, take the Mahdi, and carry him to Cairo in a cage, I believe. Oh! but they are great warriors, and the Mahdi's days are numbered."

"Is El Obeid in the Mahdi's hands, then?" asked Harry; for the last time he had heard news of that part of the country it had been still held by the Egyptians; and Mahomet Achmet, or the Mahdi, as he professed himself to be, had been repulsed with such heavy loss when he attacked it as to oblige him to sheer off, this being his first defeat. But he had returned in the January of that year, and taken the place after a fortnight's siege.

"Yes," said the sarcastic reis; "he holds it just for the present, till the warriors of Hicks Pasha find it convenient to walk across and take it from him."

After the disappointment at Berber, Harry did not feel the same confidence in finding his man that he had previously done. He began to be disheartened, and to think luck was against him; and to settle the matter quickly was a more important matter than ever it had been. If El Obeid was taken by the Mahdi, the insurrection of the Soudanese against the Egyptian yoke must be a very serious thing, and the country would be in a disturbed state for a long time, so that the Nile route would be closed against travellers, and passage across the desert to the sea would be equally difficult. If then he caught his man and recovered the will, he would not be able to get out of the country with it.

He had little doubt that Sheikh Burrachee's signet ring and the parchment in the silver case would, properly used, find him safe conduct to his uncle, if living; but the getting back again he suspected would be much more difficult, for his fanatical relative would probably want to keep him when he had got him.

But as Khartoum was a so much larger and more important town than Berber, so much greater difficulty was there in tracing an individual; and perseveringly and assiduously as Harry pursued his investigations, he could learn nothing. Most of those of whom he made inquiries were probably as ignorant as they professed to be; but there were some who, at the name of Daireh, looked at the inquirer with a quick suspicious glance. One of these replied with a verse out of the Koran, another with a proverb, a third said he never meddled with other people's affairs, and walked quickly away.

After three days of fruitless inquiry, Harry was obliged to have recourse to the plan which he wished to avoid as long as he could—that of applying to the authorities.

So he inquired for the house of Slatin Bey, to whom he had a letter of introduction, and went to deliver his credentials.

Experience in transacting business on his former

journey up the country had taught him how to expedite his reception, and a judicious application of baksheesh caused him to be introduced to the great man without too great delay.

Slatin Bey read the letter, and received him courteously, motioning him to a seat on the divan, and ordering him a chibouque to smoke, and coffee.

Harry knew that the great man must not be bustled, so he sucked at his long pipe with apparent complacency and indifference to all external matters, and said that he was an Englishman, who had come from London to bask in the sunshine of the Bey's presence.

"England is a great country, and London is a great town—twice as large as Cairo. I am honoured," said the Bey. "And you need no interpreter? that is pleasant."

"I speak but badly, but I can understand and reply," said Harry.

"It is well," said the Bey; "and if you have a message for the Governor it is best delivered without an interpreter."

"I have no message; neither, though a merchant, have I come to trade," said Harry, when after a few observations on fleets, armies, and Mr. Gladstone—in which the Bey evidently tried to pump him—he thought he saw an opening. "My business is a private one. A man named Daireh, a native of Alexandria, went to England as a boy, and was brought up to be a lawyer. He has fled with documents, for the want of which I cannot obtain property which is mine by right, and I have traced him to Khartoum; and I request your Highness's omnipotent aid to find him, and induce him to make restitution of what is valueless to him, but of great importance to me."

The Bey smoked a little while in silence, and then said—

"If these documents are of no use to him, why has he taken them?"

"He took them to extort money for their recovery," replied Harry. "But he had committed other crimes which obliged him to fly the country in a hurry, and before he had time to make profit of the papers."

Another long pause of silent smoking, and the Bey observed—

"It is a difficult matter, and he will be hard to find."

Harry was prepared for objections, and had learned the best arguments for their removal. He placed a purse containing the sum which his friends in Cairo had estimated sufficient on the divan, and said—

"I know that legal expenses are great in all countries, and it is only just that I should bear the charge."

The Bey bowed and clapped his hands.

"Send Abdullah here," he said to the attendant who appeared.

Abdullah came in; an old man, with an ink horn and other writing materials, worn in a case stuck into his girdle instead of weapons, who prostrated himself, and was questioned. He remembered the name of Daireh, and knew there was something wrong about him. But he must consult his books and examine certain sbirri, or policemen.

So Harry had to go away, with the promise that he should have fuller information next day. He did not for a moment expect to be satisfied so quickly as that, nor was he; but still he was infinitely more lucky than most people who have to deal with Turkish or Egyptian authorities, for at a third meeting, and with a little more baksheesh to subordinates, he got at the facts; and very disappointing they were.

When the Egyptian army, now under the command of Hicks Pasha, was being gathered to the camp of Um Durma, where it was at present situated, Daireh had been very energetic in trying for contracts to supply the troops with various requisites, and had ingratiated himself with many of the Egyptian officers, so he came and went freely past the sentries at all hours, always having the password. One of the English officers, however, chanced to see him one day in company which aroused his suspicions, and he had him watched, and shortly afterwards a couple of spies were taken, from the papers found on whom, as well as from the confessions they were induced to make—not, I fear, by arguments which would be approved of in more civilised lands—it became evident that Daireh was in communication with the enemy, and had kept him posted as to the number of the troops, their organisation, and their probable movements. Orders were immediately issued for the arrest of the traitor, who, however, had disappeared, having doubtless taken refuge with the Mahdi.

This news was a terrible blow to Harry. He had tracked the man all these thousands of miles, and here, just as he had his hand upon him, he had slipped away again, and was now farther off than ever.

There seemed to be but one chance left—to employ the signet ring, to apply to the principal dervish of Khartoum, and seek out his uncle Ralph, the Sheikh Burrachee. He was most likely with the

Mahdi, or else with Osman Digna out Red Sea way; and, in the former case, he would help him to recover what he wanted from Daireh, who was pretty certainly with the False Prophet. But it was extremely distasteful to him to have recourse to such an expedient. His uncle was a renegade, and if England espoused the cause of the Khedive, which, after the experience of interference with Arabi's revolt, it was very likely that she would do, he would be in arms against his country.

It was certain that he would not desert the man, Mahomet Achmet, whom his cracked brain accepted as a prophet from Heaven, for any patriotic consideration, for he was a wrong-headed Irishman as well as a fanatic, and a man with a grievance to boot, and would glory in drawing his sword against England. And if he joined him and sought his aid, Harry Forsyth might find himself in the awkward fix of acquiescing, if not taking part, in war against his countrymen, or of losing his head. And he had a sort of foolish weakness for his head, which fitted very comfortably on his shoulders, and did not want transferring to any other pedestal. And then, suppose, after all, the Sheikh Burrachee were serving with Osman Digna on the other side of the Soudan! He would be farther off his object than ever after he joined him.

He revolved all this in his mind as he walked moodily through the bazaar, where the products of all countries were displayed, not excepting the merchandise of Manchester and Birmingham, when he heard voices in loud altercation, and, looking up, he saw a group of men whose gestures showed them to be strangely excited about something.

An Arab, who stalked along, his hand on the hilt

of his sword, and scowling on the bystanders, seemed to be the object of this commotion.

"Stop him!" "Seize him!" "The spy!" "The rebel!" were the cries; but the Arab passed on like a lion through a crowd of wolves.

Then an Egyptian soldier, bolder than the rest, seized him by the sword arm, and in a second half a dozen were upon him. But in the next he had shaken himself free, and his bright blade flashed in the sunlight, and down went the first aggressor on the causeway, which was flooded with a crimson stream.

Pistols were pulled out, carbines unslung, as the motley crowd rushed to the spot. Pop, pop, pop; at least half a dozen shots were fired. One bullet whizzed unpleasantly close to Harry's nose, another smashed in amongst the bottles of an apothecary's stall, from which an assortment of odours arose, attar of rose and assafœtida being the most prominent. What billets all the other bullets found I know not, but one severed the Arab's spine, and avenged the Egyptian.

By the time Harry got up to this latter, he saw that a man in European clothing was by his side, kneeling on one knee, and trying to check the flow of blood which pumped out of a wound in his neck.

"Is there a human being here who is not a jabbering idiot?" he cried in English. "Keep back, you fools, and let the man have a chance to breathe."

"Can I be of any use?" asked Harry, pushing to him.

"That's right, come on," said the surgeon, as he evidently was. "Lay hold of this forceps, and hold tight—that's it—while I cut down a bit and tie it lower down. No good, I fear; there are too many vessels severed. By George, how sharp those fellows keep their tools!"

He was right; it *was* no good. In five minutes the Egyptian soldier died under his hands. Upon which he rose up and walked on to where the Arab lay, to see if anything could be done for him; but he had hardly moved since the shot struck him.

"A bad business," said the doctor to Harry, who had followed him. "We have not got many soldiers in our force brave enough to lay hold of an Arab, and can ill afford to lose one of them in a stupid affair like this."

"Are they such cowards?" asked Harry. "But I say," he added, as he looked in the other's face, "is not your name Howard?"

"Yes, it is."

"Don't you remember Forsyth at Harton—your fag?"

"Remember little Forsyth! of course I do. But you don't mean to say—by George! now I look at you I see a sort of a likeness. But I should never have known you."

"I expect not. When you left I was thirteen, and I have altered a good bit since then. But you were eighteen or thereabouts, and have not changed so much."

"That's it; though I have had plenty to change me, too. But how do you come to be here, and in that toggery?"

"Well, it is rather a long story," said Harry, "and I would sooner tell it sitting down somewhere out of the sun. What are you doing here—in private practice?"

"That is a long story, too," cried Howard, laughing; "and I would also sooner tell it sitting out of the sun. Come to Yussuff's, where we can wash this mess from our hands, and get anything we want."

Yussuff's was not far. It was a convenient establishment, where you could get a meal, or a bottle of wine, or even beer, if you would pay for it, or simply take a chibouque or narghile, and a cup of coffee or a sherbet.

"Try the lemonade; they make it first-rate here," said Howard; and Harry took his advice, and swallowed a big glassful of nectar, which no iced champagne he had ever drunk could beat. And then they washed their hands and rested on a comfortable divan while they interchanged confidences.

Howard had been a bit wild, perhaps, before he passed the College of Surgeons, and did not see any opening afterwards; he had no money or professional interest. So he had gone into the Turkish service, and, thinking himself ill-treated, had passed into that of the Khedive, and had lately volunteered to accompany Hicks Pasha's expedition.

"I have made a regular hash of it, as usual," he said; "for my great wish is to study gun-shot wounds, and for that purpose I should have taken service with the Mahdi; for almost all our fellows are hurt with spears or swords, while all their wounded are shot. But now tell me what extraordinary chance has brought you out here."

Harry told his story, leaving out, however, all that part about his uncle, the Tipperary Sheikh, who was now in all probability in the ranks of the enemy Hicks Pasha's force was about to attack.

When he had done, Howard said—

"I remember that fellow Daireh; he would have had a short shrift if we had caught him! It was unlucky, though, that he was found out before you came; he could not have done us much more harm, and the finding him here would have done you a great deal of good. By George! you are a nasty fellow to have for an enemy, Forsyth! What a sticker you are—a regular sleuth-hound. Fancy following your enemy to the very end of the world! Such a little innocent chap as I remember you, too. I don't think I bullied you much, did I? By George, I should have thought twice about offending you if I had known what a Red Indian I had to deal with!"

"I did think you rather a beast sometimes," said Harry, laughing; "and I took it out of the next generation, when I had a fag in my turn. But there is no revenge or vice in my present journey; it is simply to get my money. I had been a good bit of the way already on other people's business, and that put me up to coming on my own. Do you remember Kavanagh?"

"Very slightly; he was a little fellow—Brown's fag."

"He is not a little fellow now!" said Harry, laughing. "I should say he would weigh down the pair of us."

"And you can talk the lingo!" said Howard, admiringly. "It is very few words that I have been able to pick up. But what are you going to do now?"

"That is just what I was wondering when that row took place, and sent all my ideas and reflections spinning. I must sleep on it."

"Look here," said Howard, presently. "The chances are that that fellow Daireh has gone to the Mahdi's headquarters, which are at El Obeid. Now we are going to El Obeid; therefore come with us there."

"A capital idea!" cried Harry, hope dawning

once more in his breast. "There will be a chance of catching the fellow, after all, that way. But how can it be managed? Will Hicks Pasha be bothered with me?"

"He does not want any useless mouths, it is true," said Howard; "but I expect that he will be able to make some use of you. An Englishman who has shown sufficient energy to make his way out to Khartoum, and who can understand and speak Arabic, and that at an age when his sisters and their she friends would call him 'a nice boy,' and patronisingly teach him the newest waltz steps, is sure to be available in some capacity, especially for a leader with the resources of our chief. At any rate there is no harm in trying, and if you come with me I will introduce you. You need not tell him your story, you know, unless he asks you for it, because it is rather long, and he is very busy. Later, over a bivouac fire, it may interest and amuse him. Just say who you are, what you can do, and offer your services, and I do not doubt you will find yourself a man in authority over a certain number of Egyptians."

"What sort of soldiers do these Egyptians make? They did not do much good against us under Arabi."

"No; and we have a lot who ran away at Tel-el-Kebir here. They are no good. The Egyptian rule has been a curse to the Soudan, and the Egyptian troops are the greatest curs that ever tempted a brave but unarmed people to throw off the yoke. But suppose we go to the camp."

CHAPTER VIII.

KAVANAGH'S CHOICE.

CAPTAIN STRACHAN was an old naval officer, who lived in a rather retired spot on the borders of Somersetshire and Devonshire. His house had a verandah round it, and one warm afternoon he was sitting at a table under this, spectacles on nose, tying artificial flies. A young son of twelve sat by him rapt, holding feathers and silk, which latter he had previously drawn through a kid glove containing cobbler's wax, and wondering whether he should ever attain to the paternal skill in this manufacture.

Mrs. Strachan and two of her girls were round another wickerwork table a little farther off, indulging in afternoon tea, their books and needlework put down for the minute. Presently the sound of a horse's hoofs was heard upon the gravel beyond the garden hedge, and Mary, the eldest girl, jumped from her low basket chair, exclaiming—

"Here he comes!"

Everybody looked up, expectant; even Captain Strachan laid down his work—and those who have ever endeavoured to manufacture an artificial fly know what *that* means—as our old friend, Tom Strachan, walked up the path towards the group. As he did not look very pleased, his mother concluded the worst, and said—

"Never mind, Tom, if you *have* failed; very few succeed the first time, and you have two more chances."

For Tom had been in for the competitive examination, and had now ridden over to Barnstaple to forestall the country postman and learn his fate.

"But I have not failed, mother," said Tom; "indeed, I am pretty high up in the list—better than I expected."

"Well done, my boy!" cried Captain Strachan. "Not that I had any fear for you, because I saw you reading steadily at home when there was no pressure put upon you. And those were the fellows who always passed in my days. But I am glad it is safe, all the same, and we will have a bottle of that old Perrier-Jouet for dinner on the strength of it. But I say, Tom, you look as grave as a marine at a Court-Martial. No wonder your mother thought you had scored a blank."

"Well, the fact is, my friend Kavanagh has not had my luck. It is awfully hard lines, for he has only missed it by twenty marks. It is a bad job."

"Aye, it is a pity," said Captain Strachan. Reginald Kavanagh was a general favourite in the family, with whom he had twice been to stay in the holidays. "A pity for him and a pity for the service. He was cut out for a soldier if ever a lad was. Well, I hope he will study hard now, and succeed next time."

"That is the worst of it," said Tom. "He has no second chance, for he has no money to live upon till the time comes. I told you about that will which has been stolen or lost; that was the only thing he had to depend upon, and he has got to earn his bread."

There was a general murmur of regret. Mrs. Strachan particularly pitied him for having no mother to console him, though her husband thought that this was a redeeming feature in the case. If he had to bear her disappointment as well as his own it would be a great deal worse, he said, and no young fellow of spirit wants to be pitied.

"Besides," he added, "there is this to be thought of. Suppose he had succeeded, he would not have been in a very pleasant position. A subaltern trying to live upon his pay is placed about as uncomfortably as a lad can be. For my part, I am not sure that I would not sooner be a full private, if I must take to soldiering at all."

"But your other friend, Forsyth, who went out to Egypt to find the man who was supposed to have the will—has nothing been heard from him?" asked Mary.

"Nothing to help," replied Tom. "There has been one letter from him, and he was as hopeful as ever; but he had only got as far as Cairo. Of course, if he succeeds Kavanagh will be right enough, but what is he to do in the meantime? He has no relative to go to, you see."

"We would have him here for a spell if it were likely to do him any good," said Captain Strachan.

"Thank you, father. It will be kind to ask him, but I know he won't come. He has never been sanguine about Forsyth's recovering the will, and I know had made up his mind to face the situation if he failed in this. He would feel that coming here would only make it more difficult afterwards. He expected to be spun, and I have no doubt has fixed his plans."

Although his friend's failure damped Tom Strachan's pleasure in his own success, it could not entirely quench it, and the family party soon grew more cheery.

Of course the publication of the list was a terrible facer for Kavanagh, and when he saw the certainty of his failure his heart thumped hard and his brain reeled for half a minute. But when the mist cleared from his eyes he drew a long breath, shook himself, and lit a cigar. He did not bother himself with "ifs." *If* he had read this subject a little more, and that a little less, he would have got so many more marks. *If* those questions he had particularly crammed in such a subject had been set. *If* there had been three more vacancies, &c. Neither did he regret his former want of application, which he had done his very utmost to remedy the last year. Nor did he give way to a passion of vexation about the missing will, or repine at Fate. "What's the use?" he said to himself when these thoughts recurred to him; and he smothered them as he walked towards his room—this was in the chambers of a brother militia officer who played at being a barrister and lived in the Temple. As he was a sportsman and an Alpine climber, he did not live very much in London, and finding that his subaltern, Kavanagh, was going to lodge in the capital for the sake of reading with a crammer, and having a spare bedroom which he did not want, and was thinking of letting off if he found a friend whose coming in and out would not bore him, to take it, he proposed that the lad should do so. If he liked to pay him £20 a year he might; if not, it did not matter. For he had taken a great fancy to Kavanagh, who, indeed, was a general favourite. When Royce, the owner of the chambers, was away, Kavanagh had the sole use of the sitting-room as well as of the bedroom; and when he was in town it was much the same thing.

They breakfasted together, but Royce spent most of the day at his club.

He was in London now, and Kavanagh wished he was not, for he did not want consolation, advice, or offer of help. He knew that he had to work out this business for himself, and the less said the better. Royce was not in now, that was one consolation. Kavanagh went up to his room, and began overhauling his clothes. He selected an old pair of corduroy trousers which he had used for shooting, with a coat and waistcoat which had been worn with them, and a pair of boots bought in the country ready made, on an occasion when he had been obliged, by an accident to his wardrobe, to supply himself in a hurry. A much-worn check shirt, with collar attached, and a black silk handkerchief, with a pair of worsted socks, completed the lot of clothes which he laid upon the bed, and for which he then changed what things he had on. These he packed up with all his other clothes in several portmanteaus and carpet bags. He next placed his tall hat away in its box, and, having completed these arrangements, put on a wideawake, went out, and called a four-wheeler. Then he went upstairs again, and returned with a tin uniform-case on one shoulder and a portmanteau in his hand. It took him three trips to bring all his goods down and stow them on and in the cab. When at last he had accomplished it, he was stopped as he drove off by one of the officials, who said—

"Halloa, my man, where are you off to with Mr. Kavanagh's luggage?"

"I am Mr. Kavanagh," he replied.

"I beg your pardon, sir," said the man, touching his hat, as he recognised him.

It was not very far that he took the cab, only across to Holywell Street, where he stopped at an old clothes shop, and dismissed the astonished cabby, after having carried all the luggage inside, a young man with a hooked nose helping him quite as a matter of course.

"Now, then," said Kavanagh, "what are you going to give me for all these things, clothes, uniform, portmanteaus, cases, and all. Of course they will go dirt cheap, but don't overdo it, or I shall call a cab and go on to the next establishment. I don't mind the trouble of packing up again."

"Theresh no one in the street gives so good a prish as me," said the man, turning over the different articles, and beginning to depreciate them. There was no sale for uniforms; those shirts were thin in the back; that coat was too big for most customers, and so forth. Kavanagh cut him short—

"I don't want to know all that; come to the point, and say what you will give for the lot."

"What do you ask?" counter-responded the Jew.

"Twenty pounds; and that's an alarming sacrifice."

"Twenty pounds! Did any one ever hear the like! Twenty pounds for old clothes!"

"Why, you would sell the portmanteaus and tin cases alone for ten, and that overcoat for three."

"You think so, my tear young man? Tear, tear, how little you know of the trade! I'll give you five pounds for the lot, and then I doubt if I shall make any profit," and the dealer looked determined.

"Say ten pounds, and it's a bargain," said Kavanagh.

"No, I say five, and I mean five. Take it, or leave it."

"Well, to have done with all bother, we will make it seven pounds," cried Kavanagh, who was amused with his first attempt at making a deal of the kind.

The Jew compressed his lips and shook his head.

"Very good, then," said Kavanagh, dragging one of the portmanteaus towards him, and beginning to pack it. "I will try my luck over the way there. I see it is so close a cab will not be necessary; I can carry the things across. Sorry to have troubled you."

"Here, stop a bit," said the Jew. "Say six pounds, and that is a more generous offer than you will get anywhere else."

Kavanagh went on with his packing.

"Well, six ten, and that will swallow up all my profit, I fear, but I'll risk it for once. Well, come, seven pounds then, since you must have it."

So Kavanagh left goods and chattels, which had cost about seventy pounds, behind him, and walked out with a tenth part of that sum in cash.

Then he went down the Strand till he came to a pawnbroker's, where he disposed of the rings, studs, and pins which he possessed, thus adding a further ten pounds to his capital.

His next visit was to a watchmaker's, where he was known, though the owner of it did not recognise him at first in his shabby clothes.

"You see I have come down in the world, Mr. Balance," said Kavanagh.

Mr. Balance put on what he meant for a grave and sympathetic face.

"To wear a gold watch and chain would be absurd in my altered circumstances. Are you willing to change them for a stout silver one which will keep as good time, and pay me something for the difference?"

"Certainly I will, Mr. Kavanagh; but, dear me, sir, pardon my asking; your guardian, Mr. Burke, was such an old customer. I hope sir, there has been no unpleasantness between you."

"None whatever; only he has died, poor man, and his will, in which I know that I was well treated, cannot be found. So you see I must not indulge in gold watches."

"Dear me!" said the old man, to whom Kavanagh had gone for his first watch when quite a little boy, and upon whom he had called whenever he was in town since; to get the second handsome gold hunter now in question; to have it cleaned; to buy some little knick-knack, or merely for a chat. "Dear me; I do hope all will come right; I am *sure* all will come right."

"I hope you are a true prophet," said Kavanagh, cheerily. "But now, how about this silver watch?"

He chose a good strong one, with a chain to match, and handed over the gold, Mr. Balance giving him twenty-five pounds besides.

"I say! this is too much!" cried Kavanagh. "It only cost forty pounds when new."

"And is worth thirty-five now," said the watchmaker. "I shall make a good profit out of the bargain, I assure you."

Kavanagh pocketed his new watch, held out his hand, which the old man grasped, across the counter, and walked away murmuring, "Good old chap!"

It was still early in the afternoon, so to complete all his business at once he walked back to the chambers, took his sword, which he had not parted with, packed it up in brown paper, and directed it to Tom Strachan. Then he wrote this letter:—

"DEAR TOM,—When I joined the Militia I hoped that it was a stepping-stone to the Line, so I would not have a tailor's sword, but indulged in the expensive luxury of a good one. Accept it, old fellow, with all sorts of congratulations and good wishes. 'The property of a gentleman, having no further use for it,' eh? I must poke my way to fame with a bayonet, if I am to get there, instead of carving it with a sword. Thank your people for their kindness to me.—Yours, &c."

"By-the-by," he soliloquised, when he had stuck and directed this epistle, "I have not sent in the resignation of my commission yet." And he took half a sheet of foolscap and wrote out the formal notice to the Adjutant of the 4th Blankshire at once. Then he said, "There is nothing else, I think, but to post the letters and send the sword off by rail; and then go in for new experiences."

It was a good bit of a new experience for him to carry a parcel through the streets of London, and book it himself, but in his present costume he did not mind doing it one bit. Indeed, he felt quite light-hearted; knowing the worst was much better than the anxiety of the past few weeks. And then there was another matter. Having been used to a good allowance, and possessing naturally somewhat fastidious tastes, he had not been very economical, though, as he hated the idea of debt, and would rather have blacked shoes for a livelihood than have imposed on his generous godfather and guardian, he had not fallen into actually extravagant habits.

When Mr. Burke died, and the will was not forthcoming, and he was thus placed face to face with actual impending poverty, Kavanagh had the sense, the manliness, and the honesty, to do violence to his tastes and feelings, by guarding against all unnecessary expenditure. But to a free-handed and generous disposition this is a very hard task; and when the end came, and he cast up his accounts, he found to his dismay that he owed more than the balance of his allowance, the last sum paid to him, would cover.

It was not much, and would not have been pressed for, but Kavanagh, though rather weak about his personal appearance, had a pound of manly pride to an ounce of girlish vanity, 'and would sooner have gone in rags than owed money to a tailor. The money he had obtained that afternoon would entirely clear him from every liability, and leave him with a few pounds in his pocket; and this relief made him quite light-hearted, in spite of the final tumble of his house of cards.

The question was—where to dine. He knew lots of restaurants and chop-houses, but even in the most humble of the latter, where the floor was saw-dusted, his present costume would excite remark. He had from boyhood been particular about his dress, and his collars and waistcoats had incited some of his friends to call him a dandy, so his scruples may have been exaggerated.

At last he saw several better-class artisans go into an eating-house in Oxford Street, and following them he did very well. The table-cloth was stained with brown circles from the porter pots, and was otherwise dirty; the forks were pewter, and there were no napkins; but the meat was as good as you would get anywhere, so were the vegetables, the beer also; and the cost was about half that of the most homely chop-houses he had hitherto patronised.

His dinner done, it was about the time when the theatres were opening, so he went to the gallery door of one of the principal of them, and after waiting a little while, amongst the good-humoured crowd, he surged upstairs with them—many stairs they were, and steep—and got a good place close to the chandelier. The warmth and light from it were rather too obtrusive, but did not prevent his taking an interest in the performance, which was shared by his neighbours in the most intense and hearty fashion. The women sobbed at the pathetic parts, while the men set their teeth and turned white when the villain temporarily got the best of it, and both sexes roared with delight over the comic scenes. Likewise, all sucked oranges; therefore Kavanagh purchased and sucked an orange, and ingratiated himself with his female neighbours by politely offering them that fruit!

And between the acts, when the young men in the stalls, in their white ties, and white kid gloves, and nicely parted hair, stood up and languidly surveyed the house through their opera-glasses, Kavanagh had a sardonic amusement in the recollection as he thought that a fortnight before he had sat in that fourth stall in the third row, in evening dress, with a gardenia in his button-hole, and had similarly inspected the inferior beings around him. Froggy Barton occupied that seat to-night. Kavanagh took a squeeze at his orange, and thought he could hit Froggy with the skin. But of course he refrained from trying. Only he did look so sleek! "What much wiser people we are than the swells!" Kavanagh thought. "We enjoy ourselves without being ashamed of it, and we endure crowding and semi-suffocation without getting ill-tempered!"

But he soon had enough of it, in spite of his philosophy, and after the second fall of the curtain was glad to get into the fresh air.

When he reached the Temple he found Royce expecting him, and directly he entered he got up and shook him by the hand.

"I did not see the list till six," he said, and then I came to chambers in hopes of finding you, and getting you to come out somewhere. You have not been moping, I hope."

"Moping! Not a bit of it," replied Kavanagh. "I am not going to cry 'I take a licking!' because Fortune has caught me a couple of facers without a return. I have been to the theatre, and enjoyed myself vastly, I assure you."

"To the theatre! you; in that dress!" exclaimed Royce.

"Oh, I went to the gallery. I have accepted the situation."

"Come and sit down and light a pipe," said Royce. "I won't bore you with unavailing regrets. Tell me what you are going to do, and if I can help you at all."

"Thank you; I have thought it probable I should fail, and have debated with myself deliberately what course is best to adopt. I have come to a conclusion, and no one can help me. My first thought was that if I failed to be an officer I would be a private, and the more I have thought it over the more convinced I have become that that would suit me better than anything else. I have never learned a trade, so I could not be a skilled artisan, and a soldier's life would suit me better than that of an ordinary day labourer, whose work requires no head-piece. As for spending my days in an office, a warehouse, or a shop, it would be like going to prison for me. In short, I am going to enlist, and have also determined on the branch of the service which is to reap the benefit."

"Cavalry, I suppose; Lancers, Dragoons, or Hussars?"

"Neither. I fixed on that arm at first; the uniform attracted me; the sword is a noble weapon; and to ride is pleasanter than to walk. But these advantages are more than counterbalanced by the lot of accoutrements a horse soldier has to clean, and the fact that at the end of a day's march he has to attend to his horse before he can look after himself."

"A great many gentlemen's sons go into the Artillery."

"I have settled upon the Infantry, and intend to-morrow morning to offer my invaluable services to the Foot Guards. You look surprised."

"Well, yes," said Royce. "To tell the truth I fancied that you would be anxious to get to India; there is more chance, you know, of promotion that way."

"I have thought out that. But, to tell the truth, unless there were a prospect of active service I should prefer to remain in England, for this sole reason. I do not give up all hope of that will turning up, and if it should, I want to be in the way of getting early information, and looking after my interests."

Royce sat in silent thought for a little while, and then said—

"I see what you mean, and upon my word I do not know how to advise you better."

And after a little more chat they went to bed.

Next morning, when Kavanagh was dressed, he turned to his bath with a sad conviction that his morning ablutions must in future be of a much less satisfactory nature, and he sighed, for this went more home to him than almost anything. "Ta, ta, tub!" he said, as he closed the door.

He found Royce already in the sitting-room making the tea, and they breakfasted together.

When the meal was over, Kavanagh rose and said—

"By-the-by, there is my gun; it is a full-choke, and a remarkably good killer if one only holds it straight. It was a present, and I did not like to sell it. Will you have it as a memorial from a fellow to whom you have been uncommonly kind? Good-bye, and thank you for all."

"Good-bye," said Royce, in a voice which he had a difficulty to keep steady. "I hope luck will turn for you soon; but I feel sure it will. And if you have forgotten anything, or I can do anything for you, mind you come to me, or write if I am out of town. Good-bye again."

Kavanagh wrung his old captain's hand and hurried down-stairs, leaving him with a ball in his throat and moisture very near his eyes.

"Thank goodness that is over!" he murmured, as he left the Temple. "Now for the barracks."

Instead of offering himself to one of the outside recruiters, he went straight to the Orderly Room, and told a sergeant waiting outside that he wished to join. So he was brought before the Adjutant almost at once. He stood six feet in his stockings, and measured forty-one inches round the chest, so there was no difficulty about his acceptance. They jumped at him like a trout at a May fly.

He gave his real name, Reginald Kavanagh. "If I were ashamed of what I am doing, I would not do it," he reasoned. And besides, he wished to be traced with the greatest possible ease should the missing will be found.

Of course the life at first was extremely hard, and the companionship of some of his comrades very distasteful to him, but he took care not to show it. And others were as good fellows as ever stepped, and with them he made friends.

The fact of his knowing his drill thoroughly made matters easier for him, and he soon learned how to clean his arms and accoutrements, make his bed, and so forth. And by dint of unhesitating obedience to orders, even when foolish, and never answering or arguing with superiors, he got a good name without subserviency.

CHAPTER IX.

THE ARMY OF HICKS PASHA.

IT may have seemed to you that Harry Forsyth took the death of the Egyptian soldier rather callously, seeing that he was not used to such scenes, and that he ought to have been a little more impressed. But you see he had resided in Egypt, and been some way up the Nile before; and in hot countries people not only live a good deal, but die a good deal, in the open air, so that he had seen human bodies; and more than once, in the course of his journeys, he had come upon one such lying much as you will see that of a dog on the mud of a tidal river at home at low water.

It is astonishing how soon we grow hardened to such spectacles. And then, unless he has become exceptionally cosmopolitan, a Briton finds it very difficult to reckon an African, or even an Asiatic, as *quite* a human being. Of course he knows that he is so, just as much as himself. He knows, and perhaps vehemently asserts, if necessary, that even the lowest type of negro is a man and a brother, and not a connecting link between man and monkey. But he cannot *manage* to feel that he is of the same value as a European, or to look upon his corpse with a similar awe.

In the early days of the Australian colonies, an officer in a Scottish regiment quartered out in that hemisphere caught a native robbing his garden, chased him with a club, and hit him harder than he intended, so that the man fell down and never got up again, for which the officer was sorry, though held justified. About that time bad news from home oppressed his spirits to such an extent that his soldier-servant, who was much attached to him, and was allowed considerable freedom of speech in consequence of his value and fidelity, thought fit to remonstrate. He attributed his master's lowness of spirits entirely to his brooding over the accident, and said one morning when he had brushed the clothes and brought the shaving-water—

"I ask your pardon, meejor; but it's sair to see you take on so aboot the likes of that heathen body. A great traveller I was conversing with last night, and a respectable and trustworthy man, sir, told me that there's thousands and thousands of them up the country."

He thought that his master was fretting over the wanton destruction of a rare specimen, a sort of dodo!

Howard and Forsyth left Khartoum and strolled towards the plain where the Egyptian army lay. A town of tents, well pitched indeed, and dressed in parallel lines, and kept fairly clean—the English officers, though they had had all their work cut out, had at length taught the Egyptians that—but wanting in all those little embellishments which distinguish an English or French encampment, especially if it is at all permanent. No little flags to mark the companies; no extemporised miniature gardens; no neat frames to hang recently-cleaned accoutrements on. The sentries mooned up and down, carrying their rifles as if they were troublesome, heavy things, they longed to throw down, that they might put their hands in their pockets.

In one block of tents, however, which they passed through there was a great difference.

The sentry stood to his front and shouldered arms, as he saw Howard approach, smartly and with alacrity. The men were cleaning their arms as if they took pride in the task, not like paupers picking oakum; others were laughing loudly, or playing like schoolboys, and Harry noticed they were all black.

"These niggers look much finer fellows than the rest," he observed.

"I should think they were!" replied Howard. "These are Nubians, and I wish we had more of them. They hate the Arabs, too, and that is another good thing."

"What a lot of camels!" exclaimed Harry, as, passing over the top of a little hill, they came in sight of lines and lines of those ships of the desert, lying down, kneeling, standing; "and how strong they smell. One might fancy oneself in a menagerie."

"Yes; Hercules himself could not have kept that quarter clean; the Augean stables were nothing to it. But look at these fellows we are coming to now. You seem to be a bit of a military critic; what do you think of them, and how do you like their mounts?"

They were now passing a small camp on the further side of the mound they had crossed. Three rows of tents, and aligned with each on the reverse flank a line of horses picketed—small, almost ponies, thin in the flank, wiry, but extremely rough. There had been no pains taken in grooming them evidently. As for the men loafing or swaggering about, those who were fully dressed were so stuck all over with arms—pistols, swords, daggers—that one wondered if they were suddenly attacked what weapon they would have recourse to first, and if they would make up their minds in time.

"I am no critic at all," said Harry, laughing, "though every Englishman thinks he is a judge of horseflesh, and I fancy those might possess endurance, if not up to much weight. As for the men, they seem to fancy themselves more than the Egyptians; but a more villainous, bloodthirsty, thievish-looking set of scoundrels, it has never been my luck to see herded together."

"You are not far out," said Howard, laughing. "I should not like one of them to come across me if I were wounded and helpless, and had anything worth stealing about me, let me be friend or foe. But they are useful for scouting, and there are only three hundred of them. They are called Bashi-Bazooks, you know."

"Yes," said Harry; "from *Bash*, a head; *ba*, without; *zook*, brains. So called, as the 'Old Skekarry' said, because they live on their wits: *lucus a non lucendo.*"

"My dear fellow," remonstrated Howard, "have I come all this way from conventional England to the wilds of Africa to hear once more that dreadful quotation? Go on; give us *Sic vos non vobis*, and follow it up with *Tempora mutantur nos et mutamur in illis*, or any other little House-of-Commons delicacy; only don't say *et nos*, as some of the senators, who cannot, alas! be flogged for it, often do."

Harry apologised, and they now approached the English officers' quarters, the Egyptian flag marking that of the General commanding the expedition.

"Wait here a little," said Howard; "I will see if

the chief is disengaged and able to see you," and he entered the tent.

Harry sat down on a rude lounging chair he found just outside under the shade of a palm tree, and tried to reflect, not with any great success. He was thoroughly bewildered with the events of the morning, following the variations of hope and despondency produced by the near approach to the object of his journey, and then finding it elude him, which had occurred twice in the last few weeks. Without knowing it, he was becoming a practical fatalist, inclined to do what seemed best at the moment, and let things slide, forming no plans for a future which was so very uncertain. Not a bad state of mind this for a hot country, where worry of mind is especially trying. Perhaps that is why Asiatics encourage it so much.

It was not long before Howard came to the tent door and beckoned Harry in. On entering, he saw the General seated at a table covered with writing materials, finishing a despatch for which an orderly was waiting. He was dressed in a sort of loose tunic, with pantaloons and riding-boots, and the sword which trailed by the side of his chair was straight. A pith helmet stood on the table before him, and altogether he looked like an Englishman, and not at all like a Pasha, as from the name Harry somewhat absurdly expected.

Presently Hicks Pasha looked up, and Harry at once recognised one who is born for command. There was no mistaking the bright eye, which seemed to look *into* the man it rested upon; the firm and manly features, the *will* expressed in the strong nervous hand. But it is in vain to attempt to explain this, which at the same time everybody can understand. The schoolboy with his master, the soldier with his officer—every subordinate knows instinctively if it is of any use "trying it on." Not that he looked like one who would be harsh or tyrannical. On the contrary, his face was lit up by a courteous smile as Howard introduced his newly-found friend.

"Glad to see you," said the General, offering his hand. "The country is in a disturbed state for travellers, and I fear that you will hardly get out of it without some risk. The river is still open to Berber, and you might get across from there to Suakim. But I cannot promise to help you much."

"It is not my object to get out of the country at present," said Harry; "quite the reverse. I thought that perhaps you might be able to make use of me in some way, and wished to volunteer my services. I can make myself understood in Arabic, if that is any use."

"Well, we have an interpreter," replied Hicks Pasha. "If you had served we might be glad of you, but you are too young for that."

"I learned my drill as a volunteer," said Harry, "and I have been successful at Wimbledon as a shot."

"Well, but I cannot put you in the ranks with natives," said the General, laughing, "and I cannot take you about as a sort of animated machine-gun. Can you ride?"

"Yes," replied Harry, who indeed had a very fair seat on horseback.

"I might make use of you then to gallop for me, or to go out with the scouts, as you speak Arabic. Well, we will attach you as a volunteer cadet to a company *pro tem.*, at all events. An Englishman is always useful to control the fire in action. But you must understand I do not guarantee you any pay; we will put you on rations, and if your commission is made out and confirmed I will do my best to obtain arrears for you; but you must take your chance of all that."

Harry said that he quite understood, and only asked to be allowed to accompany the expedition to El Obeid in any capacity. And then the interview was over, and Harry left the tent, feeling quite as grateful as he had expressed himself, and glad also to serve under such a chief.

It is curious how little things turn our minds in one direction or the opposite. Twenty-four hours before, Harry Forsyth had no sympathy whatever with the Turks and Egyptians, while he thought the wild tribes of the Soudan fine fellows, and worthy of the independence they sought to establish. Indeed, he had seen too much of the shameless corruption and cruel extortion of Egyptian officials to feel differently.

And now, because he wanted to get to El Obeid on the chance of catching Daireh, and because English officers of position and experience commanded an Egyptian army, and the General of it had a "presence" which inspired him with confidence and respect, he was ready to take up arms in defence of a cause which had nothing, so far as he knew, to recommend it, except that a certain amount of civilisation, the wearing of trousers and petticoats, banking, railways, and steam navigation were on one side, and a very primitive mode of life with nudity, or getting on to it, on the other. True, that there is the question of the slave trade, and that iniquitous business is kept up entirely by the Arabs, but that very important matter had no weight at that time with Harry, who merely knew that the slaves he had met were almost as free and much better off than the Fellaheen or peasantry of Egypt.

"You must now come and make the acquaintance of my particular chief," said Howard, as they left. "You must know that I am an irregular volunteer like yourself; at least, my appointment as surgeon requires confirmation."

And so they went to the medical quarters, and Harry was introduced to the head of that department, who took a professional view of the advent of the new-comer, and observing that he was very young for the work before him, asked if he was acclimatised.

But when he learned that he had got through the hot season without any serious illness, he concluded that he had as good a chance of standing the campaign as any one. That same evening, Harry made acquaintance with the other English officers, to the company of one of whom he was next day posted in orders. And then came the matter of getting uniform, a horse, and a sword, which was accomplished at once, without much difficulty in the shops of Khartoum; and he found himself once more Europeanised.

There was no time for delay, as the expedition was to set out in a few days. The seniors received Harry kindly and cordially enough, but they were extremely hard worked, every man having to do the duty of ten. They were full of high spirits and confidence, however, sure of defeating the Mahdi, recapturing El Obeid, and conducting the campaign to a satisfactory conclusion, and the men caught a great deal of their spirit.

The mass of them had fought under Arabi at Tel-el-Kebir, and had there conceived a great idea of the prowess of their conquerors. English officers they imagined could not be defeated, and led by them they felt certain of victory. They were also much inspirited by the martial music with which the air was always filled. The bugle bands were really good, and some of the native airs lively and harmonious, but the constant beating of their tam-tams would have been somewhat trying to a nervous person, to whom quiet was the first condition of happiness.

Plenty was found for Harry to do, and as he showed zeal, alacrity, and intelligence, he soon became a favourite. "Send the young 'un" was often the decision come to when a matter requiring promptitude and gumption, and which the seniors could not well leave work in hand to attend to, had to be done. The great ambition of a subaltern in any capacity, civil or military, should be that his superior may learn to trust him; and Harry Forsyth succeeded in that.

He was happier now than he had been for a long time, for he was too much occupied with his new duties to worry about Daireh and the missing will. And if a shadow of melancholy came over him, it was when he thought of the cottage at Sheen, and the anxiety his mother and sister would be in on his behalf. He wrote a long letter home, giving an account of all his proceedings and his present occupation, and sent it off the day before the march across the desert commenced.

At length the camp was struck, and the army was on the march—7,000 infantry, 120 cuirassiers, 300 Bashi-Bazooks, and 30 guns with rocket battery. There were some 1,000 camp followers, and 6,000 camels and horses. At first the route of this seemingly never-ending cavalcade lay along the Nile bank.

Then it was committed to the desert. One hundred and eighty miles of trackless, parched waste lay between them and El Obeid. The first few days had indeed been weary work; the ground was full of broad, deep cracks, for it had been under water when the Nile rose, and on the river receding the fierce sun had had this effect upon the mud. Mimosa shrub also grew thickly in parts; and it was important that the men should not straggle, for that was the opportunity the Arabs were on the look-out for, and so many fearful disasters had already occurred from this very cause. For the soldiers, if the fierce children of the desert rushed upon them unexpectedly when they were in loose formation, were as helpless as sheep, though, when in a compact body, and under the immediate eyes of their English officers, they could fight steadily enough, as was proved at the battle of Marabia in the spring of that same year, when they inflicted very severe losses upon the Arabs, whom they totally defeated at little cost to themselves.

But though the march had been toilsome, the river was near at hand, and the worst enemy of the desert, *thirst*, was not to be dreaded. But now they were to leave the Nile behind them, and depend for their water supply entirely on the wells, which were understood to be at certain places on the line of march, though these were often found to be at much greater distances than had been represented.

The progress was very slow, for they had to march in square—the leading battalion in line, the rear also in line, the right and left faces moving in fours, or in column, according to circumstances. In the centre were the camels and other baggage animals, with the two things which were as necessary to existence as air to breathe—ammunition and water.

When, through inequality of ground or any other cause, the lines bulged, or the columns were broken, it was necessary to halt till all closed up again, and this of course delayed the march very much. Ten miles a day were the utmost they could accomplish without running most unjustifiable risk. The irregular cavalry now proved of extreme value; preceding the army, scattered out in front and on each flank, they were bound to come upon any ambushed enemy in time to gallop back and warn the main body, who would then be able to close up, and present a front on every side, which the enemy would find no opening to break in at.

On the fourth day, as the troops were passing over a plain of sand which stretched away to the horizon all round, without a shrub to break the monotony, only here and there a block of rock, or the skeleton of a camel, showing where some wretched overtried animal had sunk under the too great presumption upon his wonderful powers of endurance, the scouts gave notice of Arab approach, and a figure could be seen coming over the summit of a sand-hill, thus proving that the ground, though apparently flat, was undulating.

Field-glasses were turned towards the object, which could then be recognised as a man mounted on a camel, and the distance beyond him was eagerly scanned for the host of which he was assumed at first to be the precursor. But no one else appeared; he was quite alone, and he came directly towards the troops.

As he was well mounted, and they were moving to meet him, it was not long before he was quite close, and then it could be seen that he was dressed in robe and turban, with a shawl round his waist, and that these garments, as well as his face, were stained with blood. And he leaned forward on his camel, as if well-nigh exhausted with wounds and fatigue.

When the officer out with the scouts met and accosted him, he demanded to be led to the chief, and when he was accordingly brought before the General, he said—

"I am the Sheikh Moussa. Neither I nor any of my tribe have acknowledged the Mahdi, whom we hold to be a False Prophet and impostor. Whereupon he sent a body of troops to attack the village where seven families of us dwelt. They came at the rising of the moon, and set fire to our huts, but we flew to arms, and thrice drove them back, slaying two for one. But they were ten to one, and at each onset we were fewer and more weary. At last the fight turned to mere slaughter. I sought my dromedary and fled, in hopes of vengeance. They have slain my wife, my children, my slaves; there is a blood feud between the Mahdi and me. Then I remembered that the Turks led by Englishmen were at Khartoum, preparing for an attack upon my enemy, and I said, I will seek the English Turk, the Hicks Pasha, and I will say, 'I would be avenged upon my enemy, but I am alone, and what can one arm do? I have a sharp sword, I have a far-killing gun, I have a blood feud with your enemy. Let me fight in your ranks.' I rode part of a night, and a day, and a second night; I had only filled my water-bottle once. It ran dry; my wounds grew stiff. I said, 'I shall never reach Khartoum, I shall die unavenged. It is Allah's will; praise to Allah, and the One Prophet, for whom I am. When lo! the English-led Turk army has risen up and gone forth to meet me. It is Fate."

He had a drink of water given to him, and then the General asked him if he knew El Obeid well.

"Every street, every corner of the ramparts," he replied. "Did I not take part in the defence when the Mahdi—may his grave be defiled!—was driven from them with slaughter?"

"You may ride with us," said the General. "Look to his cuts, Howard," he added, seeing him close by, with a sponge and a bandage already in his hand.

It was a sparing drop of water that was used, and that was presently drunk with avidity, defiled as it was. Howard declared the cuts to be mere flesh wounds of no consequence.

"I am the most unlucky fellow that ever was!" he exclaimed; "I never do get any gunshot wounds, hardly."

The Sheikh Moussa certainly proved an acquisition that day, for he took them a route diverging somewhat from that which they had been following, and so cutting off some three miles of their journey to the wells where they were to halt till the moon was up. And three miles when the water is running low are a matter of tremendous import to the traveller in the desert. After that the General often sent for the Sheikh Moussa to ride with him on the march; and he questioned him, and compared his answers with the maps and plans he had. And the more he was tested the more genuine did the man appear. The tribe, too, to which he claimed to belong was known to be friendly, and not as yet overawed into owning allegiance to the Mahdi.

And so the square dragged slowly on from well to well through the long scorching mornings and the bright moonlight nights, and was swallowed up in the desert.

CHAPTER X.

SENT OUT SCOUTING.

It is one of the first principles of warfare that an army should always keep up communication with what is called its *base*, that is, the safe place from which food, ammunition, stores of all kinds, and fresh men to supply the place of those who fall, can be sent to it, and to which the sick and wounded may be returned. But as there is no universal rule in anything, and people have often to do what they can, rather than what they know to be best, it so happens that columns have sometimes to be launched into an enemy's country without any communication with seaport, town, or friendly frontier, so that they are entirely self-dependent, with no resources beyond what they have at hand, and liable to be attacked on all sides.

This is termed being "in the air," and is a very great risk, which is only voluntarily incurred for the sake of gaining some equally great advantage. In civilised warfare failure under such circumstances means surrender; in expeditions against barbarians it involves utter destruction.

Hicks Pasha's little army was now thus isolated, and, after several days' march across the desert, matters began to wear a very serious aspect. As has been said, ten miles a day were the utmost that could be accomplished, and the distance between the places where water could be obtained increased as they advanced.

Water was carried by camels in tanks with galvanised linings, which kept it fresh, and free from the nauseous taste which it gets from the skins in which travellers generally have to keep it. It is true that there is an earthenware water-bottle, which is in much request, and the inhabitants of a town on the Nile earn their livelihood by manufacturing them. But the porousness of the clay, which keeps the contents so deliciously cool, makes them very brittle.

In these tanks sufficient water could be carried for twenty-four hours, which meant at the present rate of marching but ten miles. There came an occasion when, at the end of the first day's halt from the last well, an order was given to put men and horses on a half ration of the precious fluid. Considering that the full ration was very insufficient, this caused much suffering, especially as, there being no moon, night marches were out of the question, and the parched troops had to toil through the sand in the mornings and evenings, though they were forced to rest and get what shelter they could in the hottest part of the day.

That night Harry was roused from a dream of plunging in the river at Harton, which, however, refused to cool or wet him, but seemed to turn to hot sand at his touch, by a shot and then a volley, a little in their front. He started to his feet and found Howard standing beside him.

"Some stupid mistake of a sentry, very likely," said he. But presently the outposts came running in with three of their number missing, and two others with slight spear wounds, and reported an attack of the enemy. The force stood to its arms at once, and as it bivouacked in square, in the order in which it marched, every man was in his place without delay or confusion, and there was no danger of surprise, and some of the men would keep firing uselessly into darkness, and it gave their officers some trouble to stop them. This was done, however, and the waste of ammunition was left to the Arabs, who kept up a dropping fire till dawn, wounding a poor camel by chance, but unable to do much damage by starlight from the distance at which they kept.

"No gunshot wounds for you at present," said Harry, when he rejoined the surgeon.

"I don't want any," replied Howard. "I could not attend to a poor fellow after treating him, in any satisfactory way, on the march, and without water. Do you know, I am tempted to drink the contents of my medicine bottles."

"Then you *must* be thirsty, poor fellow. But, I say, do you call this being under fire? There! something struck the ground which I fancy must have been a bullet."

"Yes; they are making very long shots, but as some of them get into our neighbourhood, I suppose one may be said to be so. Why?"

"Only because I have never been under fire before, and I expected to be in a funk."

"There is time enough; I daresay you will get a satisfactory test of your nerves before long. But courage is a comparative thing, depending very much upon circumstances. I, for example, am a non-combatant, and though I have little dread of infectious diseases, which many heroes would shrink from risking contact with, I hold all lethal weapons in strong dislike. And yet, if there were a barrel of beer in front, though it were guarded by the best shots in Boer land, I would have a fight for it."

"I should think you would!" cried Harry. "Beer! How can you be so cruel as to mention the word?"

But though the Arab fusillade was almost innocuous, it harassed the troops, keeping them on the alert all night. And when, with the first streaks of dawn, the dreary march began, all traces of the foe had disappeared. All the morning dragged along, till fatigue and the heat of the sun compelled the mid-day halt. Then forward again till dark; and no wells reached! Hardly a drop of water left for each man! Several had dropped and died in the course of that day's march, and several horses. The bugle bands, which had been so cheery in the start, were silent now; the poor fellows were too parched to blow their instruments. Even the tam-tams were silent. Not that either would have been prudent, for though, doubtless, they were never lost sight of by the enemy's scouts, there was no advantage in publishing their whereabouts.

Harry was on outpost duty that night, and when the firing was renewed, which happened soon after dark (though no enemy had been sighted all day), he, not being hard pressed, would not withdraw his men. The stars were very bright, and objects were distinguishable at about thirty yards distance; perhaps further by Harry, who was particularly clear of vision, that being the reason, possibly, of his fine shooting. The Arabs got closer to the rocks, amongst which the outpost was situated, with sentries at intervals connecting it with the square. Harry felt savage with thirst, fatigue, and this aggravating annoyance, and was strongly tempted to try and make an example. He took a rifle from one of his men, and began stalking carefully in the direction of the flashes; not directly towards them, of course, which would have been trying to meet the bullets, but on the flank.

Crouching down under a sand ridge, he got pretty close, crawled a little nearer on his hands and knees, and peered forwards. There was a flash and a report quite near to him, and then Harry could plainly distinguish the man kneeling up, withdrawing the old cartridge from his Remington. He levelled his rifle, but could not see the fore-sight, so as to align it with the object. For a moment he was nonplussed, but suddenly remembered having read of a dodge for night shooting, and resolved to try it.

He had in his pocket a small box of matches, and, taking one of these, he broke the end off and rubbed in on the fore-sight very gently, careful not to let it explode, and succeeded in making the little projection so luminous that he could align it with the back-sight and the Arab's body. Then he pulled the trigger, and saw the dark figure leap forward and fall prone. Saw it, indeed, but only in a fraction of a second, for he stole back to the sand ridge, slipping in another cartridge as he went.

There he lay still a minute, listening and peering. Presently a tall figure, which looked gigantic in the dim light, bounded close to him, with a gun in his left hand, and a spear in his right. He had evidently made a rush in the direction of the flash, and now stood, looking right and left for the man who had fired. Harry almost touched him as he pressed the trigger, and the savage lay at his very feet. "I'll have his spoils any way," thought he; so he picked up the spear and Remington, and got back to his men as fast as he could. The Arab scouts, bothered by these two shots, were probably uncertain about the movements of the troops, and thought they had shifted their ground since they had marked them down, and possibly had flanking parties who might surround them. For they withdrew to a distance, fired a few shots in the direction where Harry *had been*, which was quite away from the main body, and the outpost too, and then gave no more trouble for that night.

In the course of the next day the water gave out entirely, and there was not a drop in the army beyond what some few far-seeing, self-denying men, had hoarded in their gourds.

Harry had not been one of these, and when the mid-day halt came he thought he was dying, and fell down in the glare of the sun, senseless. When he returned to life he found himself under the scanty shade of a mimosa tree, supported by the strong arm of a man whose sun-burned face and flowing beard, the loose robe which he wore, and the silk scarf which surrounded his tarboosh, with the pistol and dagger thrust into a shawl round his waist, seemed to betoken a native of the country; but the kindly eyes were those of an Englishman, as were the murmured words, "Poor lad! poor lad!" which fell on his ear. His brow was deliciously cool, and his throat less parched; and he recognised that it was the man whose wonderful journey to Merv had so enthralled him when he read of it who had now spared the water, which was life, to damp his brow and give him respite; and he was certain that it was Mr. O'Donovan, the newspaper correspondent, now accompanying the army of Hicks Pasha, who had saved his life.

Howard, who came up at the moment, was almost awe-struck at the sacrifice.

"I have known one man allow his veins to be drained to supply the life-blood which might be infused into the veins of his friend; but what was that to sparing water *now!*" he said.

The patience and discipline of the men during this trying time were admirable; there was no grumbling, no repining against their leaders; and just fancy how the sturdy Briton would have growled!

The officers did their best to cheer them up, assuring them that they were certain to reach the wells that afternoon, and always bearing an air of confidence in the future before them. But when they were alone together, and looked into each other's eyes, it was evident that they thought they were in a very desperate position.

However, let them reach and carry El Obeid without too great delay, and all would yet be right. Their assurance to the men concerning the wells was verified; and when they approached the mud-holes which bore that name, discipline for once broke down. First the Bashi-Bazooks urged their fainting steeds to a gallop; then the infantry broke from their ranks and hurried forward; and had the enemy come down in force at that moment, they would have had an easy prey. But, oh horror! the puddles were choked with the putrefying bodies of men, horses, and camels, who, wounded in a recent fight near the spot, had crawled hither to drink, and die.

Thirst, however, overcame disgust; the contaminating carcases were dragged away, and many plunged their faces in the filthy pools. Others had the self-control to dig or scrape holes for themselves, and wait till a purer water had percolated into them, when they slowly satisfied themselves and their faithful horses, and then managed to collect a supply for the next march.

Wonderful was the effect of the water, when at last a sufficiency for all had trickled out. The musicians found their instruments, and played once more; the outposts stepped off to their stations with alacrity; and all felt as if El Obeid had already fallen.

But several days' more terrible marching, with insufficient water, and many a death from sheer hardships, fatigue, or sunstroke, were to elapse before they neared the fortress. At last, however, the time came when, on starting at dawn, the guide assured the General that he should see the sun set behind its walls. After four hours' march one of the senior officers called Harry.

"You and your nag look pretty fit," he said; "that comes of being a light weight. Is your water-bottle full?"

"Yes," replied Harry; "I have not touched it since we left the last wells."

"That is right; I want you to take six men out scouting. You see that rocky hill, with trees, out to the north?"

"Yes."

"The General wants to know if the enemy are behind there in any force. Go cautiously; and if you see no one, pass through the wood, and have a look on the other side of the hill; you can see from here that it cannot be very extensive on the top. But if you find Arabs in the cover, try to draw them; and if you succeed, and they are in force, come back at once. But should they keep in cover, so that you cannot tell whether there are half a dozen or a considerable body, skirt round the hill, and see if there is any sign of a camp, or a large body of the enemy concealed by it. Be cautious, so as not to get cut off. I have selected six of the best mounted Bashi-Bazooks, in case you have to make a bolt for it. Of course, you see the importance of knowing what we have in our rear before attacking the place."

"All right, sir," said Harry; and in another minute he was trotting across the plain, followed by his six picturesque, irregular horsemen.

Of course he did not go fast, as it was most important to reserve the powers of the animal that carried him for the emergency of having to gallop for his life, which it was not at all improbable that he would be called upon to do; but half an hour's steady trot, the ground being fairly free from obstacles, and not so yielding as usual, brought the party to the foot of the hill.

Harry ordered his men to extend, and they threaded their way among the rocks in a line, working cautiously up towards the belt of trees. When they were within a hundred yards, however, a couple of shots were fired from the cover, and the bullets came pattering against the rocks.

Harry had impressed upon the men beforehand what to do in such a case: to retire slowly, halting to return the fire at intervals; and they did it pretty fairly, though not quite so steadily as could be wished. And when they were down on the level plain, a couple of them showed a decided inclination to try the mettle of their steeds in a race in the direction of the column, but Harry managed to stop them; and, withdrawing a little, the party dismounted, and fired a few ineffective shots at the Arabs, who were mounted, and came down towards them.

There were but eight in the party, and Harry could see no more behind them, so he concluded that it was clearly his duty to skirt the hill and see what was on the other side. Besides, seven to eight was not such prodigious odds as to justify bolting without a bit of a fight, he thought.

So he got his men together, and, drawing his sword, told them he meant to charge the moment the Arabs were at the bottom of the hill, so as to overthrow them by the impetus before they could get any pace on, and trotting quietly on with this object, he got within thirty paces, and then, cramming his spurs in, went at them as they got clear of the declivity. And he showed good judgment, in spite of his inexperience; for he bowled one enemy over with the force of the shock, and a Bashi-Bazook on his right served another the same, and got a slice at him as he rolled over, which made the number of combatants level.

But, unfortunately, the other Bashi-Bazooks did not charge home, but swerved, wheeled, withdrew a little, and began firing wildly. Harry was engaged in single combat with another Arab, who could have given him any number of points in sword-play, and presently made a drawing cut at him which would infallibly have taken off his head, had not his horse at that very quarter of a second suddenly fallen, shot dead by one of his own men.

Seeing their officer down, the Bashi-Bazooks fairly turned and galloped as hard as they could go, the Arabs who were otherwise disengaged racing after them—five pursuing six; for the man who had been ridden down had got a broken thigh, the second was killed, and the third was now dismounting in order to polish off Harry comfortably as he lay on the ground.

But our friend, though he was pinned down by the body of his horse, which lay on his left leg, was not hurt, and his right arm was free. He drew his revolver, and when the Arab stood over him he shot him in the breast. The man fell—but not dead—across Harry, with whom he grappled, seeking to clutch him with the left hand by the throat and sabre him with the right. But Harry caught his right wrist, and a struggle took place, in which each strained every muscle.

In his efforts, Harry got his leg from under the dead horse, the sand being loose; but as he did so his enemy got his sword-arm free and cut him over the head—not with much force, for he was weak and in a cramped position, but sufficiently to inflict a nasty wound. It was an expiring effort; he fell over helpless, the blood gushing from his mouth, and Harry had no need to give him another barrel, which he was prepared to do, but rose to his feet to survey the scene of conflict. The Bashi-Bazooks and their pursuers could be seen in the distance, still going at a great pace. The horses of the broken-legged and the two dead Arabs were careering about; his own head-dress had fallen off, which was a serious affair, though the afternoon was waning.

But before putting it on he bound his head with a strip of cotton torn off the garment of the Arab at his feet, for the cut on the scalp was bleeding freely. Then, feeling very thirsty, he took the man's water-bottle, but it was empty. So, picking up his sword, he moved over to the other dead Arab and tried his, and with better success; there was a refreshing draught in it, which Harry was thus able to benefit by without infringing on his own supply. Then he considered that he must get out of sight somewhere before the Arabs returned, which they were sure to do, to look after their missing friends. He had now no horse, and to make his way on foot across the open plain by daylight was to ensure being seen by the returning horsemen and cut off.

The best place to hide in would surely be the wood, where he felt certain that there were no more Arabs, or they would have come out to join in the chevy. He would lie there till nightfall, and then endeavour to make his way to the column, though he did not feel like taking a long walk just at present.

As he was going up the hill, however, he saw the Arab with the broken leg lying helpless. The string which held his water-bottle had broken, and the gourd lay beyond his reach. The man glared like a wild beast when Harry picked it up, and clutched at his waistband, but there was no weapon in it.

"Don't fear me," said Harry in Arabic, holding out the gourd, which the other snatched viciously; "I am an Englishman, and the English never hit a foe when he is down, unless he is very obstinate and unreasonable, and insists on biting or kicking."

But the wounded man made no reply. It is to be feared that he only thought either that the speaker was a great liar, or else that his countrymen were great fools. It was evident that, so far from being touched, he would be the first to betray the secret of Harry's hiding-place to his returning friends if he knew it. So as Harry did not like to shoot him through the head, or draw his sword across his throat, he made a detour as if going across the desert, and did not commence the ascent until he was out of the other's sight. It was not very steep or very high, but Harry had some difficulty in getting up it. He felt very weak, giddy, and queer, and had hardly got to the wood, and sunk down under the shade of trees behind a big black boulder, than he lost consciousness, for he had bled more than he knew for, and it was that which turned him faint.

How long he lay without consciousness he did not know; and I daresay that you have noticed in story-books that people never *do* know. Indeed, it would take a very methodical person to look at his watch just as he was going off in a swoon, and refer to it again as he came to. Harry Forsyth certainly never looked at his watch, but he snatched his water-bottle, for one effect of loss of blood is to cause intense thirst. A quantity of liquid being taken out of the body, Nature seems to point out in this way that the loss should be supplied; you know she is said to abhor a vacuum. If he had had all his senses about him, he would merely have taken a sup and held it in his mouth some time before swallowing it; but he was half dazed, and did not know where he was, and he yielded to the instinct of thirst and took a long, deep draught. For the present it was the best thing he could have done, for the effect was that he sank into a sound restoring sleep, which must have lasted many hours, for when he woke again the night was far advanced, and there were streaks of dawn in the east, and it was quite two hours to sunset when he had begun his nap. The wound in his head smarted, but otherwise he felt stronger and more refreshed, only hungry. He had crammed some biscuits into his kharkee jacket the day before, and these he ate, washing them down with what remained in the water-bottle, which he emptied without much compunction, as he reckoned that he would easily strike the trail of the column and come up with it in a short time.

They had reckoned before he left that it was three hours' march at the longest to the wells within sight of El Obeid, where they were to halt for the night, and he thought that he surely ought to be able to walk, alone and unencumbered, at least as fast again as the square moved, and he had little fear of not being in time for the attack. The place could hardly be carried by a *coup de main;* they would have to breach the walls with artillery first. Of course he might be cut off on his road; that was a risk which could not be helped or avoided.

Directly he could see his way, he retraced his steps down the hill, and went round the base to the side where he had had the skirmish; but he did not look to see whether the dead Arabs had been buried by their comrades, or to inquire after the welfare of his friend, the enemy with the broken leg. No, he stole along that part as quietly as he could.

The orange, purple, violet, old gold flashes shone wider and higher, but the only way in which Harry heeded them was by keeping the point, at which it was evident from the intensity of glory that the sun would rise, at his back, for he knew that El Obeid lay due west of his present position. It was true that he had a compass attached to his watch chain, but for some unknown cause the thing had struck work a fortnight back, and now the black half, which ought always to have turned to the north, perversely remained where you choose to place it. But, after all, the sun in the morning and evening, and the polar star at night, will put you somewhere in the right direction, *when you can see them.*

As for hitting off the exact track by which he had come on leaving the column, he could no more do that than on the sea, for there were no marks to guide the eye, and the surface of the plain was the same as water. One dead camel's skeleton is uncommonly like another, and they lay about in various directions, showing that caravans converged to or diverged from El Obeid by different routes. When the sun burst forth with all that inconceivable grandeur which drives artists who visit the country to despair, and causes untravelled gazers on their pictures to accuse them of exaggeration, when their efforts have as a fact fallen far short of the reality, Harry's eyes scanned the horizon in every direction for an enemy, but he was alone on the sandy expanse.

No! what were those black figures moving along the side of yonder dune? His hand went to the butt of his revolver as he saw them. But he was presently reassured; they were only vultures and eagles overgorged by the fruits of war; the only beings besides wolves and hyænas, who pluck them.

CHAPTER XI.

A GLIMPSE AT A TRAGEDY.

As the power of the sun increased, Harry Forsyth found that his renewed strength was but partial, and though considerable compared to his weakness before that long sleep, was by no means up to his powers twenty-four hours previously, before he got that cut down through his scalp and lost all that blood. And soon the thirst began; but thirst was his familiar now, and he had learned to bear it as we do what is constantly recurring and inevitable.

But as time passed on the thought would intrude upon his mind. Was he going in the right direction? El Obeid, indeed, must lie to the west, if the guides were to be depended upon, but would not the General diverge very likely on approaching the place? It could not be told beforehand from what side he would find it best to attack it, and Harry might be going quite away from his friends. Still, if he once caught a glimpse of the town, he should feel fresh confidence, for then he would certainly get round to the army, somehow, and in time for the attack. But this last consideration was not so important a matter with him as it had been some hours before. He did not feel particularly keen after fighting just now. A beefsteak and a pot of porter, and then to turn into a comfortable bed, with a lump of ice on the top of his head, would have formed his programme of perfect bliss. And yet, if his friends were in the thick of it, he would like to be there, and take his share in what was going, too.

Pshaw! he must not get nervous, he said to himself. Unless the guides were treacherous, he must sight the minarets of El Obeid soon *Unless the guides were treacherous!* Was there a chance of that? Experience showed that there was always. And that professed friendly sheikh, who had come in with his scratches and told such a plausible tale, was he to be trusted?

Hark! What was that? Dropping shots away to his right front. Again, others; and now a volley; more single shots, increasing to a continuous roll of musketry.

"They are at it, and I am not there!" Harry cried aloud, as, forgetting fatigue, weakness, even thirst, he pressed forward in the direction of the firing. What surprised him most was that he heard no report of the Krupp guns, no whish of rockets, no continuous grinding of machine guns. Why did they not use their artillery?

Half an hour brought him to rocks, herbage, and palm trees, and here were empty preserved meat cans and other *débris*, showing that the force had bivouacked there the night before. And here, too, deep down in a rocky dell, he found a well of clear, bright, sweet, cool water! He flung himself down, plunged his face in the delicious liquid, and sucked in large draughts of the life-inspiring elixir. When he could drink no more he filled his water-bottle, and then, removing his pith helmet, he unbound the bandage which he had tied over his head. It had of course stuck, and the attempt to remove it was painful, but by wetting it freely he got it off, and then bathed his head and face, saturated his pocket handkerchief, and tied that on as a fresh bandage.

Then, much refreshed, he again hastened forwards, guided by the sound of the still continued firing. The character of the country was now completely changed. It became hilly, and the hills were precipitous and covered with inky black rocks, which lay so thickly about that it seemed as if a shower of enormous aerolites had fallen there.

Harry threaded his way amongst these, some way up a ravine, which wound to the right. The firing now seemed quite close; indeed, he could see smoke floating up to the clear sky. But surely El Obeid could not be there, in the middle of a mountain pass, commanded on all sides by higher ground! The army must surely have been attacked on the march.

He turned a corner, from which the valley ran for some distance straight, and came suddenly on volumes of smoke, pierced by incessant flashes of fire, not a thousand yards in his front, while every now and then a spent bullet came pattering against the rock behind which he crouched, trying to make out whether those nearest him were friends or foes.

Firing was also going on from the higher ground to right and left, and one or two of these points were visible from Harry's present position. He had no field-glass, but he carried a small pocket telescope of great power, and adjusting this, and holding it steadily with some difficulty against the rock side, for the field of vision was very small, and his hand shook with excitement, he made out that the men holding these were certainly Arabs.

And presently some wounded men of those engaged in the valley to his front falling to the rear, and coming within five hundred yards of him, and clear of the smoke, he perceived that they were Arabs too. And then the fearful truth broke upon him. The spent bullets which fell towards him came from his friends. The army had been enticed into the defile, round which the Mahdi's troops were posted. When it was hopelessly entangled, a body of Arabs, which had lain in ambush for the purpose, had closed in upon their rear to cut off retreat, and these were the men now in front of him.

Though he felt convinced that this must be the state of the case, Harry did not give up all hope that the Egyptians might fight their way through, though with severe loss, to the other end of the defile, and to ascertain this he went back, and then began mounting the higher ground, trying to work round to the front of the position. This he had to do very cautiously, to avoid falling in with groups of Arabs, whom he was perpetually sighting. Indeed, to get near the edge of the rocks commanding the defile without being observed was impossible, but by making a wide detour he kept clear of them. And thus, after the lapse of some hours, and with occasional difficult climbing, he reached a lofty point, from which he could distinguish the sides of the ravine held by the Arabs and the pall of smoke which covered the doomed square, fighting like a lion at bay, surrounded by the hunters.

For eagerly as he searched with his telescope in every direction he could perceive no line of advance or retreat; every point appeared to be barred by the enemy. There seemed to him only one hope; if General Hicks could hold on till nightfall, perhaps he might push through backwards or forwards under cover of the darkness.

So the hours passed, and the fusillade did not

cease; only slackened at times to burst out again, till the sun sank down in all his glory, and the heavenly splendour of the after-glow bathed the sky, just as if all on earth was peace, goodwill, and happiness, and men had ceased to strain all the powers and talents which the God of Mercy has bestowed upon them for their mutual benefit to one another's destruction; then sudden darkness, and silence broken only at long intervals by a fitful splutter of musketry.

Harry had marked a little cave, where two boulders leaned together, and into this he now crept, for the air was cold. Here he lay, thinking with agony of his friends below there. How many were now living, and what chance had they of getting clear if they had survived thus far?

And his own position, was that any better? Nay, they indeed would die fighting, but he would either probably perish of want, or be barbarously murdered in cold blood. He still wore his uncle the sheikh's ring on his finger, and carried the silver case containing the parchment in his breast, but since he had thrown in his lot with the Egyptian army, his faith in those talismans had become weakened. Why, he did not know; it was an illogical feeling, for, of course, the circumstances had not altered. Probably it was because it is impossible to trust to two diametrically opposite sources of aid at the same time.

Then his thoughts wandered to home, and his mother and sister, and their terrible anxiety at his long silence, and how they would not know whether or not to mourn him as dead. And then he dropped asleep.

He woke at dawn, wondering how he could have slept when his comrades were in such sore straits.

Had they got away? In answer to his thought, the firing recommenced as before, and in the same quarter, answering " No ! "

All day long the noise of battle lasted, and Harry watched in vain for a change in the situation.

At one period a body of Arabs came up and crossed the mountain from his rear, and he only just had time to conceal himself in his rocky hole to escape observation.

But they pushed on, and went down into the fight; doubtless carrying ammunition. How Harry got through that long day he could not remember. He made his water-bottle last, but he had no food beyond one biscuit. But anxiety for some time prevented his feeling hungry There seemed no change in the situation, except that the volume of fire diminished perceptibly ; and the cloud of smoke becoming thinner, he could, from one point, just distinguish something of the square. It was still existing, then, and might, perhaps, cut through that night, though it had failed to do so on the preceding.

When darkness fell, Harry crept back to his hole, and again he slept. But he awoke before dawn, roused by the cravings of hunger. It was of no use to stop where he was, and at the first glimpse of daylight he commenced his descent towards the plain, not by the way he had come, but on the opposite side, in the direction he calculated the remains of the army must take if they succeeded in pushing through.

At the foot of the hill, in a rocky, barren-looking dell, not at all the place where you would expect to find it, he chanced upon a spring; and after drinking and replenishing his gourd, he sat down to try and collect his thoughts.

And as he sat there he saw a solitary figure coming towards the spot. It was a camel, with an Arab on his back. Harry concealed himself behind a boulder and watched. The poor beast could hardly move, and, in spite of all urging, presently fell. The rider took certain articles from the saddle, and came to the spring, where he sat down, after drinking; and, pulling out a lump of bread, began to make his breakfast. The sight made Harry feel ravenous; he was determined that he would have a share of that bread. He would probably have been justified in potting him with his pistol, which he might easily have done, for he was almost certainly a hostile Arab with despatches. But he might belong to a friendly tribe, and if he were an enemy, Harry could not murder him like that.

He had a Remington rifle, so Harry must pounce upon him, or he would not have a chance. He did it rather cleverly, and the meal of the Arab was suddenly interrupted by finding the muzzle of a revolver within a yard of his head, while, at the same time, his rifle, which rested against a rock beside him, was thrown to some distance.

"Throw away your sword and pistol, or I will shoot," said Harry. "But do that, and share your bread with me, and I will not hurt you."

"My hygeen is dead; I am weary and wounded; and the chance is yours," said the Arab. "What have I to do but to submit? It is fate," drawing his highly ornamented and damascened pistols from his waist-band, for he was a considerably dressed Arab, this one. These he laid aside; then he took out his sheathed scimitar, but appeared to hesitate.

"How do I know," he said, "that you will not kill me when I am completely disarmed?"

"Why should I?" replied Harry. "Could I not have shot you from behind the rock?"

"Fool you were, not to!" cried the Arab with the bound of a wild beast, springing up, flashing the blade out, and uttering the taunt, which in his own idiom was but a couple of words, simultaneously.

So quick and sudden was the movement that it might well have deceived the eye and paralysed the nerve. But the very start made Harry press the trigger with his forefinger. Even so, and only a yard off, he was as likely to have fired over his shoulder as to have hit him. But he did not. The point of the scimitar just left the scabbard as the owner of it went down on his back motionless as a wax figure.

Harry was perfectly bewildered; he was not conscious of having fired; yet, there lay the Arab, with his face blackened with the powder, and a small hole in the forehead just between the eyes.

I hope you will not think the worse of Harry Forsyth for what he did next. War makes the feelings very callous, for the time being, at all events, with regard to certain things. Besides, Harry had had nothing but biscuits to eat for one hundred and seventy-two hours, about, and not many of them. He pounced upon the bread and devoured it. What to do next?

The conviction had now forced itself upon him that there was no hope for the Egyptian army, but that it was doomed to certain destruction. There was no possibility of surrender; it was war to the knife, for the Arabs neither took nor gave quarter. And thus his mind reverted to the object of his throwing in his lot with that body, which he had in a great measure lost sight of in the company of Howard and the excitement of a totally new life. But, after all, he had not come out to Egypt and the Soudan to fight, but to discover Daireh and, if possible, gain possession of the will.

The only chance for him to accomplish this now was obviously through finding his uncle, the Sheikh Burrachee, and to do this he must follow the course he had pointed out: find a dervish or fakir, and show the ring and parchment. Of course the efficacy of these might all be the delusion of a crazy brain, but he must take his chance of that. It was certain, however, that he would never get the chance of a hearing in his present costume. The helmet, the uniform karkee jacket, would insure his being shot or cut down by the first follower of the Mahdi who saw him. They must be discarded, and the dead Arab lying hard by would supply him with a disguise. For, instead of going nearly naked, like so many of them, this man had a smart turban and a long garment, which came a good bit below the knees, bound round his waist with a sort of shawl of gay colours.

So, after having taken his life and his breakfast, Harry now proceeded to despoil him of his clothes.

There was a fair supply of cartridges in a bag which the ill-fated Arab had worn over his shoulder, so Harry took that and the rifle, and presently he came out of the glen in complete Arab costume, his European clothes being made into a bundle and shoved under a rock. The only article of dress he had retained was a light linen waistcoat, in which were pockets containing the silver case with the parchment, his watch, and his money. The dead man's pistols, though ornamental, had flint locks and were heavy, so he left them, but the scimitar he stuck, together with his own revolver, in the waist-shawl, and the rifle he slung over his shoulder.

Then he went to the hygeen, or camel, hoping that water might revive it, but the poor beast was past that—its eyes were already glazing.

All this time the roll of musketry in the distant ravine still continued, and with a heavy heart he turned from the spot, and went out into the wilderness.

His idea was boldly to accost the first living being he met, and ask the way to El Obeid, intending to represent himself as a merchant whose caravan had been attacked and robbed by Nubian blacks. He knew that he would be recognised as a European by his speech, and probably arrested as a spy, but then would be the time to test the efficacy of his uncle's talisman. It might be inefficacious, or he might perish in the desert before he met any one, but he did not give up all hope of a better fate. His being sent out on that scouting expedition, wounded, and so prevented from rejoining the ill-fated column, was so extraordinary that he felt that his hour was not yet come. For it almost seemed to him as if a miracle had been performed in his behalf.

He had not gone a hundred yards before he noticed several black specks in the distant sky. Nearer and larger they came, till he could distinguish two eagles and five vultures hovering lower and lower, till at length they settled down in the dell by the spring which he had just left. And he shuddered. How soon he might lie, helpless and dying, and watching these loathsome birds of prey swooping towards him!

His idea was to keep bearing to the west, which was the direction in which he knew that El Obeid lay, unless indeed he had passed to one side of it, which he did not think probable, or he should most likely have seen it from the mountain-top. Any other high ground he came to he would ascend, so as to get as wide a view as possible. And so he tramped on towards the declining sun till it sank; then he lay down in the solitude and darkness, and fatigue gave him sleep.

When dawn awoke him he was beyond the sound of the firing, or else it had ceased. And though he knew well enough that this was no good sign, the silence was less harrowing. He resumed his weary march till the sun reached its full power. There were some stunted bushes a little out of his track, and he made for them, hoping to find water. In this he was disappointed; so taking a sparing pull at his water-bottle, he crawled under one of them, seeking its shade. There was a slight rustle, and a snake rose on its tail, and darted at him with its forked tongue, but, just missing him, glided away.

Harry then looked more carefully, but there was no other, and he rested. Another escape! Did he, then, bear a charmed life? After about an hour, he grew restless. The sand in that part lay in high ridges or dunes, some of them at least a hundred feet high, and he hoped that on surmounting the next beyond him he would come in sight of the town, or at least of some oasis, with water and human habitations, and with each recurring disappointment he became only the more eager to reach the sand-hill beyond. But he was becoming very faint, and the wound in his head throbbed to agony. He was at last so "*beat*" that he was on the point of letting himself sink down on the sand to struggle no more, when suddenly there, straight before him, lay the object of his desires! Surely not a mile off, but say a mile and a half, rose towers, fortifications, minarets, palm-trees, and, most grateful sight, all this was reflected in a broad clear sheet of water.

"El Obeid!" he cried aloud, forgetting everything else in the joy of the moment.

He had never heard that it was on a lake, and thus his wildest expectations were surpassed.

No need now to torture himself by refraining from his water-bottle. He seized and drained it, and then falling on his knees he thanked Heaven for this deliverance. For though, when considered calmly at a distance, he had recognised the perils which would attend his adventure in entering the place, which was now the headquarters of the Mahdi and his fanatics, they seemed as nothing compared with the immediate prospect of perishing of want and thirst, alone, in the desert. Rising to his feet again he hurried onwards, but the place was much farther off than it had first seemed, for when he had gone on for a full twenty minutes, with speed inspired by hope, he seemed to be no whit nearer.

On again, plunging through the loose sand, reeling, staggering. A little more effort; he must be nearing it, though it did not seem so; another ten minutes, say, and he would be able to plunge into that delicious water! And so he fought on, when suddenly all vanished.

He rubbed his eyes and looked again. Had sudden blindness fallen upon him? No, he could see the sand-hills as plainly as possible. But the city, the fortifications, the minarets, the water, which were so distinct a minute ago, where were they? All turned to sand? That could not be. He was giddy, and must have altered his course without knowing it.

He looked all round him, bewildered. Sand, sand, sand, and nothing else. Then the truth flashed across his memory: the mirage! Towers and water were as unreal as the magician's money in the "Arabian Nights' Entertainments," which turned to paper in the drawer where it was. For the first time Harry was stricken with utter despair; without water, without food, alone in the trackless desert, exposed to a fierce sun, he fell, and lay motionless for awhile. Then up and on blindly, in what direction he knew not. His tongue swelled; his throat seemed choked and breathing was difficult.

Soon he lost consciousness of everything but a sense of distress and pain; and after awhile even that left him, and he fell senseless.

CHAPTER XII.

ABDUL ACHMET.

A BODY of twenty Arab warriors mounted on camels was crossing the desert, and as they rode in Indian file, and from ten to twenty paces apart, the string was a long one. Probably they did not belong to a tribe that had taken part in any of the numerous routs, assaults on strong places, and massacres, which had supplied so large a portion of the Mahdi's troops with modern arms of precision, for those of them who carried guns had those long-barrelled, short-stocked weapons, which are familiar to us in pictures, and which are so admirable from an artistic, and so worthless from the Wimbledonian, point of view. But the majority carried spears instead of guns, and they were all armed with swords and pistols.

Whatever the actual number of days and hours which elapse between the dates of an Arab's birth and death, his life seems a short one reckoned by sensations and incidents, for he spends so very large a proportion of it in sitting on the hump of a camel as it toils across a country of maddening sameness. The distances he has to travel are so vast, and his means of progression so limited!

Perhaps that is the reason why, when he does come across an occasion of excitement, he is so terribly in earnest. He is months and months without the chance of an emotion, accumulating explosive forces all the while; and when he at last goes off, he does it like dynamite.

And yet, perhaps, the child of the desert, if he visited our shores, might point to a ploughboy plodding up and down, with one foot in the furrow, from dawn till dusk, and ask if *his* task were lively. Or, still more forcibly, he might take us into an office in a dingy city street where copying clerks sat at their monotonous work, and put it to us how many minutes in the week we supposed *they* lived.

But still, though it might be difficult to deny that he had reason on his side, there is a certain dreariness about the endless sandy plains which renders it difficult to imagine it possible for a human being to spend his days in traversing them without going mad.

But these present travellers did not seem to mind it. Some of them solaced themselves with the chibouque, as they sat with the comfort which can only be acquired after years of practice on the humps of their camels; the others, though silent and quiescent, did not look bored.

Presently the one in front was attracted by an object a little out of his path, and turned to examine it more closely. Then he spoke to his hygeen, which knelt down, whereupon he dismounted, and went up to the figure of a man lying on the sand. There had been a great deal of fighting and carnage, beyond the ordinary blood-feuds between the different tribes, going on for some months in the country, and the bodies of men were as commonly found as those of camels used to be. So it may seem surprising that the Arab should have taken the trouble to dismount for such a trifle.

But this body was dressed, and had weapons—was worth despoiling, in fact. This particular child of the desert was not more greedy than others; he was a man in some authority, and rich according to his own ideas and those of his people. But still, one does not like to see articles of value unappropriated, and one might as well have them as any one else. Such sentiments might animate you or me, let alone a gentleman who had been brought up to regard all human beings who did not belong to his own particular set much as we look upon beavers, foxes, hares, grouse, pheasants, as creatures that are provided by Providence for our sport or profit.

The body lay on its breast with the arms stretched out; the head a little turned, so that the right cheek lay on the sand. And when the Arab bent over it, it did not look, he thought, quite dead. Well, if he were not, a man with such a good gun as that ought to be when a better man wants it. But still, it has been shrewdly observed that there is a deal that is human about human nature. The Arab might not improbably be in the same position some day, and would he not then require aid himself? And then the Koran enjoined true believers to succour the distressed who fell fainting in the desert; and this was an educated man, who read his Koran; and a religious man, according to his lights, who obeyed its precepts when he happened to remember them, and temptation to the contrary was not too strong. If he had known that the property before him belonged to a pig who did not believe the Prophet, it might have been different; but he could not tell that, and he turned Harry Forsyth over to give him a drink of water.

As he did so he saw the ring on his finger, and his humane intention vacillated. He had a fancy for a ring like that. Never mind; he would compromise matters, he thought—take the ring, rifle, and cartridges first, and give him a drink afterwards. But when he took the hand for the purpose of drawing the ring off it, and saw the stone close, he started back with the exclamation, "Allah is great!" and let the hand drop.

"He bears the signet!" he said to his followers; "and he lives. We must not leave him. We must take him on to El Obeid."

"The Fakir's Oasis is close at hand," said another; "let us bear him there. The holy man will know best what to do with him, and the shorter the journey the better for his life."

"You speak the words of wisdom, Meouf," said the leader; "let us lift him on to your camel; it has the easiest pace."

A cynic might imagine that Meouf knew this, and that his claims to being a good Samaritan were affected by the fact that he would have the trouble of carrying the helpless man, and his wish to do so for as short a distance as possible. But we won't be cynics, and we'll give him all the credit for his forethought which we can.

The Fakir's Oasis was less than an hour's ride off for a good camel. Harry, when some water was poured down his throat, showed decided signs of life, though not regaining consciousness. He was lifted on the camel, and carried forward, his property being scrupulously respected with one exception. The leader of the party considered that, as he was an invalid, and therefore, for the time being, a non-combatant, he could have no immediate use for a Remington rifle, or the cartridges belonging to it, and these he therefore made free to borrow for an indefinite period. It was a small fee for him to pay, after all, for his life.

The oasis they were taking him to was one not known to European travellers, and indeed but few native merchants were aware of its existence, for it was out of the usual caravan routes to El Obeid, from which place it was not more than two hours' journey distant. It was a little patch of fertility in the midst of a plain of undulating sand, and appeared a hundred-fold more luxuriant from the contrast. There was actual herbage on which some goats were feeding; a small patch was even under cultivation, and corn grown there. Fine acacias lent a grateful shade, but not equal to that afforded by a splendid fig-tree which overhung a deep cool well.

The oasis received its name from its having long been the residence of a fakir who was accounted a sort of prophet, and commanded great reverence. His successor, Abdul Achmet, who now lived there, was also in high esteem among the followers of the Mahdi, to whose cause he had given his adherence.

There were three houses, all inhabited by priests or dervishes, of whom Abdul was the chief, and a small mosque, all built of sun-dried bricks, which, retaining the look of clay, are habitually termed by European travellers *mud*. But this gives rather a false impression, as a mud hut properly consists of wattles with mud plastered all over them, which is a different thing from one regularly built, though the bricks are sun-dried instead of being baked in a kiln. What is the use of having a tropical sun if you do not make it do some fire-work for you beyond nearly roasting you to death?

Abdul Achmet received the party, several of whom he knew, under the shade of his fig-tree. Harry Forsyth was carefully handed down from the camel and laid before the dervish, and the signet-ring was shown to him. Whereupon he said that it was quite right to bring him on to him, and that he would take care of him; and he had him carried into his house and attended to.

The travellers watered themselves and their camels, and were then treated to dates, pipes, and coffee. They rested thus in the oasis, and benefited, it is to be hoped, by the companionship of their clerical entertainers, till the hottest part of the day was passed, and then, once more mounting their camels, went on their way to El Obeid—an easy march for the evening.

Days passed before Harry Forsyth was conscious of anything; then for weeks he had no sense of life but pain and weariness, with intervals of blissful rest. He had no doctor but the first lady who ever practised —Dame Nature, who sometimes, strange to say, pulls her patients through almost as well as if she had a diploma. But he was well nursed, and there is a great deal in that.

At length there came a time when he knew that people moved about and talked, and that he took food and was very weak; but he did not know where he was, nor cared. He had visions, and half knew they were visions; sometimes these were rather pleasant but more often very much the other way. What was the matter with him? As no medical man diagnosed his case, it is impossible to say, though that he was for some time in a high state of fever we may safely assume. He had gone through a good deal, and had had a cut through the scalp of his head right down to the skull. At last he woke one day after a long sleep and recognised his nurse, whom he took to be a demon—a very nice, amiable one, with gleaming white teeth, who grinned from ear to ear with pleasure to see him better.

At last it dawned upon him that it was absurd to suppose an evil spirit would sit there fanning the flies away, or would put cooling drinks to his lips; and he jumped abruptly to the opposite conclusion, that there were such things as black angels, and this was one of them. Though perhaps nearer the mark, he was not quite right yet, for his kind and careful nurse was but a negress — a slave from the interior. Black, white, or brown, women are always more patient and tender when anything is really the matter than men, bless them!

It was rather a shame to have called her Fatima, because that leads one to expect rather prettier lips and a fairer complexion; not that this incongruity ever struck Harry, even when he came to know it, which was not for some time yet. For by that time he had come to associate his nurse's homely features with all that was pleasant and solacing.

He did not know where he was, nor had he any clear perception of past events. He had been very uncomfortable, and there was a dim impression upon his mind of past misfortunes, but he had no care or curiosity with regard to past or future; he was at ease for the present, and that was all that he felt signified.

One day when he opened his eyes after a doze, expecting to see Fatima, he found in her usual place a tall man, with a long white beard, and shaggy white eyebrows, which contrasted curiously with his dark skin, giving him something of an unearthly appearance.

"Oh, long-expected one," he said, when he saw that Harry noticed him, "to whom Allah hath at length restored some degree of understanding, know that you are welcome and among friends. This writing found upon you tells me that you are he of whom the Sheikh Burrachee has often spoken, the Feringhee destined to bring his benighted and hitherto accursed race to the acceptance of the true faith. The sheikh is beyond Om Delgal, far away up the Bahr el Abiad, amongst the heathen whom the All-bountiful One has given to the True Believer for bondsmen. But he will return when the Mahdi—his name be revered—shall need his services. Then shall you join him with renewed health and strength. In the meantime, I, a humble servant of Allah and his Prophet, and one whose eyes have been opened to the divine mission of the Mahdi, which the Turks—may their tongues swell—are slow to receive, even I will expound to you the mysteries of the only True Faith, and from this day forth consider my house, and what poor goods I may possess, as your own."

Harry Forsyth quite followed this speech, and knew that the Sheikh Burrachee alluded to was a relative whom he had seen at some time, and was to rejoin. For anything recalled to him by words he remembered at the time, though it passed from his brain the moment afterwards, neither pleasing him nor distressing him. His mind was like a lake, and ideas suggested in any way resembled clouds passing rapidly above it, reflected for a minute on the surface, and then gone. It was rather a curious thing that what Arabic he had picked up had not passed from him; on the contrary, it sounded more familiar to him than it had done before. Probably that was because of his surroundings at the time of recovering consciousness, and of Arabic being the first sound which fell on his ears.

He replied coherently enough to his fakir host, though his voice was very feeble. He thanked him for his present hospitality, and for the care he had taken of him during his illness, and he expressed the pleasure it would give him to see the Sheikh Burrachee when he came back from the Equator.

And then Fatima brought him food, which he turned to like a baby to its bottle.

From that day Abdul Achmet paid him constant and long visits, reading long passages from the Koran, and expounding to him that, as Mahomet had been sent to convert idolaters, and had accomplished his task, so now the Mahdi had been appointed to teach the truth to Europeans and other civilised races. The means to be employed were the same in both cases, and were simple, consisting merely of the extermination of all who would not be convinced.

"The great and indeed only object is the overthrow of infidelity," he explained; "and if all infidels are killed there will no longer be such a thing."

"Q. E. D.," replied Harry Forsyth, in a tone of assent which pleased the fakir mightily.

"Q. E. D." was not intelligible to him, but it sounded very well indeed, he thought.

Sometimes Harry listened to these long tirades, and sometimes he did not, the latter reception of them being very much more frequent than the former. But he looked politely attentive, and that was sufficient. He was the best listener when Abdul Achmet entered into personal details concerning his heroes, in which he occasionally indulged; as when he told how the Mahdi was brought up as a carpenter at Dongola; how he first came to know of his mission; of the holy men who had taken up his cause; and of his residence and education amongst them. And then he described his miraculous success, and what a boon even in the present life the spread of his authority would be. In proof of which he recounted the extortions and cruelties of the Turks, and how the taxation of the Soudanese was so excessive as to ruin the country itself, while the bribes exacted by the officials who were appointed to rule the country made it impossible to obtain justice. He also waxed very indignant over the unnatural folly and wickedness of those Powers who sought to interfere with the slave trade, which he looked upon as a perquisite provided by Providence for the Arab race. Indeed the fakir showed himself to be a man of some thought and shrewdness, and some people to hear him speak might have fancied that secular interests, such as improving their condition in life by throwing off a burdensome yoke, and maintaining the considerable profits which they derived from imposing such yokes on other people, who happened to be black and to have thick lips, and woolly hair, had something to do with the aptitude shown by the Soudanese to accept the new religion. But Abdul Achmet was an honest fanatic, and neither intended to insinuate this nor thought it.

On the whole, Harry much preferred to hear his black nurse Fatima talk. She told him about her childhood, when she remembered playing about among trees and in long grass with other little darkies; and their fright when they heard the lions roar; and how once, when she had wandered away alone, she saw two fiery eyes glaring at her from a bush, and ran home, expecting to be pounced upon and eaten all the way. And she described her parents' hut, with a low entrance, into which the family had to crawl on their hands and knees. Then, while she was still quite little, her tribe declared war against another tribe, and all the young men went out to battle, and were defeated, and fled back to their village to make a last stand in defence of their wives and children. And she described a night attack, and the horrors of a massacre, the burning of the huts, and the carrying off of the younger women, the youths, and children; how they were sold to Arab merchants, and underwent a fearful desert march; and how she cried for her mother at first, but was bought by a man who treated her kindly, and was happy, and forgot her native language and habits. All this she told in a simple, artless way, and when she found that it amused her invalid she repeated it again and again. But his interest did not flag for the repetition. He was like a little child who has a favourite story, and cries, "Again!" when told it, preferring it to risking a new one, which might not prove so good.

And time flew by, and Harry Forsyth remained in this state of semi-imbecility, free from anxiety about his mother and sister at home, forgetful of all but his animal comforts and the superficial interest he felt in such prattle as this. His bodily health improved before his mental activity; perhaps it was owing to the freedom from worry consequent upon this lethargic state of mind that he was able to pick up some strength.

But he became able to move about and help himself, and wander out to the fig-tree over the well, which the delighted Fatima thought extremely clever of him.

One day, as he sat in his favourite spot, thinking of nothing in particular, a body of horsemen rode up to the oasis, and the leader of it dismounting came up to him, and held out his hand English fashion, though he spoke in Arabic.

"Harry," he said, using the English accent for the name, however, "you remember me?"

Harry looked at him in a troubled way, and pressed his hand on his forehead.

"I told you that you would come to me, for the inward voice, which never errs, declared it to me," he went on. "Struggle as you might, you could not avert your destiny. Our family is called to do a great work. I have commenced it, and it will be yours to complete it. I am growing old, but I can still strike a blow for the cause. May Allah grant me to die when my right arm is powerless: to die on the field of battle, in the moment of victory, with my face to the foe! Yes, you are clearly destined to lead the hosts of Islam. Have you not come out to me alone, leaving home and friends? Have you not traversed the desert without guide, still alone; and though struck down by an unknown hand, have we not met? Have you not miraculously learned the language of the country to which destiny called you? Were you not brought when found, to all appearance dead, to the fakir, Abdul Achmet, the one man of all others I would have directed you to? And the blind fools of Europe would call this chance, as they do everything which they cannot attribute to their own forethought or cunning."

"Yes, I know you," said Harry, at length; "you are my uncle Ralph, the Sheikh Burrachee. But I think I have been ill, and everything is like a dream to me. Were there not a signet-ring, and a paper in a silver case, and jewels of value which you gave me?"

At that instant Abdul Achmet came out of the mosque, and the Sheikh Burrachee advanced to meet him, leaving Harry more bewildered and disturbed in mind than he had been since he was brought to the oasis; and that night he had a relapse of fever. It did not prove serious, however, and when it passed away his mind was clearer than before, though he still seemed like one in a dream, and the past events of his life appeared to him as having happened to some one else.

On the morning after his arrival the Sheikh Burrachee left, but some weeks afterwards he returned with an escort and an easy-paced hygeen to take Harry away with him. He took the announcement of the journey with the placid indifference which now characterised him, only at the moment of starting he showed reluctance to part from his black nurse, Fatima. But whether the sheikh bought her, or only borrowed her, it was arranged that she should go too, and Harry was perfectly reconciled. The hygeen's motions were wonderfully smooth for a camel, and the journey was made easy to him; but still it was trying in his weak state and after so long a confinement.

But it did not last long, and then they reached a town of flat-roofed houses, and entered a spacious courtyard with a portico round it, through which were the living-rooms. There were soldiers here and there under this portico, some of them wearing the turban, but the majority having a skull-cap of blue and white on their heads, and a sentry over the gate had one of them too. Those who wore the bernouse, and most of them did, had similar blue and white patches sewn on different parts of it. These were the Mahdi's colours; I don't know why, for he was never a Third Trinity man, and had no right to their blazer. Like his impudence! It is true that the colours were generally in dice, not regularly striped. Some of the soldiers did not show the colours, but that was because they had nothing to put them on unless they painted their bodies. Passing through a large room with a divan round it, and pushing aside a curtain at the farther end, you came upon another and smaller court, which was a garden with a fountain in the middle, well filled with date and other palms. There was a portico round this too, and this was destined to be the place where Harry Forsyth was to pass the greater part of his life for some time, for it was the dwelling or private part of his uncle's establishment.

Crazy renegade as he was, the Sheikh Burrachee had some old ideas of comfort which the wild life he had led had not dissipated, and being a rich man for the country where he was and the people he had adopted, he could indulge any little fancies he had; and he had made his house both handsome and comfortable.

According to the simple ideas of the natives, indeed, he was possessed of enormous wealth, and this reputation went some way towards the superstitious regard in which he was held. This was the place which Harry now entered, and reposing on a divan, low, with soft cushions on it, and close to the portico, he looked upon the green leaves and listened to the trickle of the fountain, while Fatima brought him a glass of delicious lemonade, squeezed from the fresh-plucked fruit; and the fatigues of the journey were forgotten, and he fell into a long and refreshing sleep. His curiosity, however, had not been one whit aroused; he took everything as a matter of course. Perhaps he was a character in the " Arabian Nights," and not Harry Forsyth at all—who could tell?—all seemed so strange and unreal.

CHAPTER XIII.

AN UNEXPECTED MEETING.

GRADUALLY Harry Forsyth came back to real life, as it were. First of all he had an uneasy feeling that something was wrong, but he wanted a word or an event to strike the key-note of his memory. His uncle never spoke of home matters; he was kind, and even affectionate, but was much away. He would come out into the large courtyard in the early morning, mount the horse which was held ready for him with an activity worthy of a much younger man, and scour off at a gallop with a troop of his wild retainers racing behind him. He might come back that evening, or not for a week.

And when he was at home he was very busy, seeing different people, who came and went in a great hurry, and writing despatches, which mounted orderlies, or what answered for such, were always in waiting to carry. And when they were together he talked of the wild life of the desert; of the sport to be had further up in the Black Country, but never of England.

He spoke Arabic always, even when they were alone, and never lapsed into his native tongue. Yet his face and the tone of his voice disturbed Harry, causing him to make an effort to get his mind clear.

At length, one morning he awoke with a distinct remembrance of his mother and sister, and the knowledge that he was far away from them in a foreign land, and had not had any communication with them for a long time. And he felt a strong desire to relieve their anxiety, and let them know he was alive, and also to have news of them. But he could not remember what he had come to this part of the world for.

He knew that he had wanted to trace his uncle; but why? He had come out to Egypt in the service of a firm of merchants, and the name of the head of it was Williams; he was confident so far. But had he not returned home since then? And why had he sought out his uncle? Surely not on business connected with the firm, and certainly not because he had turned Mohammedan and wanted to live like an ostrich.

A little longer, and his connection with Hicks Pasha's force, and the disastrous termination of that expedition, came clearly back to him; and with it the necessity of keeping silent about the matter, for he now wanted to get away to a civilised place like Cairo, at all events, if not to England. For though he did not know that the British Government had taken up the Egyptian quarrel, and that war had actually been waged between them and the Soudanese in the neighbourhood of the Red Sea, he knew that an officer of the late expedition would be looked upon with suspicion, if not treated as an open enemy.

Neither was he sure how his uncle would bear the disappointment if he found out that he had been in the ranks of his enemies—the Egyptians. Though he need not have worried himself about that, for the Sheikh Burrachee would only have thought it the method which Destiny had taken to bring him to him.

As Forsyth's mind grew sounder his body kept

pace with it, and he was able at last to mount a horse and take short rides; and it amused him to saunter about the bazaar occasionally, though it was not a very extensive or grand one; indeed, the poet who wrote " Man wants but little here below," would have been pleased to see how completely an Arab, as a rule, verifies his theory.

One day he (Harry, not the poet) was puzzled by some round balls of a frothy appearance, which he could not make out; could it possibly be soap? What sale could there be for such an article? The shopman might just as well have offered straps and stay-laces to the population around him. But it did not smell like soap, either; indeed, the odour was extremely unpleasant.

"That is not an object worthy of your attention," said the owner of the shop, who sat on a cushion in the midst of his goods. " I have a preparation for the hair which is infallible for restoring it if it falls off from age or sickness, for example, and which is as agreeable to the nose as beneficial to the scalp. Those balls of mutton fat are only fit for the poor who can afford no better."

"Oh, it is for the hair, then," observed Harry; "and what makes it look all frothy like that?"

"It is prepared by chewing, and women are employed for the purpose; they cheat me sometimes, and swallow a portion. But deign to come up, oh illustrious one, and partake of a cup of coffee or a glass of sherbet and a chibouque, and allow me the unparalleled and illustrious honour of showing you my poor goods."

Harry consented, not that he wanted to purchase anything, but because something about the man's face struck him as familiar, and he was anxious to remember where and under what circumstances he had seen him before.

"I have here a French pistol, a revolver with six chambers, which I can offer your Excellency almost for nothing, with ammunition to match. It is a weapon which will save your life a hundred times by its accuracy and the rapidity of its fire; and what says the wise man? 'Life is sweet, even to the bravest.'" And all the time he was talking, Harry Forsyth kept thinking, "Where have I seen him? What circumstance does his face recall?"

As he left the shop his eye fell on a bale of goods yet unopened, and on it he read the name DAIREH!

It acted like a match on a gas-jet. He had come out to seek the will, and Daireh was the man who had abstracted it!

And as he walked home, he remembered everything which had been a puzzle to him. Being still weak, he now grew as much excited as before he had been apathetic, and had his uncle been at home he would have gone to him with the whole story at once. But the sheikh was away, superintending the drill of certain European ruffians in the Mahdi's service who were to man some Krupp guns taken from the Egyptians, and Harry had a forced respite in which to collect his ideas and frame them in the manner best calculated to gain his uncle's attention and assistance.

And now his anxiety about those at home who had no doubt long mourned him as dead grew more poignant, and remembering his uncle's affection for his sister, he regretted not having confided in him and begged him to get a letter conveyed to some point sufficiently civilised to have a post. He tried to find out from Fatima how long he had been laid up at the fakir's residence, and at first she was puzzled. But at last she gave him a clue.

"The Nile had risen and gone back," she said, "when you were brought to us as dead. It rose again, and fell again, and now it will soon rise once more."

Two years! Was it possible? Nearly two years! And he wondered whether his people had gone into mourning for him, or if they still hoped on. He next made inquiries about Daireh, setting Fatima to gossip for him and tell him the result. He seemed to bear a shockingly bad character, and to be very unpopular. The fact was that he was a money-lender, and his extortions caused him to be hated.

Harry was glad of this, since it promised to make his task easier.

The Sheikh Burrachee returned, and was rejoiced to find his nephew so much improved in health.

Harry took the first opportunity of opening his budget.

"Do you mind my speaking to you in English?" he said. "I have got to say things which I should find it difficult to explain in a foreign language, which I have very imperfectly picked up, and which may not have idioms answering to the English."

"I do not love the English tongue," said the sheikh, using it, however. "But what things do you allude to?"

"Family matters, affecting my mother and all of us—you, perhaps."

"When I last went to England," said the sheikh, "I took a final farewell of all relatives, and of everything belonging to the country from which I shook off the dust on my feet, you only excepted, for I saw that you, too, were called out of the seething hot-bed of corruption, which is called civilisation, to the natural life of man. Why disturb the ashes of the buried past?"

"I love my mother," replied Harry; "and you, her brother, once loved her too."

His uncle bowed his head. "True," he said; "speak on."

"And besides," added Harry, "justice is justice all the world over, and crime should not prosper. Richard Burke, your brother, died at his home in Ireland. He had made two wills, one leaving the bulk of his fortune to his step-son, Stephen Philipson, and another, and later one, made on the occasion of Philipson turning out badly, leaving him a modest allowance, and bequeathing the bulk of his fortune between his sister and Reginald Kavanagh. This will, which would make my mother and Beatrice comfortable, as they have been brought up to esteem comfort, was not to be found; neither was the other. A dishonest clerk, forced to fly the country because a forgery he had committed must soon be discovered, stole them both out of the lawyer's office where he was employed, for the purpose of levying a sum for giving them to one or the other of the parties interested. But the police were too close on his traces, and he had to fly without a chance of making use of either document. He was an Egyptian, and went home; but not feeling safe at Alexandria or Cairo, and having connections in the Soudan, he came to this country. If both wills are destroyed, part of the property comes to you."

"And the cause has need of funds!" exclaimed the sheikh. "But how shall we find this dog?"

"I saw him the other day in the bazaar; his name is Daireh."

"Daireh, the money-lender, against whom I have had so many complaints, but who always manages to have the law on his side?"

"The very same."

The Sheikh Burrachee clapped his hands; an attendant came. "Bring hither Daireh, the Egyptian usurer," said the sheikh; "and keep him guarded in the outer court."

The Arab inclined his head and departed without a word.

It may seem to you that Harry Forsyth had recovered his wits very rapidly, and this, indeed, was the case. Up to a certain point his progress had been very slow, but that once passed he had come to himself almost at a bound. But as for his clear statement to his uncle, that he had prepared beforehand with great care, writing it out and learning it by heart, feeling that it was necessary to be as concise as possible.

A thoughtful expression came over the Sheikh Burrachee's face, quite different from the wild faraway look which now ordinarily characterised it.

"And so Richard is dead," he murmured to himself; "and Mary has known poverty in a land where there is no kindness for the poor; where all is hard and cold, and people can no longer love or even hate. And this fellow has robbed her. By my beard he shall smart for it!"

When the sheikh swore by his beard the matter was serious, and if Daireh had heard him he would not have walked along between the guards who arrested him with so impudent an air. He had so often been had up, and had got the best of his accusers, that he felt quite safe. For he knew well the customs which had the force of laws in the country, and took care not to violate them, though straining every point to his advantage. And the Sheikh Burrachee was just, and however much he might sympathise with the complainant, would not allow his judgment to be affected by his feelings.

It was indeed a rough-and-ready justice, not always consistent, and such as would not meet entire approval from any civilised persons; he went on the principle that when he could not do what he would, he did what he could, to set things straight according to his judgment and the evidence before him, adopting the habits of the people with whom he had identified himself, who had not the horror of physical pain—for others—or the employment of it to elicit truth, which we have.

He rose from the divan by the garden where he had been sitting with Harry, and, beckoning to the latter to follow him, proceeded to the outer and larger hall, where he took his seat, with his nephew at his side. And hardly had he done so when Daireh was brought in. He salaamed with a confident air, which expressed, "Who will find me tripping? It would take a clever fellow to do that. They are willing enough to agree to my terms when they want to borrow, but when I claim my own, there is all this bother and outcry, and I am dragged before the sheikh forsooth!"

But he looked more serious when the Sheikh Burrachee said to him—

"Daireh, where are the two wills you stole from Barrows and Fagan, the Dublin lawyers, when you ran away from their employ?"

Surely such an incongruous question was never put in an Arab town in the heart of Africa by a sheikh dressed in bernouse and turban, with a jewel-hilted yataghan at his side, sitting cross-legged on a cushion. No wonder Daireh was flabbergastered; such a thunderbolt out of a clear sky has seldom fallen upon any man.

"Your Mightiness is mistaken," he stammered. "I have lived, earning an honest livelihood as a poor merchant, at Khartoum and Berber, Alexandria and Cairo. But what is Dublin? I know it not."

"Is that your photograph?" asked Harry Forsyth, suddenly, in English.

"No!" replied Daireh, startled into answering in the same language; and the moment he did so he could have bitten his tongue out for vexation.

The sheikh took the likeness in his hand; it was unmistakable.

"Here is your portrait, and it was taken in Dublin, for it bears that name upon it. Also you know English," he said.

"I learned that language at Alexandria," replied Daireh, more firmly now he had collected his wits; "and I had a brother very like me who went beyond the seas, and may have lived in the place you speak of, for I never heard of him again."

"You speak the words of Sheytan, the father of lies," said the sheikh sternly; "where are the stolen documents?"

"I never heard of them, your Justice; and I know

not what you mean," replied Daireh, striving, but with indifferent success, not to tremble.

"Hassan!" called the sheikh, and a tall, stalwart black stepped forward, with a courbash in his hand. "Twenty lashes to refresh his memory."

"Mercy, great sheikh; oh, favourite of Allah, have mercy, and listen to me!" cried the wretch; but without heeding his cries four men seized him and flung him on the ground face downwards. Two held his legs, one his arms, and a third put a knee on his back between the shoulder-blades to keep him in position. It was all done in a twinkling.

Then Hassan stepped up, courbash in hand, and measured his distance. The courbash is a fearful whip made of hippopotamus' hide, a stroke from which is felt by a bullock as painfully as a cut from an ordinary whip is by a horse.

It whistled through the air, and came down upon the naked flesh of the victim, who screamed with the pain as if he would break a blood-vessel. The wild men in the hall gathered round, their eyes sparkling and their teeth gleaming with enjoyment and laughter. It was good fun to them to see any one flogged, but a money-lender and extortioner, that the punishment should fall upon such an one, was indeed a treat! And Daireh too was particularly disliked. Then the currish way in which he took his licking added to the sport. The little civilisation they had was very superficial, and did not go nearly deep enough to repress the instinct of cruelty.

Another and another lash, and the fellow's howls, yells, and cries for pity were hardly human, but seemed rather those of some powerful spirit in pain. Harry felt quite faint and sick, and looked down so as not to see what was going on. But he could not close his ears, unfortunately, and he counted the strokes, longing for them to be over. He feared being mastered by his feelings, and pleading for the wretch, so displaying a compassion which would be considered by the Arabs as a most despicable weakness, and it was part of his plan now to gain their respect, and appear to enter into his uncle's plans.

No, it served the rascal right; let him have that, and more too. Only he had rather not be present. Eighteen, nineteen, twenty. The screams subsided into a whimpering and wailing, and when Harry looked up he saw Daireh on his feet again, his eyes bloodshot, and his features convulsed with pain and terror.

"Where are the wills you stole?" asked the Sheikh Burrachee, unconcernedly, as if nothing had occurred since he last put the question.

"They are at my house, your Mightiness; send some one with me, and I will give them up."

"I rejoice that your memory has returned; it is one of the choicest gifts of Allah," said the sheikh. "Go with him and get the papers, and bring them back with the prisoner."

"A bad speculation from the first!" reflected Daireh, as he was escorted through the streets, his woe-begone appearance and gingerly gait exciting much mirth and mockery amongst the juvenile population. "I wish I had left the accursed wills alone. And what son of Sheytan is this who has traced them, and had my likeness in his pocket? A detective? No; no English policeman would win upon this mad fool of a sheikh—may the vultures tear his heart out while he is still alive—to treat him like a son. He must be one of the parties interested in the last will. What wretched luck that I did not meet him in a fair way, and make a proper agreement with him! But it is too late for that now. If I could only be revenged upon him, upon all of them—sheikh, torturer, mocking demons, and all! Ugh, how sore I am! If it were but all over! but I fear they may torment me further. I had almost sooner they took my head off at once rather than put me to more of that agony. But no; I hope they won't do that either. There is a remedy for every evil but death." With these reflections, fears, and impotent rages tormenting him, Daireh reached his house, and from a box, which contained what he had of most value, produced the required documents which had cost Harry Forsyth so much anxiety, toil, and suffering to come at. He was strongly tempted to destroy them, and so glean some little vengeance; but the certainty of perishing in fearful pain if he did so deterred him, and when he was brought back, he delivered them to the sheikh, wrapped in the oilskin in which he had carried them about him until he had a fixed residence where he could deposit them in tolerable security.

"Are these the right wills?" asked the Sheikh Burrachee, handing them to Harry.

"I think so," replied the latter, as he looked them over and examined the signatures; "indeed, I feel certain that they are."

"Then," said the sheikh, "since after all it was but infidels, and not true believers, that this rascal robbed, the justice of the case will perhaps be met by fifty lashes of the courbash, those he has already received being allowed to count. Dog!" he added, indignantly, as Daireh, flinging himself on the ground, wallowed, gasping and crying for mercy, "tempt me not, if you are wise, to treat you according to your deserts, but know that you are treated with extreme leniency."

And so saying he rose and withdrew to the inner garden court, whither his nephew gladly followed him, and here they refreshed themselves with pipes and coffee.

But the screams of the miserable felon told with what energy Hassan was performing his duty, and Harry thought the punishment would never be over. If it seemed long to him, you may be certain Daireh thought it an age, and indeed he believed that mortal endurance had reached the acme of suffering, and that one more stroke must drive the soul from the body, some time before the last had cut into his palpitating flesh.

But it takes a good deal to kill, and when all was over he was alive, though unable to stand, and when spurned from the courtyard into the street, managed to crawl and drag himself home, where he obtained the draught of water, the want of which had been his chief torment since the stripes ended.

"And now we have recovered the will, uncle, how are we to send it to my mother?" asked Harry when the distracting cries extracted by the courbash had ceased. "The old one I will destroy, as should have been done before. The money will add to her comfort, but news that I am alive and with you will make her happier still."

This last was a skilful touch, and, I fear, Harry was becoming a bit of a cheat. For, though tidings of her son's own safety would undoubtedly be the best news Mrs. Forsyth could receive, the fact that he was domiciled with her crazy brother would as certainly not add to her satisfaction.

"Keep it safely for the present," said the sheikh, after smoking some time in thoughtful deliberation; "we shall find a method of transmitting it. Great events will occur soon. The authority of the Mahdi being established in the Soudan, we shall sweep Egypt like the simoom, and Cairo and Alexandria once in our hands, we shall find no difficulty in communicating with Europe. Or, perhaps, it may be done more quickly by Suakim, should the forces of the Mahdi's lieutenant, Osman Digna, recover from their check," he added, musing and thinking aloud rather than addressing his nephew.

Harry longed to ask what check, but it was part of his newly-formed system not to ask questions or show curiosity, but yield himself passively to the course of events, and watch his opportunity. For the same reason he would not propose taking the will home himself, feeling certain that so obvious a course would be suggested by his uncle himself if he could feel it was practicable. But it was evident what he was driving at now; as his nephew picked up health and strength he began asking him about his connection with the volunteers, and whether he had paid attention to the theory as well as the practice of shooting.

And though Harry pretended not to understand, and parried the questions as well as he could, he saw very well that he wanted him to take an active part in the training of Soudanese soldiers in the use of the Remington rifles which had fallen into their hands.

For never in the history of war had a nation been armed so completely by its enemies. The Egyptians sent out armies with weapons of precision and improved artillery, and they fortified towns, where they massed vast stores of ammunition, suited to both rifles and guns. The soldiers of the Mahdi rushed upon their feeble foes with sword and spear, totally annihilated army after army, and collected the rifles. Then they took the towns and possessed themselves of the cartridges. Napoleon the Great used to say that war should support war; but this was going a step further, and making war supply the means of waging war. The only drawback was this, that the more elaborate the weapons which you put into a soldier's hands, the more skill he requires to use them effectively; and this skill can only be acquired by proper training.

But the Mahdi had never taken the precaution to send any officers to Hythe, and amongst the miraculous powers which he was said by some of his followers to possess, that of creating ready-made musketry instructors was apparently not included. The consequence was that his men were extremely bad shots, and wasted their ammunition in an almost incredible manner. What mischief they were enabled to do, especially with the artillery, was principally owing to the lessons they received from European scoundrels who had been forced to fly from their own countries by their crimes, or reckless adventurers who did not care for cause, nationality, or anything else, so long as they were where fighting and a chance of plunder was going on—men who would have made most excellent mediæval heroes, and would have had a good chance of living in song and story had they not been born a few centuries too late.

Amongst all these the Sheikh Burrachee was an

exception. He was a genuine crack-brained enthusiast, sane and even shrewd enough in many things, but quite crazy upon certain points. Convinced, to begin with, that it was the duty of every Irishman to hate the English, he had imaginary private wrongs of his own to avenge. On the top of all that, he had become a thorough Mohammedan in his sympathetic feelings and habits, and quite sincere in his adoption of the cause of the Mahdi. The appearance of England in the field, which would have caused many to hesitate, was a spur to his enthusiasm, since it offered him an opportunity of having it out with the foes of his predilection,

Harry Forsyth had no idea whatever that England had engaged in hostilities in the Soudan. When he last had any information, she was firmly determined to do nothing of the kind, but to let the Egyptian Government get out of the difficulty in the best way they could. Indeed, it was the last thing he would have guessed. But still he knew well enough that English interests were firmly bound up in Egyptian, since any disturbance of the Government at Cairo might endanger the route to India, and therefore that to assist in any way the enemies of Egypt was to act indirectly against his own country; and he was determined to be of no use, even if he made believe to espouse the cause which his uncle had made his own. And this he suspected more and more he would have to do, if he was to get an opportunity of leaving the country.

His uncle had hinted at an impending advance upon Egypt; if he could join that, and once reach the Nile, surely he would find some opportunity of slipping down the river, and joining the Egyptian troops, who would receive a relic of Hicks Pasha's army with open arms. Then he would get to Cairo, and find friends to assist him to reach England with the will in his pocket.

He did not fear that the Arabs would be able to penetrate far into Egypt proper, for there were probably some English troops still at Cairo, and more would be sent there on the first intimation of danger. The will, by-the-by, had now taken the place which the parchment given to him by his uncle had formerly held, and he seldom laid it aside, not knowing what might happen from day to day.

His health, meantime, became re-established, and he grew rapidly stronger, while his mind was perfectly clear now. At times, indeed, he had violent neuralgic headaches, but these recurred less and less frequently, and he had every prospect of soon losing all ill effects of that wound in his head.

But the stronger and better he became, the more restless he grew. The only amusement he had to pass the time in was riding. He had always been very fond of horses, and now he had a good choice, and as the two he had fancied most had not been often backed, they took some riding; and that was exercise and amusement both. But the bits and the saddles were not to his fancy: the former too severe; the latter heavy, with high peaks before and behind. But one cannot have everything, and he was grateful to be able once more to sit a horse and enjoy a gallop at all. And to watch the wild cavalry at their exercises on a broad plain outside the town was a pretty sight, though it seemed to him that their performances were too much of the circus order.

"Can the English dragoons or hussars do anything

like that?" the Sheikh Burrachee asked him one day, when they were together watching a body of horsemen who were supposed to be skirmishing.

They pulled up their horses to a dead halt from a gallop with their cruel bits; went, not over the head, as it seemed they must, but under the body of the animal; fired a shot from that position, and remounted anyhow—one by the neck, another over the tail; a third ran alongside his horse for some way, using him as cover, and then vaulted on his back without checking the pace.

Harry was bound to confess that, to the best of his belief, no British regiment, light or heavy, could rival such equestrian gymnastics.

"No," said the sheikh; "they learn to stick on while the horse keeps his footing, but these cannot be thrown; for should the horse fall, even, he jumps at once to the ground."

"But surely he must reach it head or shoulder first sometimes," objected Harry.

"No," replied his uncle; "he turns a somersault and alights on his feet. The European is as far behind the Asiatic in horsemanship as in everything else which is manly and not demoniac. The use of the sword, for example. The dragoon has a straight weapon, with which he is taught to cut or thrust. If he does the former, and the blow is not parried, he may knock his opponent down, but he seldom inflicts a dangerous wound. If he gives point, he may kill his man indeed, but his weapon will often become so entangled that he is for some time unable to free it, and he remains defenceless against another attack. But with his curved blade of temper, which will not shiver and which takes a razor's edge, the warrior of the East neither strikes nor gives point, but presents the half-moon-shaped sword at his opponent, holding it still if galloping, pushing it forward if motionless, and will so slice off limb or head, or cut deep into the body, without useless expenditure of strength, or the chance of losing even the momentary control of his weapon. I have seen an Arab meet an enemy in full career, and slice his head clean off in this way, with hardly a perceptible movement of the arm."

Having no knowledge on this subject, Harry assented without any mental reserve; but concerning the military utility of acrobatic equestrian performances, or of their being available at all in the hunting field, he entertained the very gravest doubt. But they were good fun to watch, for all that, and one, that of vaulting into the saddle while the horse was in motion, he practised, and to a certain extent caught the knack. He also went in for throwing the spear, which the natives could do for ten yards or so with great force and accuracy; and though he did not make very good practice, it proved an excellent exercise for his muscles after his long confinement.

The Sheikh Burrachee was delighted to see how his nephew took to these martial exercises, and at last he put the question to him point-blank, whether he would not assist in teaching some of the men the use of the Remington rifles they had captured.

Harry, having thought over the best course to pursue in such a contingency, consented with apparent alacrity, but said that he hoped his shortcomings would be excused. His uncle, not knowing how much that hope covered, replied that he must not take the Kor Dofan for Wimbledon, and the most elementary instruction would be esteemed extremely scientific.

So the very next day Harry found himself with a squad of five hundred men to instruct.

" Delightful task, to rear the tender root—to teach five hundred Arabs how to shoot !" he said to himself, when the lot were handed over to him. There was one consolation: do what he would, his instructions to so large a number, without assistance, could not avail much : but he wanted to do nothing at all.

His uncle was not present ; he had no one to check him, able to judge whether his instruction was good or bad. So he stuck some stones up for butts, at about twelve hundred yards, and set them all firing at them. He judged that by this he would in the first place accustom them to firing at a comparatively innocuous distance ; and in the second, that they would waste a good deal of ammunition.

" His honour rooted in dishonour stood ;
And faith unfaithful kept him falsely true,"

in the words of Tennyson's famous conundrum.

CHAPTER XIV.

TRINKITAT.

THE *Alligator* troopship came tearing along the Red Sea, sending the spray flying from her bows, and churning up the historical water with her screw, just as if it were ordinary commonplace sea-water, without any sacred, classical, or poetical associations! The men gathered on the forecastle and the officers on the poop were alike gazing hard at a town of brilliant whiteness, which became more distinct every minute.

"And that is Suakim," said one of the group of officers. "It looks very clean at a distance. What is it made of, doctor?"

Doctor MacBean was a middle-aged man who liked the society of young ones because he had one little weakness: he was very fond of holding forth, and young men were more inclined to listen patiently to him than older ones. He was a naturalist, a sportsman, and had been a great traveller. There are men who go through Greece, as they would through Surrey, gleaning nothing; but the doctor was not one of them. If he were only a day in a place he learned all about it, and what he learned he remembered. So that to be in his company was to have an encyclopædia conveniently at hand, from which you could learn what you wanted to know without the trouble of turning over the leaves. For the rest, such a *boy* past forty there never was—ready for anything for sport or fun, even to a spice of practical joking; and with all this a grave Scottish face which imposed upon those who had not found him out. But in matters of information he was trustworthy, his passion for fact overcoming his love of mystification.

"Suakim is built of madrepore," he replied to the above question; "very curious. Houses and mosques all of the same materials as these reefs we are now coming to."

"Madrepore—why, that is a sort of coral—isn't it?"

"Yes, it is coral."

"That's queer though. My shirt-studs are made of coral; fancy a town built of shirt-studs!"

"Shirt-studs are quite a secondary use of the article; the principal being to help babies cut their teeth. Have you got your coral still, Green?"

Green was a very young subaltern, who had not been to a public school, and was somewhat easily imposed upon.

"No," he said; "at least not here. It is somewhere at home, I believe."

"That is right; you will want it when you come to cut your wisdom teeth. You know, I suppose, that you cannot get your company until you have done that?"

"I knew I had to pass an examination," said Green, not convinced that this information was quite *bonâ fide.*

"Of course, but this is in addition to that. When a vacancy occurs, you send in your certificate of having passed in tactics, and then you are ordered to go to the Veterinary College, and there they look in your mouth."

"But I am not a *horse!*" exclaimed Green.

"No, but the rule applies to other animals," said his tormentor, gravely.

"I know you are chaffing me," said Green, and indeed the roars of laughter were alone sufficient to show him that.

"But all the same, it is curious that a town should be built of child's corals."

"That is why it has been selected as a good station for infantry," said a young fellow amidst a chorus of groans.

"I tell you what it is, Tom," said one of the captains; "I will not have you in my company if you do that again. The man who would make a bad pun and a hackneyed pun in such beautiful scenery as this, would—I don't know what enormity he would *not* commit. Come late on parade, very likely."

"Oh, no!" said Tom Strachan, for the lieutenant was no other then our old friend, "I hope I know better than to infringe on the privileges of my superior officers."

A general grin showed that Strachan had scored there; for Fitzgerald, his captain, was noted for slipping into his place just in time to avoid reprimand, and no sooner. But he could not make any reply without fitting the cap; so he grinned too.

"Is Suakim an island?" he asked.

"Not now," replied MacBean. "When I was last here it was, but since that Gordon has had a causeway made to the mainland. There, you can see it now," he added, as the vessel steamed through a gap in the outer coral reef.

"I wonder whether these passages in the reef were made by cutting the coral out to build the town," said another.

"No," replied the doctor. "Their origin is rather curious. Sometimes, in the wet season, torrents rush down from the mountains to the sea, and the fresh water kills the polypus which makes the coral, and so stops the formation of it just there, and makes an opening. This theory is confirmed by the fact that all such passages through the reefs are immediately opposite valleys."

"The town looks like a large fortification; I suppose the dwelling-houses are behind the walls."

"No, those are the houses; and what look from here like loopholes are the windows. The place is worth looking over, though you won't have much time for that, I expect, nor yet for boating amongst the curious coral caves, or looking at the queer creatures which serve for fish and haunt them, until you have chawed up the Hadendowas and got Osman Digna in a cage."

"Not then, I hope," said one of the seniors of the group. "I hope they will send us across to Berber, when Osman's forces are swept from the path."

"I doubt if they will," replied the doctor, shaking his head. "It will be frightfully hot in a couple of months."

"It is the only way to save Gordon."

"I fear you are right, but I hope not. But here is a boat coming off to us."

It was a man-of-war's boat dashing along with the smart, lively stroke which can never be mistaken. It was alongside presently, and almost the moment it touched, the naval officer they had seen in the stern sheets stood on the quarter-deck; a harlequin could not have done it more quickly.

"It is a mistake your coming in here, sir," he said to the commanding officer; "you are to go to Trinkitat."

So the chance of closely investigating a coral town, and seeing how closely or otherwise it resembled a similar sort of colony in an extravaganza, was lost for the present for the First Battalion of the Blankshire, who growled. And yet, oh fortunate ones! if they but knew it, they gained two more comfortable meals, and one comfortable night's lodging, by having to go on.

For they did not anchor in Trinkitat harbour till it was too late to land that night. The delay caused a last rise to be taken out of poor Green, or rather a final allusion to a long-standing one. When the battalion got its route for the Soudan, the lad was as keen to see active service as any one of them, and it was a severe shock to him when one of the most mischievous of his brother officers pretended to discover that one of his legs was crooked, which would incapacitate him, he feared, from marching across the desert.

"You would knock up in an hour's march, and have to be carried, you know," said the tormentor; "it would never do."

"I am sure my legs seem to me all right," urged poor Green.

"Well, of course, I may be quite in error," candidly admitted the other. "We will ask a doctor."

So Doctor MacBean was called in, and he made an examination of the accused limb.

"Dear, dear!" he said, "however were you passed for the army? The *scarsal bone* of the *fons ilium* is all out of drawing."

"But you won't tell, doctor?" pleaded poor Green; "it does not inconvenience me in the least, I assure you."

"Not now, perhaps," said the doctor, nodding his

head; "but after a long march in sand, it might be serious. I am very sorry, but I must do my duty."

But, being much entreated, the doctor was persuaded to try what an invention of his own, which he spoke diffidently of, would do. So Green's leg was done up in splints for twenty-four hours, and then plaistered up. And after a bit the doctor saw so much improvement that he agreed to say nothing about it, and so Green sailed with the rest.

"How is your *fons ilium*, Green?" he was asked that evening in the saloon.

"Hush!" he whispered, anxiously; "the colonel will hear you! I am all right. I'll walk you ten miles through the deepest sand we meet with for a sovereign."

"Thank you; no amount of sovereigns would tempt me to accept the responsibility of putting your scarsal bone to so severe a test. But I am glad it is so much stronger; very glad. I would not have the regiment miss the aid of your stalwart arm on any consideration. Never shall I forget the way you delivered that No. 3 cut which caught Mercer such a hot one the other day, when you were playing single-stick on the deck. I say, by-the-by, have you had your sword sharpened?"

"Yes!" replied Green, with enthusiasm. "It has a good butcher's-knife edge upon it; so the corporal said, who ground it for me. It is quite as sharp as my pocket-knife."

"I am not quite so soft as they take me for," he added, confidentially, to Strachan presently.

"Of course you are not, my dear fellow," said Tom. "I doubt if it would be possible."

"Now that MacBean, the doctor, you know: did

you hear what he said about the fresh water coming down from the hills in the rainy season, and making gaps in the coral because fresh water killed the insects that make the coral?"

"Yes, I heard him," said Strachan, wondering what fault Green could find with what seemed to him a very lucid explanation.

"As if I was going to swallow that!" said the other. "The rainy season, indeed! Why, every one knows that rain never falls in Egypt."

"But, my dear fellow, this isn't Egypt for one thing, and it rains sometimes everywhere, I expect," said Tom, who was somewhat tired of imposing on the innocence of Green, who was a very willing and good-tempered lad. "Do you know you remind me of a very old story of a sailor-lad who returned home to his grandmother after a cruise in these very waters. It may be familiar to you."

"I don't remember it," said Green.

"Well, it is really so apt that I will tell it."

"'What did you see that was curious, Jack?' asked the old woman. 'Well, granny, there were flying fish; they came right out of the water and flew on the deck, and we picked them up on it.' The old woman laughed and shook her head. 'What else, Jack?' 'Why, I wish you could see the sea at night in them parts, granny; where the ship disturbs the water it all sparkles, and you can see her track a long way, like a regular road of fire.' 'Ha, ha! go it, Jack. What else?' Jack's budget of fact was exhausted for the moment, so he had to take refuge in fiction. 'Well, when we were in the Red Sea, you know, we hauled up the anchor, and we found a carriage-wheel on one of the flukes. A queer old wheel it was. And the chaplain, he looked at it and found the maker's name, which was that of Pharaoh's coach-builder. So he said there was no doubt it belonged to his army, when he followed the Israelites after they had gone out of Egypt.' 'Ah, now you are telling me what is worth listening to!' cried the old woman. 'We know that Pharaoh's host was drowned in the Red Sea, and that they had a many chariots. It is like enough you should fish one of the wheels up. But to try to stuff your poor old granny that fish can fly, and water take fire! For shame, you limb!'"

Green was a bit thoughtful, and puzzled over the application of this fable; but Strachan having to hurry off on duty, he could not question him further.

Every one was on deck by daybreak next morning, and the bustle of the day commenced. The *Alligator* was rather a late arrival, and the shore was already white with tents, large and small, circular and square, the camp being protected by an earthwork and a trench, which came down to the sea on each side, entirely enclosing it on that of the land, while on the other it was protected by the harbour and its gun-boats.

But there was not much time for gaping; launches and boats of various kinds were alongside presently, and the work of disembarkation commenced. It did not take long, for a number of little piers had been made, rude enough, but answering their purpose, and several boats could land their passengers at them at once. Then there was an officer ready to show them where to get their tents, and it was not long before the First Blankshire had added several streets to the canvas town.

They had hardly done that, however, and were

still telling off men for the various regimental duties, when they were called upon to find a large fatigue party for the public service. And now, if any men felt the cramping effects of life in a small compass on board ship, they had plenty of opportunity for stretching their limbs and getting their muscles into full play.

The sailors, for the most part, brought the cargoes ashore, and the way they worked was marvellous. They bundled bales and boxes into the boats as if the ship were on fire and they had only a few minutes to save them in; they rowed them to the strand as if they were racing in a regatta, and they got them out on the jetties before dockyard hands at home would have quite made up their minds what bale they should begin with.

And they laughed and chaffed, and seemed to think it the best fun out. Such energy was infectious, and "Tommy Atkins," without coat or braces, and with his shirt sleeves rolled up above his elbows, tried to emulate "Jack." Some of the goods they had to pile up on the shore; some to carry to the commissariat stores; and some, again, to the ordnance department. If free perspiration was the best thing for health and vigour, they were going the right way to work to obtain those blessings.

There was a lad in Fitzgerald's company, that in which Strachan was lieutenant, upon whom these new duties fell very hard. His name was James Gubbins, and he enlisted because he found it hard to obtain any other employment. And no wonder, for never was there such an awkward mortal. He broke the hearts of corporals and sergeants, and the officers of his company would fain have got rid of him. But he was perfectly able-bodied, and the surgeon was bound to pass him. Neither would the colonel help them; the man was well conducted, healthy, and tried his best. "He would make a good soldier in time," he said. Perhaps so, but the process was tedious. One lad, who joined as a recruit a month after Gubbins, learned his drill, went to his duty, was made a lance-corporal, and had the drilling of the squad in which Gubbins was still toiling at the rudiments.

He got perfect in the manual exercise, and was dismissed from recruit drill at last however, and even learned to shoot, after he had once taken in the part of the back sight of his rifle which was to be aligned with the fore sight, haziness about which nearly caused several bad accidents, as his bullets went wandering dangerously near the butts to the right and left of that where he was supposed to be firing.

By the time he passed muster he was indeed a valuable soldier, if the value of a thing depends upon the trouble taken to manufacture it. And now poor Gubbins had more to learn! It may seem very easy to turn a crank, to pump, to shoulder a box, to help carry a bale, or to push at a capstan bar, and this certainly is not skilled labour. Yet there is a way of doing each of these things in a painful, laborious, knuckle-cutting, shoulder-bruising, toe-smashing manner, and a comparatively easy and comfortable one.

And James Gubbins invariably did the worst for himself possible. I do wish that a special artist had seen him trying to help sling a mule on one occasion, and endeavouring to take a similar animal to the place appointed on shore for it on another. Words can do no justice to those scenes.

Another adventure, however, I will try to describe. A naval officer engaged in transport came up to Tom Strachan, who was in charge of half his company on fatigue duty, and said—

"Look here, do you see that steamer with a green funnel? Well, there are stores on board, for your regiment mostly. A whole lot of shells have to be landed this afternoon, and all my men are at work at that. I wish you would take that lighter, and let your fellows go off to the steamer and unload it. We should bring you the stores, as a rule, for you to carry up from the jetty, only we are short-handed."

"All right," said Tom.

The lighter was propelled by large oars, or sweeps, and James Gubbins found there was yet another trial for him in this weary world—that of endeavouring to row with one of these things. But he was so clumsy, and impeded the others to such an extent, that they pushed him on one side and told him to keep quiet.

When they got alongside, a rope was thrown up and caught by a sailor on deck, and Strachan went up a rope ladder to see exactly what had to be done. The stores were as yet in the hold, and the first job would be to hoist them out of it; so the lighter would not be wanted alongside for some time. The sailors let it drop astern, and then made it fast.

"Now then, men, you are wanted on deck; look alive!" cried Strachan.

The sergeant in the lighter looked puzzled how to get on board for a moment; but seeing a grin on a sailor's face, and at the same time observing a rope hanging from the taffrail close to him, he seized, pulled at it, and finding it firm at the top end, swarmed up it presently. It was not far to go, or a difficult operation, so the others followed.

Then they manned the crane, by which a chain with a big hook to it was lowered into the hold, as if to fish for something. And a bale having been caught, it was wound up, slewed round, and deposited on the deck.

When this had been going on a little time Strachan called out—

"Where's Gubbins?"

"Gubbins, sir," said the sergeant; "is he not here? No, he is not. Where can he have got to? Gubbins!"

He went aft and looked into the lighter; there was no one there, and he was turning away again, when he heard a voice in tremulous accents crying—

"Help! help! Do pull me up, some one, or send a boat. He will have me—I know he will! He will jump presently; and if he doesn't, I can't hold on much longer. Help! Oh, lor! Help!"

There was James Gubbins clinging to the rope by which the others had come on board. He had waited till the last, and then attempted to follow. There were two knots in the rope, one near the bottom, the other some five feet higher, and by grasping it above the top one with his hands, and above the lower one with his ankles, he managed not to fall into the water. For the lighter had floated clear of him. As for swarming up the rope without the aid of knots, he might as well have tried to dance on the tight rope.

Now to fall in the water would of itself have been a serious thing to poor Gubbins, who, of course, could not swim; but to add to his terror there was a shark, plainly visible, his back fin indeed now and then rising out of the water, swimming round and round, opening his mouth, but by no means shutting his eyes, to see what luck would send him. And good rations and regular meals, with something a day to spend in beer, had agreed with James, who had not been accustomed before enlisting to eat meat every day. He was plump, and enough to make any shark's mouth water.

The sergeant called for assistance, and Gubbins was hauled up. He got a good many bumps against the side before he was safely landed on the deck, but he stuck to his rope like a limpet, and came bundling on board at last.

And then, when he felt himself out of the reach of those cruel jaws which had threatened him for a time, which seemed to him long enough, he nearly fainted.

After this experience, if James Gubbins ever learned to swim, it would have to be after his return to England, for nothing could persuade him to go into the waters of the Red Sea. And so he missed the principal pleasure which hard-worked "Tommy Atkins" enjoyed at that period. For when the work of the day was over, bathing parade was the great feature of the evening, and the margin of the strand was crowded with soldiers, swimming, wading, diving, splashing, playing every imaginable game in the water, for, however tired they might be, the refreshing plunge gave them fresh life and vigour.

And, by-the-by, why is the British soldier called "Tommy Atkins?" I believe that there are plenty of people who use the term and don't know. The nickname arose simply from the fact that every company has a ledger, in which each man's accounts are kept. So much pay and allowance on the credit side, so much for deductions on the debit, with the balance. The officer commanding the company signs to the one, the soldier himself to the other. On the first page of this book there is a form filled in, for the guidance of any new pay sergeant who may have to make out the accounts, and in this the fancy name of the supposed soldier is printed in the place where he has to sign, and this fancy name is "Thomas Atkins." But upon the point of who was the first person to generalise the name, and how it came about that his little joke was taken up and came into common use, history is dumb.

This is a digression, and I suppose, according to the ideas of some people, I ought to ask you to pardon it, for I observe that that is a common plan upon such occasions. But I do nothing of the kind. If I thought it needed pardon I should not have made it; and you ought to be glad to improve your mind with a little bit of useful information. But you knew it all before? Well, how could I tell *that*, I should like to know.

Whether the sharks were good old-fashioned Mohammedans, who would not bite on the side of the Mahdi, or whether the number of British soldiers in the water together, and the noise they made, overawed them, they did not attempt any supper in that direction, and the men enjoyed their bath with impunity.

The work went on day after day for some time, always at high pressure, and the men got into rare good training for marching or any other kind of work. And they had plenty of water to drink, for the steamers in the harbour were perpetually at work condensing the salt water, which turns it, as you probably know, into fresh. Pipes then conveyed it on shore, where it was received in tanks and barrels. And the want of natural springs, and the consequent necessity of having recourse to an artificial supply, were not without advantage.

For the only water which can be got for troops when campaigning is very often polluted, and the men get dysentery from drinking it, whereas this was necessarily quite pure. And probably owing to this cause there was wonderfully little sickness. A terrified horse gave trouble in the landing him one day, and Tom Strachan, who was with the fatigue party which had to do it, lent his personal assistance, and with success, but he grew warm over the job.

As he was wiping the perspiration from his forehead Major Elmfoot rode up.

"Well, Strachan," he said, "how do you like this work? Do you want it over that you may begin fighting the Arabs?"

"Well, yes, sir," replied Tom. "A little of it goes a good way, and we have had more than a little. Still, we should not get on well without grub or cartridges, should we, sir?"

"No, my lad, you are right there; and I am glad to see you are a philosopher."

"Am I that, sir? Well, it is no use grumbling, but I am glad it is pretty nearly over."

"Pretty nearly over, you think it, do you?" said the major, drily. "Then the stores are to walk up to Fort Baker by themselves, I suppose."

"Have we got to ——," began Tom, in dismay.

"Yes, we have," replied Major Elmfoot to his unfinished query; "and you are to knock off this job and start off on the other one at once."

It was a peculiarity of the major's to preface an order in that way—that is, to prepare you for something quite different, and then take you aback. If you were just going to dinner, and he had a duty for you which would cause you to defer that meal, he would begin by asking if you were hungry. He did not mean to be aggravating; it was only a way he had; but it was rather trying sometimes.

Fort Baker was about three miles from Trinkitat harbour; it was erected by Baker Pasha on the second of the month which was now drawing to a close, that is the February of 1884, when he was in command of the Egyptian army which was cut to pieces by the Arabs on the fifth. There is no fresh water nearer that part of the coast than the wells at El Teb, eight miles off; so every drop of the precious liquid for the use of the troops had to be first condensed at Trinkitat, and then carried in tanks of galvanised iron on camel or mule back to the fort. Three miles do not sound like a long distance, and on good ground are not very far. But the greater part of this track lay through marshes, and for a mile it was very bad indeed. But all were in good spirits, for it transpired that this was the last of that sort of work the two companies of the Blankshire employed in it were to have for the present. They were to take their arms and accoutrements with them and remain at Fort Baker till the rest of the battalion joined them. But it was hard work to get the unfortunate baggage animals along.

"I say, sergeant, what am I to do with this campbel

now?" asked a soldier, alluding not to a clansman of the famous Highland chief, but to a ship of the desert which had sunk down in the mud, making the most horrible noises imaginable, and seemed likely to be swallowed up after a bit.

"The Johnny who understands him won't do nothing; may I lick him?"

"No, no," said the sergeant, glancing towards his captain, and with a frown at the man which was half a wink, intimating that if it could be done quietly and unofficially a little gentle persuasion used towards the Egyptian driver might expedite matters.

"What's up?" asked the captain, turning back.

"A camel that's down, sir," replied the sergeant.

Tom Strachan put the case in the form of an old nursery jingle, which he murmured for the benefit of another subaltern, Williams, who was by his side at the moment.

"Captain, captain slang sergeant; sergeant won't swear at private; private won't kick Egyptian; Egyptian won't stir up camel; camel won't get out of that; and C Company won't reach Fort Baker tonight."

The captain was equal to the occasion, however.

"Look here, you know," he said to the native driver; "if you don't make that camel go on with that load, you and your two mates will have to carry it yourselves, don't you know."

Whether the "Johnnies," as Private Smith called them, understood all this is perhaps doubtful, as their English was peculiar, but the tone and gesture which accompanied the words were very intelligible, and the Egyptian began to unload the poor bogged beast with great alacrity.

The soldiers, seeing his purpose, helped him, leaving the two other included natives to go on with other camels, and soon the goods carried by the fallen one were conveyed to a sounder place. The wallowing animal being beaten and prodded, emerged from the mud uttering unearthly cries, and was then reloaded, still objecting loudly, and on he went again.

There was no difficulty in catching the others up; other mules and camels in front were in a similar plight. These were also unloaded, and then the men pulled and pushed and heaved them out, first taking off their shoes and stockings, and rolling their trousers up as far as they could.

One man, finding that even so he got those garments sorely bemired, so deep was the slush, took them off altogether; others followed his example, hanging their trousers round their necks. But no one need have been shocked, their limbs were by no means bare, but decently clothed in long clay stockings.

"I say, Tom," said Williams to Strachan, "fancy the regiment turning out like that for Commanding Officers' parade at Aldershot!"

James Gubbins managed to distinguish himself as usual, for he let a floundering mule knock him over and roll upon him. Having to help the animal out, he seized one of his hind legs and hauled at it, with this result—

"Look at Gubbins!" cried one of his comrades; "blest if he hasn't been taking a cast of hisself in clay. Going to have a marble statty, old man?"

"You ought to have a photo taken to send home to your sweetheart, Jim."

"Pity it's the end of February, and not the beginning; what a lovely valentine he would make, surely."

"It's easy to laugh at a chap," spluttered Gubbins, "but this stuff tastes awful; and however shall I clean myself for inspection?"

"Never mind, old chap, you'll be confined to barracks, and then them Johnnies with the spears can't get at you."

"If any chap had a drop of rum instead of jaw to give a chap with his mouth full of filth, there would be more sense in it," said the victim; and it was one of the wisest remarks he had made for a long time. Some good Samaritan *had*, and administered it, and Gubbins was consoled.

"You have made these Egyptians work," said Tom to his captain.

"Yes, I flatter myself I know how to treat those fellows."

"Oh!" cried Tom.

"What's the matter?" asked Fitzgerald.

"Nothing; only if a poor sub had done it!"

"Done what?"

"Well, you know, it was one of the jokes which were tabooed by general consent."

"Get out!"

But it must be owned that though he meant nothing so atrocious as Tom Strachan implied, the captain did pronounce *fellow* like Fellah!

The fort was reached at last, and never a mule or camel left on the way. There were some salt-water puddles at the end of the worst part of it, and in these the men contrived to wash the mud off their limbs before resuming their nether garments. Ward the quartermaster was there before them; and he had a rough tent in which to receive the officers of the two companies, and he treated them to ginger-beer and tea.

Ward was an old campaigner, who had seen no end of service—been frozen in the Crimea, broiled in India, devoured by stinging insects on the Gold Coast. Strachan liked to listen to his yarns, and was in consequence rather a favourite of his. And if you are going on a campaign, it is not half a bad thing to be on good terms with a doctor, a quartermaster, or any other staff officer. They always have a bite or a drop of something should you happen to come across them when nobody else has.

"You didn't expect this kind of work when you thought, as a boy, how you would like to go into the army, eh?" he asked him.

"No," said Tom, laughing; "they don't enter into these little details in books. It's mostly feasting and fighting, with other fellows getting killed, that a school-boy looks forward to."

"Ah, the fighting is the best of it; there is something to keep you going in that. Give me the chap that will stand hunger, thirst, fatigue, want of sleep, and fever, and be as jolly as a sand-boy all the time. That's the sort for a soldier."

"But all that would be no good if he would not stand up when the pinch came."

"Of course not; but a fairly bred one—I mean English, German, French, Italian, Dutch—is bound to stand if he is properly trained and led. If he is rightly drilled it does not occur to him to run away unless his comrades do; and then, after a bit, he gets excited. Then, as to generals; I don't say that it's an easy thing to fight an army well, but it is easier than to feed it. I tell you all the real art of war lies in little details that no one ever talks about."

"Then you are not a hero worshipper Ward?"

"Not I, I have seen too much. I take no credit from men who get mentioned in despatches, win the Victoria Cross, and so forth; but there is a lot of luck in it. Heaps of men deserve these prizes just as much as those who get them. Indeed, the most deserving of all get killed out of hand, and make no claim. You see, one man does a thing with a flourish, which attracts notice, and is popular, and gets watched; and another is quiet and retiring, and afraid that if he pushes himself he may not prove as valuable an article as he has led people to expect; and a smart or plucky thing which gives promotion, or the Victoria Cross, to the first, merely elicits a 'well done, old fellow!' from his mates for the second."

"And that's worth risking a good bit for!" cried Green, with his eyes sparkling, and a heightened colour.

"Hark to Green! Good lad! By Jove, he's right!" Green blushed.

"Why are you like King Duncan's blood on Lady Macbeth's hand, Edwards?" asked Tom Strachan of the last speaker.

"I can never guess riddles," said Edwards. "Give it up."

"Because you have made the Green one red," said Strachan.

"*You* will never miss the Victoria Cross for want of cheek, at any rate," said Fitzgerald.

"I am glad of that," replied Tom, "as I have my plan for it. I mean to stick behind you the first time you go to do anything heroic, and if you get killed I shall hope to get the credit of your action."

"So you want me to be knocked on the head, do you, you young villain?"

"Not at all, sir; no one can say I would rather have your room than your company."

"What *are* the boys coming to?" cried Fitzgerald. "When I was a sub, I no more dared to speak to my captain like that than to—to walk off parade without permission," he added, after pausing to think what was the highest possible stretch of mortal impudence.

"Perhaps your captain had not your appreciation of wit," replied Tom.

"Wit, indeed! You call your bad puns wit, do you?"

Next day the rest of the troops marched in from Trinkitat, and bivouacked outside the fort. They had made a fair start, and commenced the campaign now, and the novelty of eating their evening meal in the open, by the light of a bonfire, had a charm for some of the young ones. The officers' mess of the First Blankshire was held round an oval trench. A coat thrown on the earth dug out of it served for a seat; the feet were placed in it, and the pewter plate with food on it was held on the knees. This is infinitely more comfortable than feeding in a cramped position on the ground.

Though they knew all about it before, it seemed strange to the inexperienced to lie down at night in the open, like animals, instead of going to bed, but some were so tired that, not being on duty, they rolled themselves up in the coats they had been sitting on, and courted a nap directly they had done feeding.

Those who did so, however, were presently aroused by a tremendous cheering, which made them jump up, and run to see what had happened. It was the arrival of the Sixty-fifth, who had been stopped on their return from India, and sent to Trinkitat instead of England. They had only landed that afternoon, and had marched on at once. It was not long, however, before the challenge of the sentries, and the snores of sleepers alone broke the silence of the little host, lying stretched in slumber under the faint light of the new moon. Their sleep was disturbed by showers of rain, which interfered with all but the very sound, and even these were fairly roused at last by a regular drencher, the water coming down tropical fashion, in bucketfuls.

"Halloa, Green!" said Strachan, to that young hero, whom he found standing in astonishment, drenched, but not dismayed. "Do you believe that it rains sometimes in the Soudan, now?"

"I do," replied Green, solemnly. "Books talk nonsense."

"I wish it was time to start," said Edwards, joining them. "It seems so absurd to stand here saturated, with no possibility of resting oneself, when one might be getting on."

"It is more than half-past four, and reveille is to sound at five. Let's try and light the fire again; there's a bit smouldering, in spite of the rain."

This was Strachan's suggestion, and voted a good one; and they had just succeeded in raising a blaze, when a bugle started the most romantic, melancholy, musical call in the whole category. I mean in itself, and not for its associations; and yet when one thinks how many thousands of brave men have been roused by it to go to death, it is not free from these. Number one only got about three notes start, when a second began, and presently the whole air was full of plaintive sound.

Then flickers of fire shone out, and coffee was boiled, and the men got their breakfasts. Then, after a while, the Fall-in sounded, and the different corps and detachments stood to their arms. The commanding officer of the First Blankshire went round the ranks, and spoke to the men here and there. He did not remark on the mud which still clove to James Gubbins, but he stopped opposite Green.

"Why, what is the matter, Green; where and how are you hurt?" he asked.

"I, sir?" said Green, in astonishment; "I believe I am all right."

"Why, you are bleeding like a pig!" And so he was, from his right ear.

"I must have cut it with my sword, sir, carrying it carelessly. I forgot that I had had it sharpened."

"Well, it can't be very bad, if you did not know it," said the colonel, laughing as he rode on. The bleeding stopped presently, but not before it had made Green's karkee sleeve and his sword, down which there had been a trickle, look exceedingly warlike.

"He has fleshed his maiden blade!" said Tom Strachan.

CHAPTER XV.

EL TEB.

THE force started on the march about eight o'clock. It moved in square, with camels, mules, baggage, ammunition in the centre. Also inside were the surgeons and ambulance, and some troops ready to strengthen any weak part in the course of action; there were guns, either machine guns (as guns which fire bullets through individual barrels by turning a handle—various improvements upon the mitrailleuse —are called) or Krupp guns, at the corners, manned either by sailors or artillerymen.

The square was not a square in the sense of Euclid, because two sides of it were longer than the other two. One of the longest faces led, the men being in line. The other formed the rear face, and moved also in line, turned to the right about; but when halted and fronted it would face to the rear. The side faces marched, the right side "fours left," the left side "fours right," so that when halted and fronted they too would face outwards.

The officer in command, General Graham, had two men who knew the ground well, Baker and Burnaby, to point out the best route to avoid obstacles which would break the formation, and so they moved over a flat expanse of sand, with now and then a hill overgrown with low bushes. Not far from the line of march these sand-hills were larger and more numerous, and the bushes thicker, and amongst and beyond these parties of the enemy were hovering;

to guard the infantry against a sudden attack from these, a squadron of light cavalry were spread out half a mile ahead, covering the flanks.

"I ask your pardon, sir," said a sergeant to Strachan, as they tramped through the sand, "but do you happen to know what we are going to fight about? Not that it matters, only it gives an interest like to the business."

"Oh, yes, sergeant," said Tom. "We are going to relieve Tokar."

"So I thought, sir. But then, you see, Tokar, they say, has fallen."

"I believe it has," replied Tom; "but that was the original idea. And if we are a bit late, why then we must show them how we would have relieved it if it had not been taken. The Arabs had no right to be in such a hurry. You remember the sham fights we used to have at Aldershot? Neither side was to commence manœuvring before a certain hour, when a gun fired. Well, these Arabs have not played fair, but stolen a march upon us before the proper time. But that is no reason why we should go home after all this trouble and preparation without a fight."

"Of course not, sir!"

"Well, then, they have got the wells at El Teb, and have raised fortifications to defend them, I believe, and our job to-day is to get them out of that. Then we go on to Tokar, and we shall see if they make another fight there."

"Thank you, sir," said the sergeant; "I understand quite enough now."

A puff of smoke from the bushes; another; twenty. But no bullets came, the enemy firing from too long a distance. It was like a peaceable field day with blank cartridge burning.

Trinkitat harbour was in full view, and an energetic ship there, seeing the Arabs' position thus indicated, tried to throw shells amongst them. But they, too, were out of range. Only, as shells when properly constructed burst somewhere, and these were sent over the heads of friends, their exploding short was dangerous, and after two or three attempts the experiment was dropped.

The main body of the cavalry followed in rear of the square, and to the left of it, in three lines.

"Look at those birds!" said Green to Tom, coming up to him to draw his attention. "What lots of them! They look like vultures surely, some of them."

"And they are vultures, too. What carrion have they got there I wonder. Faugh! One can smell it from here."

"Look at General Baker, what a stern expression he has got," said Fitzgerald, letting his subaltern come up to him. "What a scene those birds and this stench must recall for him!"

"Ah, to be sure!" said Tom. "This was the line of the flight of his Egyptian army a month ago, when they let the Arabs massacre them without even attempting to resist. Well, we won't do that if we can help it, will we, Green? We will strike a blow, even if we cut off our noses as well as our ears."

"There, there, don't chaff him, Strachan; you are too bad. And look to your half-company. Close up, there!"

The enemy kept up their innocuous out-of-distance popping, principally at the advance cavalry. The square was halted two or three times for a minute's rest, which the men dragging the guns must have particularly wanted, considering the loose nature of the soil. Then on again, after between two and three hours' march.

Tom Strachan could see huts, and what looked like a fort with guns; earthworks also in another part, with flags stuck upon them. Also, of all earthly things in such a spot, an old boiler, such as you may see in some Thames-side yard, where old vessels are broken up and worn-out machinery accumulates.

Here the cavalry skirmishers, having done their work, retired to their main body. Another halt, almost within rifle-shot of the position, and the men flung themselves carelessly down on the sand. Major Elmfoot was examining the defences through his field-glass.

"That thing looks like an old boiler, major," said Fitzgerald.

"And it *is* an old boiler," replied the other. "I was hearing about it the other day; there was a sugar-mill here once; that ruined building was part of it."

"Ten-shun!"

The men sprang to their feet all together. The enemy were close, and there would be serious work in a minute. A flash and a puff of smoke from the earthworks, a singing in the air, another flash and report close by, and the fragments of a shell were flying about their ears. Two more bursting right over, and a man here and there dropped.

Then the rifle-fire opened in earnest, and those who had never yet heard it learned what the sound of a bullet was like. More men were hit, collapsed, and were picked up by the ambulance.

Still the square pressed steadily on, the men stepping jauntily as if marching past. Green said to himself with joy—

"I am under fire, really under fire! And I am not half so frightened as I thought I should be."

"Mayn't I give them one back, sir?" a man asked him.

"Not yet; presently," he replied.

He had hardly spoken before the words, "Halt! Lie down!" were passed, and return fire was opened, both from guns and rifles, overpowering and almost silencing that of the enemy.

"Advance!" Up the men jumped again, and pressed forward towards the works.

The ground was broken by lumps of rock, bushes, and holes, which made temporary breaks in the ranks as the men had to give way to pass on either side of them, and then run up into their places again. Behind every rock and bush, crouched in every pit or hollow, were Arabs, who seized the opportunity to dash amongst the men, getting into the very ranks, and striking with their spears and sharp swords right and left, and on equal terms.

For the rifle, considered as a firearm, was of no use at such very close quarters; the bayonet at the end of it, or the butt, was all that could be used. The bayonet exercise is often spoken of as a bit of gymnastics rather than of practical value; but smartness in the delivery of a thrust was just everything now. In civilised warfare it may be that bayonets are seldom crossed, but when you have to deal with a barbarian foe, who places his trust in cold steel, the case is different. For the first thrust perhaps the bayonet has the advantage, for the weight of the rifle behind it sends it very quick and true, and difficult to parry. But the point once turned or avoided, the spear gets the pull, as, by drawing back the hand which holds it, the point can be withdrawn to the shoulder, and launched, without a chance of parrying, at any unguarded spot.

True, that the English soldier can also shorten arms, but it takes both hands to do that, and in the meantime the whole body is exposed; while the Arab shortens his spear with the right hand alone, and the left arm, with a round shield of hippopotamus hide upon it, can be used to put aside the bayonet thrust. Unless wounded to death, they fight on when they have fallen, clutching at their enemies' legs, stabbing while they can hold a weapon.

Such struggling as this caused the advance of the square to be very slow, for those portions of the front line which had no obstacles to enable the enemy to get amongst them had to wait while the men engaged in these single combats despatched their foes and were ready to advance again. Not that they wasted their time, for they had plenty of shooting to do to clear their own immediate front.

Nor was this the only cause of delay; the rear line of the square was also subject to rushes of the enemy, who lay in ambush till it had passed, and then dashed upon it. To meet the attack it must halt and face about, and the rest of the square must halt too, or a gap would be opened through which the determined foe would rush. Then, again, the flanks, or side faces of the square, were also attacked. These had to turn towards the front when the square advanced, not in file, or two deep, as they stood, because men moving like that must always straggle out too much, but in fours. Thus, on each forward movement, the right side of the square formed fours left, the left side of it fours right. But in this way the men would have their sides towards the surrounding enemy, and would be helpless. So when attacked they had to halt and front, thus becoming a line two deep again, facing their foes. But this required another general halt till the enemy were killed or driven back.

It is difficult to explain all this without using technical terms, but I think you will understand how absolutely necessary it was to move steadily, with the men forming the four sides of this square standing shoulder to shoulder, and leaving no openings.

If the forces opposed were about equal, no such square as this, which moves with such cumbersome difficulty, would be thought of; but when a mere handful of men have to encounter countless hordes, it is employed to avoid being attacked in front and rear and flanks at the same time, and to protect the wounded, the water, and the spare ammunition. But let the overpowering masses of the enemy once break into the centre, all advantage is gone, and the small body is worse off than it would be advancing in any other way, because the four sides would be attacked in front and rear, cut off from each other, and deprived of mutual support. The ammunition would be seized, and the wounded in the ambulances massacred, while the soldiers would just have to fight back to back while their strength lasted.

To prevent a partial irruption resulting in such a catastrophe, spare troops moved inside the square to oppose a second line, ready to repel any Arabs who broke in, and so aid their comrades to regain their formation.

The guns were at the corners of the square. While there was a clear space in front of them, and they were well served, nothing alive could approach. But suppose a hillock close in front, or a pit, full of Arabs, into which they could not fire, just under their muzzles, and they would become weak places, where the enemy could surge in without being met by the bristling bayonets, and so stab the soldiers on the right and left of the angle in their backs, increasing the gap, through which their friends might penetrate. And the enemy saw this plainly enough, and planned dodges to aid their rushes upon these corners.

There was one good thing for the British troops that day: a nice breeze swept the smoke away, and they could see their enemies' movements, and so stall off many a rush with their fire before it came to close conflict. If a thick pall of smoke had combined with the broken ground to cover the attacks of the Arabs, the losses would most likely have been heavier, and the battle more protracted.

Tom Strachan had acquired an accomplishment which promised to be useful before the day was over. He and others were practising with their new revolvers one day on the grounds near the rifle butts, where they were quartered, when the colonel rode by, and stopped to look on.

"I tell you what you should do," he said to them, "you should practise with the left hand. I have learned to shoot as well with my left hand as my right, and I believe it saved my life in India during the Mutiny. It leaves the sword arm free to ward off a cut or thrust if there are more than one at you, or you fail to shoot your man dead."

All tried it, but Strachan at least persevered, and it came quite natural to him after a while to use his left hand for that purpose. Not only that, but the determination to conquer the awkwardness he felt at first made him practise pistol shooting much more than he would otherwise have done, and he became a first-rate shot.

The weapon, however, lay in its leather case at present; he had enough to do to look after his men, and to catch and repeat the word of command amidst the din, without thinking of personal combat. He, like Green, had got an edge put on his sword. It was Kavanagh's present, and during the lull preceding the attack, he had thought of his old friend, wondered where he was, and regretted that they were not side by side that day. He and Harry Forsyth—what fun it would have been! But when the firing once commenced, he had no thought but of what he was about.

"Fire low, men! Steady! Don't shoot wildly. Harris, cover your man, just as if he were a target at home."

"Close up, there; never mind Roberts, the ambulance will look to him. Good man, Gubbins! That's your sort; can't well miss 'em at ten yards. Aim at the waist-cloth. Cease firing! Advance; *fours left* there! Close up."

Orders could not always be heard in the din; it was necessary to watch the front of the square, and move on or halt as it did, unless a particular rush at a certain point compelled those at it to take the initiative, and then others had to conform to it.

When the square got close to the right end of the curved earthwork, the troops nearest to it charged at it with a cheer, leaving a big gap in the ranks they left. Had they succeeded in carrying the place with the rush, this would not have mattered; but it could not be done. Tap a bee-hive smartly with your stick on a mild May day, and see the inhabitants swarm out at you, and you may form some idea of how the Hadendowas flew over the parapet at their assailants. Every one of them fixed his eye on an enemy, and went straight at him. Every soldier found himself with two or three opponents, and, instead of pressing on into the earthwork, had enough to do to hold his ground.

The cool, brave man, who made sure of getting rid of one with a steady shot a few yards off, and then plied his bayonet till he got a moment's pause to reload, came off well; the flurried soldier, who was not quite sure whether to stand or retire, who missed or only wounded his man, and then stood strictly on the defensive, was most likely overpowered and speared.

The greater the daring the greater was the safety, and *vice versâ*. But brave or timid, the men who had rushed out of the ranks to attack were borne back by the sheer weight of numbers. The Soudanese, however, never got through the gap that was left. The Marines inside the square promptly presented themselves as a second barrier, till the attackers, retiring in good order, fell back into their places again.

But there was some hard fighting at the point for a minute or two. Good old-fashioned cut and thrust, hammer and tongs, like cutting out a ship. Tom Strachan found himself, he did not know how, with the hilt of his sword right up against a Soudanese breast-bone, the weapon having passed right through the man's body. But there was no expression of pain in the dying face so close to his own, only hate and defiance. He was killed, not conquered.

Before he could disencumber himself from the body another Hadendowa rushed at him with uplifted spear. Tom levelled his pistol at him, and pressed the trigger; but the weapon did not explode. He had already fired all the barrels.

Another second and the spear-head would have been buried in his throat, but suddenly the Arab's arm dropped, nearly severed by a cut from Green, which caught him between wrist and elbow. The wounded man caught his spear with the left hand, and strove to stab, but before he had time he got the point in his throat, and that stopped him.

At this time Private Gubbins had a narrow escape. He fired at an Arab, about twenty yards off, and hit him hard, but he came on at him all the same, trying to spear him. Gubbins thrust at him with his bayonet, but perhaps rather timidly; anyhow he missed his body, though he wounded him again in the shoulder, and with that, and parrying, knocked the spear out of his hand. Whereupon the Soudanese caught hold of the bayonet and tried to unfix it. He could not manage that, and a tug of war commenced, in which Gubbins, being the weaker and less active, was pulled bodily out of the ranks, and would have been made mincemeat of had not some one shot the Arab through the head, while his rear rank man pulled him back. He owned afterwards that he was fairly scared.

"Thought that ere cannibal couldn't die!" he said. "Fust I shot him, and then I bayoneted him, and he only snarled like a wild cat. Fancy a chap pulling like that with one hole in his stomach and another in his shoulder! 'Taint reasonable."

They fought like that, many of them.

When the momentary confusion was over, and the square again compact, Strachan found an opportunity of slipping fresh cartridges into his revolver; the work in prospect did not look like being suited to an empty pistol. He had hardly done it before they were under the parapet of the earthwork.

Here there was a pause; the Arabs, not dashing out, the British, after their late experience, apparently not quite knowing whether they ought to break the square formation by dashing in. Not to mention that the Arabs were ticklish gentlemen to tumble over a bank into the middle of!

During this pause a stalwart, almost gigantic figure was seen walking up the slope with a double-barrelled fowling-piece in his hand. Coming to the parapet he brought the gun to his shoulder, fired right and left, and calmly opening the breech, replaced the two empty cartridges with two fresh ones, just as if he were standing during a battue, shooting pheasants and not Soudanese.

"Look at Burnaby!" cried some one, and hundreds were looking at him, expecting that at last he must fall, this dauntless traveller, keen observer, and born soldier, who courted peril as other men court safety; who spurned luxury and loved hardship; who seemed to treat the king of terrors as a playfellow.

Again he gave the enemy in the earthwork, and within a few yards of him, both barrels, and retreated a few steps down to reload.

The Soudanese followed to the top of the parapet,

but the moment one of them showed his head above it he was shot by the soldiers close below.

Directly he had got fresh cartridges in, Colonel Burnaby stepped back to his old place, and added another brace to his bag. But this combat between one man and a host would never take the fort, and the foremost line did not stand long at gaze, but ran up and clambered over the artificial bank, which was about four feet high, pouring a volley into the defenders as they did so. And now single combats again commenced, and the interior of the earthwork resembled an ancient arena.

The theoretical duty of an officer in action was suspended, for he had to fight physically and practically like the men, the only difference lying in the arms he wielded.

His sword was no longer a bâton of office, but a weapon to cut and thrust with, and the better its temper and the keener its edge, the greater friend was it to him that day. Not always did it prove true.

Captain Wilson, R.N., cut down an Arab who was about to kill a soldier, and his blade shivered to the hilt, leaving him without a weapon to ward off a cut which wounded him, though happily not severely, in the head.

Captain Littledale, of the York and Lancaster Regiment, also bent his sword over one of the Soudanese in the fort, and would have lost his life had not two of his company come to his rescue. Some of the men's weapons proved equally rotten.

" Look here, sergeant," said a fine broad-shouldered young fellow, whose face was like a sweep's with powder and dust, and whose clothes were bespattered with what Tennyson delicately calls "drops of onset," as he showed his bayonet twisted like a corkscrew, with the point bent over into a hook.

"Why, what have you been using it for, Sullivan?" asked the sergeant, taking it into his hand.

"Only prodding Johnnies, and not above three of them. It wouldn't go into the last, and I had to polish him off with the butt end. Might have smashed the stock, for their heads is uncommon hard."

"It's a deal too bad," said the sergeant. "I'll show it to the captain, and he will report it. Take Brown's rifle and bayonet, he will never want it again, poor fellow."

And indeed poor Brown was lying at the foot of the parapet with a spear completely through his body, his first and last battle ended. The spears and swords of the savages did not break or bend, or lose their edge over the first bone they touched, like the weapons of their civilised opponents.

Fitzgerald came up, and the sergeant showed him the twisted bayonet. He was not easily put out, but the sight was too much even for his placid temper.

"Keep it, sergeant, keep it. We will see if we cannot get it stuck up in Saint James's Park with the trophies of captured guns, that the British public may see the weapons soldiers are sent out to fight with. The man who is responsible for this, and the fellow who forged it, ought to be shot."

"*Forged* is a good word," said Major Elmfoot. "To pass off stuff like that for good steel is rank forgery, and a worse crime than making bad money, for here men's lives are sacrificed by it."

"I wish we had some of 'em here!" murmured one of the men.

"Aye, and the triangles rigged up," said another. "I should like to lay on the first dozen myself."

And so say all of us.

This conversation took place after the earthwork was cleared of the enemy—at least of the living enemy, for the whole interior was crowded with their dead—and while the sailors and artillerymen were turning the two Krupp guns found in it upon the retiring foe and the ruins of the old sugar-mill to which the Soudanese still clung. And the troops had a little rest while the leaders determined the direction of the next attack. And the water-bottles you may be sure were mostly drained, for the men's throats were like lime-kilns.

An officer standing on the highest part of the parapet beckoned to Strachan, who doubled up and joined the group assembled there.

"Look," said the friend who had called him, pointing to the right, "the cavalry are going to have their turn." Sure enough, there were the three lines of cavalry, advancing at a walk towards the dense hordes of Soudanese who covered the plain, some retiring slowly and reluctantly, but the majority still holding their ground.

As they drew nearer the Hussars broke into a trot, and then, when quite close, they were loosed, and swept down on the foe at full gallop, a simoon of glittering steel. Surely the grandest sight the modern world can afford; the last remnant of chivalry. For ever since the invention of firearms the infantry officer's place in battle has necessarily been in rear of his men; but the cavalry officer still rides in front, yards in front. He believes that his men are behind him, but he sees them not. Alone he plunges into the enemy's ranks, and the first shock of the encounter is his. He is a knight without his grandsire's defensive armour, and exposed to rifle bullets and bursting shells, which the old paladin knew not.

"Oh, to be with them!" cried Tom in his excitement, uttering what was in the hearts of all the group, as with eager eyes, parted lips, and breath coming short, they saw the line swallowed up in the sea of Arabs. A minute's confusion, with nothing distinguishable but the flash of weapons, and they reappeared *beyond* the masses through whom they cut their way, prostrate figures marking their track, and were now serrying their ranks, disordered in the fierce passage.

But the spectators could watch no more, for the shells failed to dislodge the Arabs from the ruined mill, and it was impossible to advance and leave any such indomitable fanatics, who cared not for numbers and despised death, so long as they could wreak their wrath upon an infidel, in their rear; and the immediate business was to turn them out of that lair.

There were about a couple of hundred sheltered by the ruin and the old boiler; and for some distance round about the ground was regularly honey-combed with rifle-pits, each of which contained an Arab, crouching down, spear in hand, only desiring to kill an enemy and die.

It was said before that they swarmed out of the fort earlier in the day like bees when their hive is tapped. Like bees, too, when angered, they only sought to sting, though they knew that the act of stinging was their own destruction. As a soldier came to the edge of an apparently empty hole in the ground, a man would spring out upon him and transfix him before he had time to offer resistance. Not that this succeeded often.

The men soon learned to approach these rifle-pits with their muzzles lowered, finger on trigger, the point of the bayonet over the opening before they came up to it. Then, if the Arab made his spring, he was transfixed; if he kept crouching, waiting for the other to pass, he was shot. A large number of the holes became the graves they looked like before the boiler was reached.

Here the massacre was horrible, for at that point the state of things was reversed, and the Soudanese were few in number, while the English were the many. And it was a revolting thing to have to shoot down and stab this handful of heroes.

But it could not be helped; they would not fly, and they would not surrender; and to endeavour to spare one of them was to insure your own death or that of a friend. It was even necessary to slay the slain, for they would sham and lie still, to spring up when the English had passed and stab one in the back; then stand with extended arms to be shot, with a smile of triumph and joy, secure of Paradise since he had sent a double-dyed infidel, a disbeliever, both in Mahomet and the Mahdi, to his doom.

The old sugar-mill and the ground about it being at length cleared, the victorious square advanced upon the wells. The whole body of Arabs were now in retreat, dismayed at last by the terrible slaughter amongst their best and bravest; for the reckless heroism which is described, though there were so many hundreds of examples of it, as to entitle it to be fairly considered as characteristic of the race, could not, of course, be universal, or they would be absolutely invincible, except by extermination.

They were brave, every man and boy of them, but the vast majority were not mad fanatics; and, indeed, a certain number of the tribes engaged did not believe in the Mahdi at all, but joined him partly because he was the strongest, and partly because they hated the Turks—and to them Turks and Egyptians were all one—and their oppressive corrupt government, and the Mahdi had thrown it off.

But they were not prepared to commit actual suicide, and did not want to go to Mahomet's Paradise just yet. So, after a certain number were killed without gaining any advantage, they grew disheartened, and retired. And then the machine guns sent their continuous streams of bullets tearing through the dense masses, and volleys from the Martini-Henrys ran the death list up still higher, and the retreat became flight.

They marched steadily on. At the wells the Arab sheiks strove hard to rally their warriors, charging alone, and, in some instances, weaponless, to shame their men into following them. But it was no use. "Tommy Atkins" was not flurried or excited now, success had made him firm and confident, and there was no wild firing. Every shot was aimed as steadily as if the charging Arab were an inanimate target and whoever came within that zone of fire was swept into eternity.

This was an expiring effort, and when two companies of the Gordon Highlanders had carried the last earthwork, with three guns and a machine gun in it, the enemy made no further resistance, but left their camp, the huts containing the spoils of Baker Pasha's army—cut to pieces by them a month ago—and the wells in the conquerors' possession.

A well is a grand name for a hole in the mud, but the water was fresh and plentiful, and there were ten of them. It is difficult to keep the bands of discipline very tight when men are flushed with victory, wild with thirst, and water is before them. So, perhaps, there was a little crowding which defeated its own object, causing needless delay in obtaining the coveted water for all. But order was soon restored, and every one served.

"Shall we go on to Tokar to-night, do you think?" Tom Strachan asked his captain.

"I hope not," replied Fitzgerald; "I want something to eat, don't you? Glory is all very well, but one cannot dine off it. Besides, it is absurd to cram too much of it into one day. If four hours' fighting, part of which was as severe as Association football playing, is not enough for one day, I should like to know what General Graham would have."

The general was not unreasonable, or he thought it better to hold the wells. At any rate, the troops remained in the position lately held by the enemy, strengthening it in parts, after the men had had a rest, and bivouacking there for the night. Provisions came up from Fort Baker, and the officers of the First Blankshire had a good mess—tinned beef, chicken and ham, sardines, and other delicacies, with biscuit and tea, with just a taste of rum apiece to top up with.

A really useful invention is that of preserving fresh meat in tins. The man who found that out, and he who discovered chloroform, ought to go up to the head of the Inventors' Class, in my humble opinion. I hope they made their fortunes. You may despise tinned food at home, when you can get fresh-killed meat and poultry not so overcooked. But go a long voyage, or even on a yachting tour, travel in wild countries for exploration, or to shoot big game, and then say.

And when they lit their pipes and lay round the bivouac fire, talking over the events of the day, what a time that was! The First Blankshire had not come off scathless as regarded men or officers. There was a captain lying yonder with his cloak over his face who would never hear the cheery bugle call again; a lieutenant was in the ambulance tent with a bullet in his leg, forcing himself to bear the pain without moaning. And of those present, several bore gashes which would have been thought nasty at home, though after being dressed by the surgeon they were accounted scratches of no signification, beyond a certain smarting and throbbing. Green had a bandage under his chin, and going up on each side till his helmet covered it.

"No," he said, when asked if it was binding his self-inflicted cut of the morning; "it's the other ear. Curiously enough, a bit of a shell or a bullet, or something, has taken the lobe off; and as it would not stop bleeding, and the flies were troublesome when I took off my helmet, which hurt, I asked a doctor to look at it, and he put this thing on to keep the lint in its place."

"You will never be able to wear earrings, if they come into fashion for men, my poor Green," said Strachan. "But what is the row with your hand, Edwards? I did not see it was bound up in a handkerchief before."

"Ah, it's nothing; only a bite."

"A bite!"

"Yes. There was a poor little Arab chap, such a game little boy, with a small spear made for him, fighting like a bantam till a bullet broke his leg and knocked him over. He lay in the first earthwork, and I tried to give him a drink, but the little rat darted up at me and bit my hand."

"Have you had it cauterised? I do believe these savages are mad," said the major. "And what became of the varmint?"

"I don't know; we had to move on just then."

"That is the worst part of these Arabs, letting their children go into the ranks so soon. I hate to see babies made into little men and women. If they must fight, let them punch one another's heads with their fists."

"I suppose, major, that as these Arabs are always fighting with one another, if there is no one else, it becomes a necessary branch of education."

"Well, at any rate," said Jones, who was learned in dogs—their training and management—and who, indeed, was known as Doggy Jones, "they need not 'enter' them to the British soldier. There are plenty of Egyptians for them to worry till they have come to their full growth."

"That is a curious thing about General Baker," said the colonel to Major Elmfoot.

"Yes, indeed, it is."

"Was he hit, sir?" asked Dudley. "I heard something of it."

"Yes, by a splinter of a shell in the face, just as we came under fire."

"But I saw him after that."

"Oh, yes; he got the wound dressed, and remounted, knowing how useful he could be, knowing the ground. But it is a nasty wound for all that, MacBean says. The strange thing is that he should have passed unscathed through the hordes a month ago, when his troops fled and left him unprotected, and the chances against him looked a hundred to one, and get hit to-day; the odds were a hundred to one the other way."

"The most curious case of that sort was Sir Charles Napier," said the major. "He was one of the most unlucky men that ever lived in the way of getting hit. In every great battle in which he took part during the Peninsular War he was severely wounded. But at Meeanee and Dubba, where he was in command, and almost everything depended upon him, and where, too, he exposed himself in a manner which made the Sindhees think he had a charmed life, he did not get a scratch."

"I wonder whether those Indian fellows fought as hard as these Arabs?" observed Green.

"Not much difference, I should say," said the major. "They flung themselves on the bayonets, and, if not mortally wounded, seized the muzzles and pressed them to their bodies with the left hand, to get one cut at their enemy and die. I don't quite see how *that* could be beaten in the way of game fighting, though these fellows equal it. I saw one do much the same thing to-day."

"And did Sir Charles Napier fight them in square, sir?" asked Green, who was of an inquiring mind on professional subjects.

"No, he met them in line, and his men had no breech-loaders in those days; not even percussion caps; only the old brown bess with a flint and steel lock, and a good bayonet on the end of her."

"But perhaps the odds were not so great."

"Quite, by all accounts. It is true that the Indians fought with swords and shields, and, after firing their matchlocks, charged home with those weapons. A swordsman requires space for the swing of his arm, so, however more numerous they may be, they must fight in looser order than soldiers armed with the bayonet, and therefore, at the actual point of meeting, each individual swordsman finds at least two antagonists opposed to him in the front rank alone. Now these Arabs, fighting principally with spears, can very often come in a much denser mass. I only give that idea for what it is worth. I think it may make a good deal of difference. The nature of the ground, also, would alter the condition of the contest. But, at any rate, I do not quite see how we should be safe against getting taken in the rear in any other than the square formation."

CHAPTER XVI.

TOUCH AND GO!

TIRED men cannot go on talking all night, even about the events of an exciting day, and one by one our friends rolled themselves up in their coats and went off to sleep. And how the unfortunates on sentry-go envied them! That was an infliction which Tantalus escaped, but it might well compare with those which have caused his name to be embodied in our language.

To feel that the lives of a number of other people as well as your own depend on your keeping extremely wide awake, when you are dead beat and have to fight against the strongest possible inclination to doze even as you walk about, is really no light trial of fortitude, though it is not reckoned amongst the hardships of campaigning. But if you are within sight of your sleeping comrades, and within hearing of their snores, it becomes doubly exasperating, and might really sour the temper if it were not for the consolatory reflection that another time *you* will be the happy sleeper, and one of the present performers on the nose will be listening to your efforts to play upon that organ.

It has been whispered that evil men when on sentry have been known to feel a grim delight in an alarm which has dissipated the slumber of their comfortable comrades, but we may surely hope that this is slanderous. However that may be, the slumbers of those who were not kept awake by the pain of wounds or by duty the night after El Teb were not disturbed, and next day the main body, after a guard had been left at the wells, went on to Tokar.

"Do you think they will fight?" asked Green of one of his seniors during a short halt.

"Sure to," replied the other. "You saw for yourself what determined demons they are, and it is not likely that they will give up a place they have only just taken without striking a blow for it."

"Do you think they will fight?" asked Tom Strachan of another, not in the hearing of the first oracle, who had moved away.

"Not they!" responded the second. "After such a licking as they got yesterday all the fight will be taken out of them."

"Which shall we believe, Green?" said Tom presently.

"It is very puzzling," replied the inquiring mind. "Suppose we wait and see before we make up our minds."

"A Daniel come to judgment!" exclaimed Strachan. "A second Daniel! We *will* wait."

"Hulloa! There's Charley Halton!" as a smart young cavalry officer cantered past with a message, having delivered which he came to exchange greetings with his friends.

One of the most enviable of mortals was Halton, a lad who might be the model for either painter or poet in search of an ideal hero. Handsome, strong, active, acquiring proficiency in all games and athletic exercises almost instinctively, a horseman with the hands of a Chaloner, and the seat of a Land, endowed with a bright intelligence which seized the common sense of things, and comprehended the meaning of an order as well as its literal injunctions, and a happy disposition which made a trouble of nothing, he was a general favourite wherever he went. He was attached as a galloper—or bearer of orders—to the General's staff, but, being employed to take a message the day before to his own regiment, he charged with them, and the officers of the Blankshire who knew him, and witnessed the charge from a distance, were anxious to know for certain what had occurred, the reports which had reached them being too contradictory for reliance.

"Well, Charley, did you eat them all yesterday?"

"Not quite; we have left a few for you. Eat them, by Jove! They were near eating us."

"Why, you seemed to go through them grandly."

"Yes, but it was like going through water, which closes on you as you go. The beggars lay flat, or crouched in holes, and cut at the horses as they passed, to hamstring or maim them; and good-bye to the poor fellow whose horse fell! We ought to have had lances, and it would have been a very different tale. But the troopers' swords could not reach the beggars, who are as lithe as monkeys. If they had run it would have been easy to get a cut at them; so it would if they had stood up. But they were as cool as cucumbers, and dodged just at the right moment. Of course some were not quite so spry as others, and got cut down; it was a case of the survival of the fittest. What acrobats they would be in time if this game lasted long enough!

"But it was like a nightmare. You know when you have a dream that you are trying to kill something which won't die; some beast of the eel persuasion. We went through them, cutting all we knew; re-formed; came back, doing ditto; through them a third time; and *then* there was no satisfaction worth calling such. The fellows were broken up indeed, and a good lot were sabred, but not so many as there ought to have been after undergoing one cutting up, let alone three. And the scattered individuals still showed fight. And we lost awfully; no wonder, for I will tell you what I saw.

"A man rode at an Arab who fired and missed him, and then seized his spear, with the apparent intention of meeting him as an infantry soldier should, according to Cocker. But when the horse was two yards from him he fell flat as a harlequin. The trooper leant over on the off side as low as he could and cut at the beggar, but could not reach him, and the moment he was past, the Arab jumped up and thrust his spear through him from behind. I never saw anything done so quickly in all my life; it was like magic.

"There was a clever old soldier who was not to be done that way; when he saw he could not get at his Arab, he slipped off his horse before you could say 'knife,' parried his spear-thrust, ran him through the body, and was up again like a shot. But it was heart-breaking business altogether; you should have seen the horses afterwards, cut about awfully, poor things; and we lost heavily in men too. The Colonel has had the dead Arabs' spears collected, and armed his regiment with them; and if they get another chance, you will see much more satisfactory business, I expect. But I must be off."

And off accordingly he went, his horse seeming pleased and proud to carry and obey him. And on went the brigade also towards Tokar.

Oracle number two proved the correct one; the enemy made no stand at the place, but streamed away at their approach, while the inhabitants came out to greet them with every demonstration of joy and gratitude.

Interpreters were few, and apt to be absorbed by senior officers, but it was gathered afterwards that the Tokarites were denouncing the Mahdi as a false prophet and heretic, whose soldiers had despoiled them of their goods, and only spared their lives on condition of their believing in him, and this condition they had thought it best to pretend to comply with, though their consciences rebuked them sorely for the pretended apostacy.

But though our friends of the First Blankshire could not understand all this, whatever officers of other corps may have done, the pantomime of the men, women, and children was unmistakable, and was only intended to express the most enthusiastic delight.

"I shall never make it out," said Green. "Have we relieved the place after all, then?"

"Cannot say; we shall find out, perhaps in general orders."

"Catch a newspaper correspondent; he will tell you all about it."

"At any rate, the gratitude of the poor people is quite touching."

"Not quite, thank goodness!" cried Fitzgerald; "at any rate so far as I am concerned; though a horrid old woman who cannot have washed for years, and who tainted the air with the rancid fat in her hair for yards round, tried to kiss me. But I dodged round the major's horse, and left her to him. In my humble opinion, we want the square formation quite as much to meet our native friends as our enemies."

Major Elmfoot got away from his demonstrative female, and rode up to the group.

"They seem very fond of us, sir," said Stacy.

"Yes," responded the major. "I wonder whether they went through the same performance when the Mahdi's army arrived."

"But they showed fight, and he took the place by storm, did he not, sir?"

"I really do not know; a spy said so. But the place does not look knocked about at all, and the people seem very jolly. I should not be surprised if the whole thing were a farce, and Tokar had not been besieged or taken at all."

"Then you do not think they are genuine in their welcome, sir?"

"I do not say that; these people have shops of a sort, I believe, and a customer is a customer all the world over."

The troops bivouacked outside Tokar, where nothing further occurred of any interest, and shortly afterwards they tramped back to the wells at El Teb, and so to Trinkitat, where they were re-embarked as quickly as might be, and steamed round to Suakim, which now became the base of operations.

And soon Trinkitat was entirely abandoned, and since no natives lived there (how could they when they had no fresh water?) the place ceased to be a place at all in any rational sense of the word.

You may have heard the old explanation of how a cannon is made: "you take a hole, and pour a lot of melted iron round it." Well, Trinkitat was a hole, and the English store-houses tents, soldiers, horses, camels were poured round it, and when they were withdrawn, nothing but the hole remained. But Suakim was a considerable place, built of coral too, and very interesting in its way to some people. And what was of more consequence, there were many good wells close by, from which water could be obtained all the year round.

Suakim itself, as has been explained before, is built on an island, but the British camp was on the mainland, within the circuit of earthworks which protected the town and harbour. It was on the eighth of March that the First Blankshire were landed at this camp. The look of the houses in the town disappointed some of them now they were closer.

"They don't look like coral at all," said Tom Strachan. "If I had not been told I should have thought they were the ordinary sun-dried brick affairs whitewashed."

"I vote we have a regular inspection of them on the first opportunity," said Edwards, "and settle the matter once for all."

"It would be kind to posterity," replied Tom.

"If you have so much time to spare, which I very much doubt," said MacBean, "you will employ it better in visiting a very pretty place and a curious. There is just a gap in the earthworks which protects Suakim, a regular breach as one may say, which has to be defended by two strong works, which the sailors have given the names of ships to—Euryalus and Carysfoot they call them. And why is the gap left? And why are the two forts made to defend it instead of filling it up? Just because the rains, which some don't believe in, make a torrent in the proper season, and this is the watercourse, and everything which barred its passage would be swept into the sea."

"I recant and apologise," said Green. "The rain quite convinced me of its existence at Baker's Fort, I promise you. But you know you sold me so often that I hardly knew what to believe."

"I never practise upon anybody's credulity in matters of that sort," said the doctor. "If a young man likes to believe that the moon is made of green cheese, I may let him; but atmospheric and scientific facts are above being trifled with. Well, if you go through this gap, which is barely a mile off, you will find a very pretty place—the wells, and sycamore trees, and dates. Just the place to spend a happy day. And if you take a bottle or two of champagne, and a *paté de foie gras*, I shall not mind if I make one of the party, and show you the objects of interest."

But such a pic-nic was not destined to come off, nor was there even any opportunity given for testing the coral theory, for there was plenty of work to be done at the moment, and on the eleventh the intending pleasure-seekers started for Baker's zereba at six o'clock in the evening.

Baker Pasha's Egyptians, though they had not proved much good at fighting, and had paid the penalty of their cowardice by undergoing a massacre which made the world thrill with horror, were very useful to the avenging force which followed so quickly on their traces. The fort they had constructed near Trinkitat had done much to help the rapid and successful advance upon Tokar; and now the zereba they had made eight miles out from Suakim, and in the direction in which Osman Digna lay with his whole army, made a good first halting-place for the English troops. A zereba, it should be mentioned, is an enclosed space surrounded by thorn-covered bushes cut down and packed round it, with old packing-cases, or anything else which will afford cover to those inside. This one was particularly strong, being further protected by a mound of earth all round it.

When the force, which was the same as before, with the addition of two hundred Marines, and a mule battery of four nine-pounders, had gone some little way, night fell, but not darkness, for a bright moon lent them her rays. Not such a moon as we are accustomed to in these latitudes, but a large brilliant orb, by whose light small print might be easily read.

"You have got the best of it," said MacBean, who rode up first to one friend amongst the officers and then to another, detailing information which he managed to pick up, he himself best knew how; but it was, as a rule, exceptionally correct. "The Highlanders, who marched out to the zereba yesterday in the heat, suffered awfully. There were five cases of sunstroke, and lots of other men had a narrow squeak of being bowled over too."

"I can easily imagine it," replied Major Elmfoot, "for it was hot enough in camp."

"It is not exactly what you would call bracing to-night, even," said Fitzgerald.

And, indeed, the air was very close, and the march over the loose sand fatiguing. But the men stepped out merrily, and joke and song lightened the way. There was an improvisatore in the Blankshire, whose comrades considered him a wonderful genius, though, as a matter of fact, his extempore effusions only consisted of taking some well-known song, and altering certain words or lines to suit a particular occasion.

But this was far more successful than original composition would have been, because it was so readily understood and caught up; and the man was really shrewd, and often hit on something appropriate.

He now trolled out in a clear, ringing voice, with every word distinct, a new version of "The Poacher":—

> "When I was bound apprentice in a village of Blanksheer,
> I served my master truly for close upon a year;
> But now I serves her Majesty, as you shall quickly hear,
> For 'tis my delight of a shiny night, in the season of the year."

And then the chorus broke out far and wide:—

> "For 'tis my delight of a shiny night, in the season of the year."

And the lads laughed at the aptness of the "shiny night," for that was evident to the dullest capacity.

Thus encouraged, he tried a second verse:—

> "As the soldiers and the sailors was a marching to his lair,
> Old Digna he was watching us, for him we didn't care;
> For the bayonet beats the spear when he rushes on our square,
> And 'tis my delight by day or night to beat the Johnnies fair."

Towards the end of the eight miles march indeed there was less singing and laughing, for throats were dry and legs weary. What, in eight miles and at night-time? Well, the next time you are staying at a sea side place, where there is plenty of sand, you try walking along it, not where it is firm, but higher up from the sea, where you sink over your ankles at every step; if you can borrow a rifle and a hundred rounds of ball cartridge and carry that too, you will be able to form a still more just opinion; but, even without that, I invite you to consider how many more miles of it you want when you have gone four. But if they were tired and thirsty they were full of spirit, and it would only have required the sight of an enemy to make them as lively as crickets again.

It was midnight when they arrived, and they bivouacked outside the zereba in the square formation, every man lying down in the place he would occupy if the force were attacked, so that if the alarm sounded, he had only to snatch up his rifle and rise to his feet, and he was ready for anything.

But they were not disturbed, and rested till noon on the 12th, when dinner was ea'en, and after it, at 1 p.m., they started once more to find the foe. As you draw cover after cover to find a fox, so in the desert you try watering-places when you are seeking game of any kind, quadruped or biped. And thus information was obtained that Osman Digna had a camp where all his forces were massed at Tamai, a valley well supplied with the precious fluid, nine miles from the zereba.

Once more was theory knocked over by experience. If there is one thing upon which most people feel quite confident about with regard to Egypt and the surrounding country, it is that the atmosphere is always perfectly clear, so that objects are only hidden from the eye by intervening high ground or the curve of the earth. For, as you probably know, anything on a (so called) level surface like the sea may be visible if the atmosphere allows it for ten miles, to a man on the same plane the shore say; but beyond that distance it gets so far round the globe we inhabit as to be hidden. Of course the taller it is the longer the top of it can be seen, as you will often perceive a ship's top masts after the hull and lower spars have vanished.

Or, on the other hand, the higher the ground you stand on the further round the earth's curve you can see; so that a man living on the top of a high mountain has a longer day than one on a flat, since the sun rises earlier and sets later for him.

But it was neither high ground nor the dip of the horizon which bounded the view of those quitting the zereba, but a thick, grey, British haze, which swallowed up everything a thousand yards in front, and out of which the Arab hosts might pour at any moment. The order of advance was different on this occasion, two squares instead of one being formed, the right under General Buller, and the left being commanded by General Davis. The guns were dragged with ropes by men of the Naval Brigade—a tug of war with a vengeance. The haze being so thick would have made it difficult to go straight for the enemy's position had the information been as uncertain as was sometimes the case, but happily it had been ascertained that if they took a south-west course they could not go far wrong, and the compass came to their aid.

The cavalry marched in rear of the square, with the exception of the scouts, who with the Mounted Infantry explored the ground in front, preventing the possibility of a surprise. Tramp, tramp, mile after mile, hour after hour, plodded the two brigades, with many a halt to enable the man-drawn guns to keep with them. But tedium and fatigue were thought nothing of. The man who would consider a five-mile walk without an object a frightful infliction would think nothing of ten with a gun in his hand, and the chance of game getting up every minute. It is the same with all sports. How far across country could you run alone for the mere sake of exercise? And how far in a paper-chase, with the hare to run down and other hounds to compete with? Think how this stimulating excitement must be intensified when there is an enemy in front of you certain to fight well, and make you do all you know to beat him. After awhile the haze grew thinner, and a range of hills loomed through it in the distance.

As the atmosphere grew clearer these became distinct, and were seen to be low, while a higher range rose above them beyond. On towards the higher ground slowly moved the two brigades, with a total front of from 400 to 500 yards, the scouts spread in a cloud before them, and these were now amongst the spurs of the lower hills.

Presently a couple of them came galloping back with the report that these were clear of the enemy, who were massed further behind, and were watching the English advance. And then a group of mounted infantry were seen returning at a slower pace.

"Look!" cried Strachan, whose eyes were remarkably good; "they have caught some natives."

And sure enough the troopers could presently be distinguished, coming on in a semi-circle, driving before them a group of men who were unarmed, and declared themselves friendly, or at least no adherents of the Mahdi, Osman Digna, or any votaries of the new Mohammedan heresy. This might be true, but the officer with the scouts thought the general had better decide so knotty a point, and so they were thus brought before him, travelling perhaps a little quicker than they were accustomed to, but otherwise uninjured.

"That's the way to run fellows in!" cried Tom, enthusiastically. "A fellow, you see, is bound to go straight when he has several rifles pointed at his head in cold blood. There goes the interpreter. I wish the colonel would just go up and hear what it is about, because he would tell the major, and the major would tell the captains loud enough for us poor subs to hear, perhaps."

"The colonel knows his duty," said Fitzgerald, "and does not intrude upon the general unless he is sent for."

"I know he doesn't, but I wish he did," replied Tom. "However, we shall get it all out of old MacBean."

And sure enough, soon after the captured natives had been pumped dry and dismissed, the doctor rode up.

"No fighting for you, my boys," he said. "The Arabs won't meet you this time, I expect, and you have had your walk for nothing. I expect that they see that the sun will lick us single-handed, and they need not take the trouble."

"What makes you say that?"

"Well, at El Teb, you know, they kept their women and boys with them, and these carried hatchets to kill our wounded with after the fight."

"That's their notion of surgery," said Tom, in a very audible aside.

"It goes more directly to its result than ours."

"Wait till you come under my hands, you young monkey! You will sing a different song then."

"I have no doubt you will hurt me more than Mrs. Arab would, doctor; but then you would cure me, you know, and she wouldn't."

"Never mind that cheeky boy, MacBean," said Fitzgerald. "Why won't they fight now?"

"Because they have sent all their women and boys away, and that, the friendly natives say, is a sure sign."

"Curious; it is just the other way on with other savage people, who send their families off when they *do* mean to fight."

"But the Arabs are only half savages; and besides they are quite unlike other people. Why, their lucky day is Friday, and their unlucky day Wednesday."

"Yes," said Tom Strachan, "and Robinson Crusoe called his savage Friday, and these fellows calls their Prophet Tuesday."

"Tuesday! What *do* you mean?" asked Major Elmfoot.

"Mardi is the French for Tuesday, is it not, sir?"

"Strachan, you are really too bad, to make such execrable puns in the middle of the desert."

"That is it, sir? I thought even my poor flowers of speech might be welcome in such a barren waste!"

Soon after this the colonel was called up to the brigadier, and when he returned he communicated what he had been told to his officers. The low hills being found clear of the enemy, it was intended to occupy them at once, and then if possible to advance upon the camp and the wells, and carry that position before nightfall. But this depended on what daylight they had, for rather than risk being overtaken by darkness in an unfavourable position, it was determined to form a zereba and wait for the advance till next day.

"It is just four o'clock," said Strachan, looking at his watch as he returned to his company; "and surely there must be a fair chance of carrying the wells before sunset, for I see a lot of the enemy on the hills beyond. Therefore I shall risk a drink," and he put his water-bottle to his lips accordingly.

"Hurrah! so will I," said Green.

"I have been fighting down the feeling of thirst for the last two hours. Do you know," he added, after a refreshing and yet a tantalising irrigation of the mouth and throat, "I have been haunted by a sort of waking dream while plodding on in silence this afternoon. There was an old man who used to bring fruit and ginger beer to the cricket-field at my school, and he has kept rising up in my memory so vividly that I could see every wrinkle in his face, and the strings which kept down the corks of his brown stone bottles as vividly as if they were before me."

"I wish they were!" cried Tom. "By Jove, what a trade the man might drive if he could be transported here just now."

"Oh! and I have often scorned that nectarial fluid," groaned Edwards, "or only considered it as a tolerable ingredient of shandy——"

"Silence!" cried Strachan.

"Don't utter that word, or I shall simply go mad. It is quite bad enough of the exasperating Green to allude to the homely pop, though one bore with it in consideration of the tender reminiscences of his childhood; but human endurance has its limits."

Those who reckoned on carrying the wells that night were over sanguine; when the rising ground was reached the progress of the guns was very slow; indeed, it was wonderful how the sailors managed to drag them on at all.

The atmosphere had now for some time become

perfectly clear; and when the infantry had surmounted the first hill they saw the broad valley of Tamai, and on the hills bounding it on the further side, corresponding with the somewhat lower range, where they stood, the enemy's lines were plainly discernible.

There were multitudes on foot, and others mounted, some on camels, some on horseback. The brigades halted, and the scouts pushed to the front, to unmask the enemy's position.

"Do you think we shall get on to-night, sir?" asked Major Elmfoot of the colonel.

"Not a chance of it," replied the chief. "But let the men lie still and have a good rest before they begin making the zereba."

So they did; even the youngest and most curious had learned by this time to husband their strength and snatch forty winks whenever they got a chance.

"They are at it!" cried Edwards presently, as crack! crack! was heard in front; and then a couple of volleys, followed by more single shots and more volleys again, and then, when the work seemed getting really hot, sudden silence. Some object had been obtained, but what it was exactly regimental officers could not know till they read all about it in the papers afterwards. However, the question of advancing that evening, which had before been answered practically, was now settled officially in the negative, and the order to make the zereba was issued. Mimosa and cactus trees, many of them seven feet high, grew thickly around, so there was no lack of material.

A position was chosen, protected on one side by a sand-hill, which made a natural rampart, and then parties were sent out to cut and bring in the cactus and mimosa bushes, and these were arranged round the space marked out, forming a prickly barrier. And at the same time the ground was cleared of cover where an enemy might lie concealed for from fifty to a hundred yards in every direction, and that was space sufficient to stop any number of Arabs rushing across it with steady rifle fire. And it soon became evident that this was no mean advantage, for heads were seen popping above the nearest bushes, on the borders of the zone which had been cleared, and it was evident that directly the scouts were withdrawn the Arabs had followed up to the English position, and were now prowling and prying around it.

As the wells could not be taken that night, and the horses could not do without water, the cavalry retraced their steps, and rode back to Baker's zereba, the point from which they had started in the morning. When they were gone the enemy entirely surrounded the zereba, which was like a ship in the midst of angry waves, hungry for her destruction. While daylight lasted the men inside watched Osman Digna's seemingly innumerable soldiers dodging about, and when night fell the knowledge that they were there unseen, and might attack on all sides at any moment, was really calculated to try the nerves. For there is nothing more unpleasant than the idea of any one pouncing upon you suddenly in the dark. But the nerves of our friends were getting pretty well seasoned by this time. Only Green, who was very frank, observed to Strachan that it seemed very lonely now the cavalry had gone. Mr. Tom, to tell the truth, had the same feeling of isolation, and even his high spirits were rather damped.

"I will tell you what is lonely if you like," he said plaintively, "and that is my last meal: it wants a companion very much indeed, and I could find plenty of room for it, and for a gallon or two of water besides."

"Yes, indeed," replied Green; "if one had a good square meal well moistened, one would feel, I think, that even the enemy were a sort of company."

But food and water had run very short, and some of the men were faint. The colonel made them a little speech; he was not an orator, but what he said was generally practical.

His remarks on the present occasion were to the following effect—

"We are short of rations, both liquid and solid, men; but you have plenty of cartridges, and the wells are but a mile and a half off, so that we only want daylight to get as much water as we please."

They got a supply sooner than was expected, however, for at half-past nine there was a bustle, and the sentries challenged; and, after a brief parley, a string of camels was admitted into the zereba, with water and other necessaries on their backs. Major Cholmondeley Turner had brought them over from Baker's zereba, and got them safely in clear of the Arabs. He belonged to the Egyptian Carrier Corps, and you may imagine how he was cheered.

The men lay down in lines two deep, leaving a space of twelve feet between the front rank and the hedge of the zereba. They wore their great coats and slept with their rifles in their hands, the officers being in rear. In the twelve foot space which was left the sentries patrolled, and there was no need to impress the necessity of vigilance upon them; the known vicinity of the enemy put them sufficiently on the *qui vive*.

All, however, was quiet till an hour after midnight, when the sleepers were awakened by a tremendous fusillade, and a storm of bullets came rushing over the zereba. But as the men were lying down, or crouching under the hedge, only a few unfortunate animals were struck by the leaden shower.

To show, however, what absurd things men will do in a panic, an Egyptian camel driver jumped, in his fright, over the prickly hedge, and ran along it *outside*, exposed to the enemy's bullets. These failed to strike him, but an English sentry inside naturally took him for an Arab trying to force an entrance, and shot him dead. The firing was still kept up by the enemy, and as some of the shots came lower, being sent through the hedges, the bivouac fires had to be put out, as their light evidently guided the Soudanese in their aim. The night was cold, and this was felt all the more after the heat of the day. And the men lay shivering, unable to sleep, and wishing for day.

As Strachan lay thus, wrapping himself round as closely as he could in his great coat, he heard a thud just in front of him, and the man lying there gave a gasp and straightened his limbs. Strachan rose and went to him, asking—

"Are you hit, my lad?" But there was no answer; he was quite dead.

This, however, was the only fatal effect of some four or five hours' incessant firing, for the Arabs kept it up for the remainder of the night.

At six o'clock the sun rose, and the enemy no longer had it all their own way. A nine-pounder was run up to the zereba hedge, and pointed in the direction from which the fusillade was hottest, and on another side a Gardner was brought to bear on a bit of cover where the Arabs clustered thickly. Ere the sun was quite above the horizon the loud sharp report of the former cheered the hearts of those who had been so hemmed in and pestered, and a second or so after there was a second bang as the avenging shell burst right among the bushes a thousand yards off. At the same time the ger-r-r of the machine gun told that its handle was turning, and its deadly missiles tearing through the light cover. The effect was immediate; the enemy cleared off like midges from a puff of tobacco smoke, and retired across the valley to their own lines.

At eight o'clock the troops issued from the zereba and advanced, as before, in two squares in *echelon*, as it is called, which means that one was in advance of the other, but not directly in front of it. If it were, and the force were attacked, you will easily see that the rear side of the leading square and the front side of the following square could not fire at anything between them without injuring one another. Or if they were on a level, side by side, it would be the same thing, the faces opposite could not use their rifles without firing into each other. But with one square a little in rear this danger is avoided, and each can support the other. Take a pencil and paper and draw two squares upon it if you do not see what I mean. Masses of the enemy could be seen crowning the hills in front and to the right, dark masses on the sides, distinct figures on the sky-line.

The route lay across dry water-courses, which were inconvenient for the square formation, the ranks being necessarily broken in descending and ascending the sides, so causing little delays while the men closed into their places again when clear. But they pressed steadily on, the Second Brigade leading. If the sun rose at six, why did not the troops march before eight? you may ask. Because the cavalry had to return from Baker's zereba, where they had gone the night before, you may remember, to water their horses. These now came to the front and spread out skirmishing. They were soon engaged with the enemy, and the firing grew very hot, forcing the skirmishers to retire, while the Arab masses pressed on. The leading square now came to the edge of a large *nullah* or dry river-bed, sixty feet deep and two hundred yards wide, thickly strewn with boulders, and having larger masses of rock rising from its depth.

This nullah was full of Arabs, crowds of whom swarmed up also to the further bank, and from these a heavy fire was poured upon the square, the other sides of which were also assailed. The First Blankshire was in this brigade, but not on the side next the nullah, and the men were firing rather wildly. For the first time since he joined Tom Strachan saw his captain, Fitzgerald, in a rage.

"You confounded idiots!" he yelled to his men, "what's the use of firing at them a mile off! What are you shooting at, Smith—a balloon? You are no use at all, Strachan; why don't you make your section reserve their fire? Steady, men, steady!"

All the other officers were making similar efforts, but for a time it was no good. Bodies of Arabs kept sweeping round some seven hundred yards off, watching their chance for a dash, and the men would keep firing at them, and, what was worse, hurriedly, without a cool aim. Indeed a good aim was not to be had, for they were only dimly seen through the smoke. And it was this probably which bothered the men; the ground in front was rough, and might conceal enemies close to them; there were swarms in all directions, and they fired at those they got a glimpse of.

Neither was the distance anything like out of range, only recent experience had shown that it required very severe concentration of fire at the closest quarters to make any impression on these brave Soudanese, and the losses which can be inflicted at seven hundred yards are slight comparatively, especially if the aim is not very cool and deliberate.

"Cease firing!" at last shouted a superior officer, and the word being promptly echoed by all, and enforced by actually grasping the shoulders of the most excited and flurried men, it slackened at length, and there seemed to be a good prospect of the unsteadiness calming down; and after all, this burst of wild firing had only lasted about three minutes. The atmosphere, however, was heavy; there was not a breath of air stirring, and the smoke hung in so thick a pall overhead, that it was impossible to see what was going on.

"Steady!" cried our friend Tom, who really had not deserved his captain's reproach, for he had been struggling all he knew to restrain his men's fire, only they got out of hand with him as with everybody else for a minute.

"Wait till the smoke clears, unless they come out of it a yard from your muzzles. Not a shot at present, or ever without a steady aim."

"That's right," shouted Major Elmfoot; "stick

to that, Strachan. No more wild shooting, men. Ah!"

There is an infinite variety of expression in the various tones of the human voice, and that simple "*Ah!*" conveyed more than I can give you any idea of. There was surprise in it and dismay, but not a suspicion of panic; on the contrary, determination was clearly expressed. The accent of the exclamation indeed was so striking that Strachan turned as sharply as if he had been struck, and at the further corner of the square he saw white teeth, gleaming eyes, tangled black locks, dark naked forms, and glittering spearheads, and—*British soldiers recoiling before them!*

As the major uttered his cry, he crammed his spurs into his horse's sides, and with one bound was among them, cutting and pointing like a trooper, and Tom found himself close to him, though whether he moved or the seething, struggling mass came upon him where he stood he did not quite know. One thing he felt sure of, that the situation was just as critical as it possibly could be. Careless, lighthearted lad as he was, he could not lead the life and pass through the scenes of the last few days without becoming familiar with the thought that every hour might very likely prove his last.

But that conviction, which would have been so terrible in cold blood, gave him little concern now; it was the feeling of *being beaten* which was such mental agony. What was his life, what was the life of any man, of a million of men, compared with defeat? At that moment he would have flung himself into the fire to secure victory for his side. I do not wish to make him out an exceptional hero, and he was not a fellow to brag, but it is certain that at that crisis he felt no fear whatever, no more than when having got hold of the ball in a football match at Harton, he had thought :

"I must have it between the goal posts, if I die for it!"

It has been explained before how he had attained a rare proficiency with his weapons; he had not fired his pistol yet, and he was as clear-headed and firm in nerve as man could be. While the chambers of his revolver were loaded he was in little danger from spearmen in front of him, for he parried the thrust with his sword, and shot the assailant *through the head*, and even an Arab is knocked out of time by that. But against a thrust in the side or the back no skill or coolness could defend him. And presently he was so jammed up by retreating soldiers that he could not use his arms, and then he was quite powerless for self-help.

It happened, by the best accounts, in this fashion. Covered by the dense smoke, the Arabs swarmed out of the nullah upon the face of the square on the edge of it. The foremost flung themselves on the bayonets; those behind pressing them on to them, the soldiers could not draw their weapons out, and found themselves hampered with dying foes, whose breast-bones were jammed against the muzzles of their rifles. If they drew back to release their weapons, the enemy took instantaneous advantage of the space yielded. When they strove to stand firm they were pushed bodily back by the dense mass surging upon them since the Soudanese in rear could push on with perfect impunity wherever the bayonets were sheathed in the bodies of the front rank. The sailors who manned the machine guns at one corner were driven back by main force with the rest, but made a desperate effort to keep back the savages, while certain parts without which the guns were useless could be removed. They succeeded, but at the cost of many lives, and then back they had to go, leaving the guns, now happily harmless, in the enemy's hands.

The confusion was frightful, the front face of the square being driven back upon the rear, and the sides jammed up with them. And then the whole tangled mass was forced slowly back, fighting its hardest. For there was no turning tail; the retreating soldiers kept their faces to the foe, and where they had their arms free delivered thrust for thrust. Marines and Highlanders fought back to back, and fought like bull-dogs. So did the Arabs for that matter; they lay tumbled over in hundreds, but others came on over their bodies. Seventy English were killed in a few minutes. Fighting thus the Second Brigade, now no longer a square, was pushed back nearly half a mile.

But now the charging Arabs came under the fire of the First Brigade, the square on the right, up to which the enemy had not been able to penetrate. This was so well directed and murderous as to check the rear masses of the Arabs, and the Second Brigade having only those in immediate contact to deal with, and relieved from the tremendous pressure, soon got on terms with their enemy again, shook them off, and recovered their lost formation.

The battle was restored; the retreat turned into an advance.

The Arabs, now driven back in turn, retired some distance and opened fire, which was not very effective. Indeed, in spite of it, the re-formed square, when it had recovered some hundred yards of its lost ground, was halted for a quarter of an hour for the purpose of serving out fresh ammunition, the men being exhorted not to waste it as they had done before. Desirous of retrieving their former error in this respect, they were as steady as veterans now, and advancing in line, firing deliberately and with careful aim, they cleared the ground in front, and fought back to the brink of the nullah where the enemy had broken their ranks, and re-captured the guns, the First Brigade moving up at the same time on their right. Savage with the idea that they had been forced to retire and leave their guns, though it was principally the sheer weight of numbers that had done it, and burning with revenge, the men set their teeth and went down into the nullah, clearing all before them. The Arabs defended every bush, every rock, every boulder; but there was no wild firing now, at thirty, twenty, ten paces, and even closer; every bullet had its billet, and the valley was cleared of the living, though every point which afforded cover, and had been tenaciously held by Osman Digna's soldiers, had its groups of corpses behind it.

Officers were intoxicated with delight at the way their men behaved after their early discouragement.

"That's the way!"

"Let them have it!"

"Give it 'em hot, boys!"

"Good man, O'Grady; there's another for you!"

"That's your sort; never pull trigger till you can blow him to smithereens."

The advance of the line was not rapid, but it left nothing living behind it. Then the First Brigade under Redvers Buller went into and across the nullah, making for the second ridge held by the enemy some half mile off, still keeping the square formation. It was well that the distance to be traversed was so short, for it was now getting on for ten o'clock, and the power of the sun was intense. The ground, too, was covered with sharp rocks of red granite, and these had become so hot as to burn the feet. But what do brave men feel in the delirium of battle? When close to the foe a volley rang out, and then from every parched throat "Hurrah!" "Hurrah!" "Hurrah!" burst forth, as with levelled bayonets they rushed upon the broken ranks before them, and the ridge was carried.

There was a second beyond it, where the Arabs still lingered, and for that again they went. But the enemy, the fight at last taken out of them, made but a feeble stand, and it was carried at the first onset. But what was that firing in their rear? Had a body of Soudanese lain concealed somewhere? Or had their dead come to life again? Neither.

One of the Gardner guns had been overturned into the limber containing its ammunition, and set fire to. This kept burning, hissing, and firing shots like a gigantic and malevolent cracker for a long time. But the Blue Jackets recovered the gun. When the victorious troops crowned the last ridge, the valley of Tamai lay below them, and there was spread the camp of Osman Digna, the object of their march, the prize for which they had been fighting. The enemy made no further attempt to defend it; they had proved to their cost that the Mahdi's assurance that the infidel guns would "spit water" was a lie.

They were disheartened, beaten at all points, and hundreds of their best and bravest lay in heaps on the hills and in the valleys to feed the vultures and the jackals. It was no retreat such as they often made, stalking slowly and sullenly from the field where they had been foiled, but a disorderly flight, a rout.

The camp was left to the conquerors, with two standards, all their ammunition, tents, stores, and the spoils of former victories, and before noon the English, without fear of molestation, were slaking their thirst at the wells.

CHAPTER XVII.

A SEARCH.

"MAY I go back to look for Strachan, sir, if you please?"

"Yes, Green," replied the colonel, "but take a file of men with you. I think there are none of these fellows left about, but some of the wounded may prove dangerous. Where did you last see him?"

"In the *mêlée*, sir, when the square was forced to retire. He was all right then."

"And did no one see him after that?"

"No one that I can hear of, sir."

"Ah, poor lad! Well, we must hope he will turn up alive. A good officer."

"Well, has the colonel given you leave to go?" asked Fitzgerald. "I knew he would, but Stacy did not care to take the responsibility, for fear anything should happen to you. You had better take a file of men of my company; they knew him best. I wish I could go, but I have too much to do. Of course, you will take a stretcher from the ambulance; it will be probably useful for some other fellow, if not for poor Tom."

Directly Green had turned from Fitzgerald, a sergeant brought a man up to him.

"James Gubbins wishes to speak to you, sir," he said, saluting.

"I beg your pardon, sir," said Gubbins when called upon to unfold his wishes, "but I heerd say as you was a-going back over them hills to look for Mr. Strachan, sir."

"Yes, Gubbins, what then?" asked Green.

"Well, sir, might I ask to go too? He was very kind to me, and I was in his ker—ker—company, sir;" and the man's voice faltered.

"Yes, Gubbins," replied Green, who appreciated perhaps more than others the sentiment which animated the poor fellow, for he himself had been a bit of a butt at first, and had been very grateful for Tom Strachan's friendship. "I am to take two men of Captain Fitzgerald's company, and you shall be one of them."

"Thank you kindly, sir."

"And pick another to go with him, will you, sergeant? a fellow with his wits about him, you know."

He did not add "to make up for poor Gubbins's deficiency in that respect," but that was what he meant, and so the sergeant understood him.

"Let me see," he said, on rejoining his company; "his servant would be the best man. Dodd! has any one seen Dodd?"

"He was killed, sergeant, just when the gun was taken."

"Ah, yes, so he was. Who to send? No, Sims, my lad; it would not do to have both idiots."

"I saw Mr. Strachan last, from all I can make out," said another man; "send me, sergeant."

"Ah, yes, Davis, you will do. Where was it though?"

"It was in the nullah, sergeant. One of the Johnnies got past my bayonet, and tried to wrestle, but I got my rifle at the port, and pushed it forward into his face, damaging the sights a little and knocking him down. And at that moment another of them jumped on my shoulders from a rock above, sending me sprawling on top of the chap I had just floored. I wriggled round and saw t'other with his spear up a couple of feet over my neck, when he tumbled over, and there was Mr. Strachan, with his sword well into the Johnny's stomach. I jumped up, and had no time to thank him, or see where he went. We was too busy."

"All right, you go at once with Gubbins to Mr. Green; he is speaking to the major, yonder. And hark! both of you. If you see an Arab lying like dead, with a weapon of any sort in his hand, run your bayonet through him first, and ask him if he is alive afterwards, for we have lost too many men as it is, and the duties will come heavy. Right about turn; quick march!"

"Well, good luck go with you," Major Elmfoot was saying, as Green started. "But I fear that he must be dead, or the ambulance would have found him and brought him in."

"I wish they would not talk like that," thought Green, as he went off, followed by his two men. "Everybody speaks of poor Tom in the past tense, from the colonel to Gubbins. I won't believe that he is dead till I see it; as for the ambulance, they have had plenty of work, and might easily miss him, if he is senseless, and unable to call out."

He went round to the Field Hospital, where the surgeons were busy at work, and applied for a stretcher. But he was told it was unnecessary to take one, there were several about the fatal spot where the hard fighting had taken place, and two others which had just brought in their blood-stained burdens were going back presently.

So the three went on their way unencumbered.

It was perfectly calm and still; the sun was getting low in the west, but its rays, though not so scorching as at mid-day, were sickening, and productive of extreme lassitude. On the first low range of hills they crossed the bodies were not numerous, and down in the valley at the foot of them they only came upon one group. A knot of Arabs retreating to their last position had evidently been overtaken by a shell bursting in their midst, and their fearfully mangled bodies showed what modern science can effect when applied in earnest to the work of war. On the next ridge the Soudanese dead lay thicker; lying dotted about singly where the Martini-Henry bullets had stopped them, or strewed in rows like the corn sheaves where the reaping machine has passed, as the Gatling guns, sweeping slowly from right to left, and pouring missiles with the regularity and continuous stream of a fire-engine, had mowed their ranks.

"I say, Gubbins," said Davis, "we fought fairly well to-day I reckon; but do you think we should have stood against such a fire as that?"

"Well, I don't know," replied Gubbins. "If there had been any cover near I, for one, should have felt uncommon inclined to make for it. I can't abide them shells and machine guns."

"No, it seems like fighting against lightning and thunderbolts, don't it?" said Davis.

But as this was an idea which required some cogitation and digesting before it could become assimilated in the Gubbins' mind, it remained without reply.

As they approached the edge of the nullah the harvest of Soudanese lay thicker and thicker, and when they got down into the dry bed of the watercourse, they had to pick their way in places to avoid treading on the corpses.

And here, for the first time, English dead lay intermingled with the Arab. There was peace between them now.

"Look carefully here," said Green, turning over a karkee-clad body which lay on its face as he spoke: it was not his friend.

"Ah, would yer!" cried Davis, presently; and there was a gasp and a cry, which might be rage or pain, as he thrust his bayonet into an Arab who, though his legs were shattered, made a cut at him with his sword as he passed. And Davis was as tender-hearted a man as ever stepped; liked playing with children; petted dogs, cats, and birds; and would risk his own life to save that of another, though a perfect stranger. He had proved it, and had the right to wear the medal of the Royal Humane Society on his right breast. But circumstances are too strong for all of us.

The search was long and ineffective.

"You are certain it was in the nullah that Mr. Strachan killed the Arab who was on the top of you?" Green asked Davis.

"Certain, sir; and that rock I showed you was the one the Johnny jumped off, I am pretty sure; though there's such a many of them, and they are so like, I wouldn't swear."

"And you had not leisure to look very particularly. But still, though you saw him here, he may have gone back for some of his men, for in dodging the enemy round stones and bushes they got scattered a bit. We had better go over the ground where we were so hard at it."

So they clambered up the further bank of the nullah, and stood again on the ground over which they had advanced, been driven back, and advanced again in the morning. Here the Soudanese lay in hundreds, piled up in places in heaps, three or even four deep, one on the top of another. And here too the English dead were terribly thick. But the ambulance had been at work for some hours, and all who had life in them were removed, while many of the dead had been withdrawn from the mingled heaps, and laid decently side by side, and apart.

Green saw that this acre of the Aceldama had been, or was being, thoroughly explored, and he returned to the nullah, where the three continued their search, examining now the outlying crevices and bushes, where individual men, stricken to death, had crawled away; or the pursuing English, observing skulking foes, had spread to clear them out, and prevent being fired upon from the rear after they had passed; and searching in this manner they got separated.

Where could poor Tom Strachan have got to? The sun was sinking fast, there would not be much more daylight, and if he were not found soon he might be left without help all night. For Green would not think of him as dead, and no more for that matter did Gubbins, though Davis had given up all hope long ago. But he did not say so.

Walking up the nullah a bit to the right, Green came to the foot of a huge mass of black rock about twelve feet high, and he thought that from the top of that he might get a more extended view of the bed of the nullah, and perhaps discern some hollow which had not yet been explored. The climbing was not difficult, and he soon sprang up. There were smaller boulders on the little plateau, and a mimosa bush, and an English officer lying on his back, with his arms extended, and his sword attached to his right wrist.

Green ran to his side; it was the object of his search—Tom Strachan.

"Dead!" he cried "Poor old Tom; dead after all!"

He knelt down and took his left arm up in order to get nearer to his body, to feel if there was warmth in it.

The arm was limp, not stiff; the fingers had been cut by some sharp weapon, and when stirred, blood dropped from them. These signs gave Green fresh hope, and loosening the karkee, he thrust his hand into his breast. Certainly there was warmth!

He raised the body a little, propping the shoulders against a stone, and taking out a flask he had brought for the purpose, he poured a little brandy into the mouth. It was swallowed. He gave him more, and presently he moved his lips and eyelids.

His first fear over, Green examined him more closely, and found that his clothes were saturated with blood from a broad wound, no doubt a spear-thrust, in the right side. Surgeons were not far, and immediate assistance might be everything, so he rose and went to the edge of the rock to call Davis or Gubbins, who must be within reach of his voice.

Shouting their names, he passed close to the mimosa bush, from the cover of which a man, with tangled locks and glaring eyes, and naked, but for a waist-cloth, sprang out upon him like a wild cat.

He had lost or broken his weapons, but he clasped the young officer in his arms, and bore him to the ground, and then, searching for his throat with his hands, sought to throttle him, while Green, keeping his chin down to his chest, and dragging at his hands, strove to prevent his design.

The movement was so sudden that he never suspected the Arab's presence till he was on him. The savage wrenched his left arm free; Green upon this got his right hand down, and managed to clutch his revolver; and just as his enemy's fingers forced their way under his chin to his throat, he put the muzzle to his head and pulled the trigger.

His helmet having fallen off in the struggle, his own hair was singed by the explosion, but he was free; the Arab rolled away from him, his head shattered—a gruesome spectacle.

Just as Green got to his feet again, his two men appeared on the rock. They had heard him call, and the voice had guided them in that direction; and while they were hesitating the pistol-shot told them exactly where their officer was.

"He is up here, and alive," said Green. "Run, one of you—you, Davis—to the place where we saw the doctors and stretchers, and tell them. Take good note of this spot, that you may not miss it. But I don't think they are a thousand yards off."

"I shall know it, sir," said Davis, and he disappeared over the side of the rock.

Green was now once more by Strachan's side, and with Gubbins' help got him into a more comfortable position. The spear-head which had wounded him, with a couple of feet of the shaft, lay close by, as if he had pulled it out before losing consciousness. The rest of the shaft also lay near, half cut through, half broken, close to the edge of the rock, and underneath that spot, at the foot of the crag, was the body of an Arab—head amongst the large stones, feet and legs uppermost—resting on the steep side.

Probably it was the man who had speared Strachan, his weapon, previously hacked nearly through, breaking with the thrust. And one of the soldiers storming the rock had shot him as he was making off. As for the disarmed man who had attacked Green, he had probably taken refuge up there after the tide of battle had swept past, intending to escape at nightfall, but the sight of a foe so close was too tempting for his prudence.

All this, however, is only conjecture; the certain fact was that poor Tom Strachan had a wide wound in the side, and that Green dared not move him much, because it made the life-stream well out afresh. There was nothing for it but to wait till medical aid arrived.

It is surprising what trivial ideas and memories, such as tags of old songs, or anecdotes more or less appropriate to the occasion, will run in our heads when we are anxious about anything, and are forced to remain in inactivity. All the time certain lines of Sir Walter Scott would worry Green, as he knelt there by his friend:

> "That spear wound has our master sped;
> And see the deep cut on his head.
> Good night to Marmion."

Over and over and over again rang the lines, till

Strachan himself dissipated them by moving his hand and murmuring. It was evident that what he wanted was water, and so Green put his gourd to his mouth, and after a refreshing draught, consciousness returned to the wounded man's eyes.

Then Green gently disengaged the sword-knot from his wrist, and, unbuckling his belt, returned the weapon to its scabbard, not without having to wipe it first.

Strachan made a movement of his hand again towards it, evidently knowing that something was taken from him. But Green showed him the sword, and said, "It is all right, I am only wiping it for you;" and the other was placid again immediately, and closed his eyes.

It was not long before the surgeon came, and they got Strachan's karkee jacket off, and bandaged him up.

"He has lost a lot of blood," said the surgeon, "and that is why he fainted, probably."

"Will it kill him?"

"Not necessarily at all. It is a nice clean wound, and all depends upon how far it has penetrated. Of course, a man cannot have a sharp instrument thrust into his body without some danger to the vital organs. The pressing matter, however, is how to lower him from this. I have got a stretcher at the bottom all right, but the sides of this rock are pretty steep for a badly wounded man to get down."

"Yes," said Green.

"But I have examined carefully all round it, and this is the best place."

And he indicated a corner where there were ledges which formed steps; and here they carried

Tom Strachan, and lowered him as gently and carefully as might be.

They could not avoid a jolt or two, which elicited a moan; but it was not far to the bottom, and there was the stretcher. Just as they had managed to get him settled the sun sank, and it was amidst the usual display of orange, crimson, and purple fireworks that they picked their way amongst the corpses which strewed the nullah. It was another job to carry their burden up the steep sides of this, but they managed it before darkness settled down on the battle-field.

At the other side, however, they were soon forced to halt, and wait for the rising of the moon. She was up, but had not appeared over the hills yet, and the ground where they were was in such deep shadow that the bearers could not go a dozen yards without stumbling either over a dead body or the inequalities of the surface. It was a weird thing to wait there in the gloom in the midst of those who had been so full of life and vigour in the morning, and were now as motionless, senseless, as the boulders amongst which they were scattered.

While waiting thus, they fancied they saw several dark figures gliding by them, and Green held his revolver ready, thinking that live Arabs were still prowling around, or taking advantage of the darkness to escape from the nooks where they had lain concealed. Presently, however, the moon topped the higher ground, and he saw one of these moving forms more distinctly, and perceived that it was a four-footed animal, not a biped. Probably they were beasts of prey stealing to the scene of carnage. It takes a good deal of the gilt off glory that the foulest beasts and birds should take heroes for carrion. And yet, after all, this is a superficial way of looking at it, for it is the qualities of the mind—courage, endurance, patriotism, loyalty, fidelity to comrades—which make the hero, and the soul is beyond the reach of vulture or jackal. As for the mere body without it, it is of no more value than an empty champagne bottle. When there was light enough they went on again, and in due time reached the ambulance. And Green, having seen his friend made as comfortable as was possible under the circumstances, returned to the bivouac of the regiment, where everybody was glad to hear that Tom Strachan was found alive, and that there was a good chance for him, for his good humour and high spirits had made him a general favourite.

"Do you know, Green, you have done a very fine thing?" said the colonel. "If you had not found Strachan this evening he would have been dead in all probability before morning. And you found him very cleverly."

And Green felt as good all over at this praise as if he had been mentioned in despatches.

The battle of Tamai was the end of the campaign. Some folk said the troops should have taken advantage of the rout and dispersion of Osman Digna's tribes to march across to Berber on the Nile, and then Khartoum would have been relieved without any further fuss. Other people, who had equally good means of judging, scorned this idea, and were certain that had such a thing been attempted every man of the expedition would have perished.

If the latter people were right, the authorities acted wisely; if the former had reason on their side, they acted foolishly. But as to which is which, it would be very rash for any one who does not know all the ins and outs, and has not the evidence which influenced those who had to decide, before him, to give an opinion. Anyhow, the expedition returned to Suakim, and the majority of the troops sailed away for different places. And Osman Digna had time to gather fresh fanatics together, and the Soudanese recovered from the shock to their superstition and conviction of invincibility which the hecatombs of slaughter had given them, and were soon ready to fight again.

And Tom Strachan was not so very badly hurt, but was soon able to be taken home to England to be nursed, and rejoined his regiment in six months.

CHAPTER XVIII.

AGAINST THE STREAM.

A SWIFT broad river, with the water broken into foaming wavelets by rocks which were everywhere showing their vicious heads above the surface; a string of nuggars, or half-decked boats, fifteen feet broad, forty-five feet long, flat-bottomed, each with a thick rope attached to the bows, and a string of men on the bank towing it under a hot sun.

Perhaps you have yourself towed a skiff on the Thames, when the current was so strong that the progress made with the oars was unsatisfactory. Well, if you have, you *don't* know one bit what this was like. In the first place, the Thames, even by Monkey Island, is still water compared to the Nile between Surras and Dal, a sixty-mile stretch. Then your skiff did not carry six tons of beef, bacon, biscuit, and other stores. It may also be safely asserted that the towing-path you walked on was not composed of sharp pointed rocks.

Those were the conditions under which certain picked British soldiers, one of whom was an old friend of ours, lost sight of for a considerable time, were dragging their nuggar up a series of cataracts. Towing always looks to me an absurd business, much as if a man were to carry a horse about, and call it going for a ride.

"Are you growling or singing, Tarrant?" asked Kavanagh of the man behind him on the string.

"Not singing, you may take your davy," growled the man addressed.

"I fancied not, though there is a certain likeness in your way of doing both which made me ask. I suppose you are growling then—what about?"

"What about, indeed!" grunted Tarrant. "D'ye suppose I 'listed as a soldier or a barge horse?"

"Don't know; never saw your attestation papers."

"Why, it was as a soldier then. I should have thought twice if I had known I was to be put to this sort of work."

"Really! why, when we were rowing, you did not like that, and said you would sooner be doing any work on your legs."

"But I didn't mean this; why, I have cut two pairs of boots to pieces against these here sharp rocks since we began it."

"Ay," said Kavanagh, "but you had already worn out some of your garments at the other game, so it was only considerate to give the feet a chance."

"Well, it's a pity them that likes it should not have the doing of it," said the judicious Tarrant.

"Well, you know, you could not pull an oar, and you *can* pull a rope," said Grady, "so you are a trifle more useful now than you were before; and begorra you had need."

"I could pull a rope if it were over the bough of a tree, and the other end round your neck," snarled Tarrant.

"Oh, the murdering villain!" cried Grady. "And would ye be after hanging a poor boy who never harmed ye in all his life?"

"Well, keep a civil tongue in your head."

"Sure, and it's myself that has kissed the Blarney stone, and can do that same. And if you had such a thing as a bottle of whisky or a pound of tobacco about you, I would make you believe you were a pleasant companion, and pretty to look at besides. But what's the use of telling lies when there's nothing to be got by it?"

"Suppose you were to pull a bit harder and talk a bit less," said Corporal Adams.

"And I will, corporal dear," replied Grady. "But sure I thought we was marching at ease."

It may be well to explain that when troops get the word *March at ease!*—which is generally given directly they step off, when they are not drilling or manœuvring, but simply on the route—they are allowed to carry their arms as they please, open the ranks, though without losing their places or straggling, smoke their pipes, and chat or sing if they like.

At the word of command—*Attention!* they close up, slope their arms properly, put away their pipes, and tramp on in perfect silence.

But marching at ease was such a singularly inappropriate expression for men who were dragging a heavy nuggar up a cataract under a blazing sun that there was a general laugh, and even Tarrant relaxed into a grin. A general laugh, I say, not a universal one, for MacIntosh, who was plodding along behind Grady, preserved his gravity.

"I don't say that silence is incumberous," explained Corporal Adams, who, since he had got his stripes, had taken to using rather fine language, "but too much talking don't go with hauling."

"Ho, ho, ho!" chuckled MacIntosh, and the corporal began to think he had said something funny. But no; MacIntosh had trodden on an unusually sharp flint, and that presented Grady's idea of what marching at ease was in a ridiculous form to his mind. So when the pang was over he was tickled.

"Eh, but Grady's a poor daft creature to call this marching at ease; ho, ho!"

A particularly stiff bit came just now. The rope strained as if it would snap; the bows of the nuggar were buried in foam, and the men hauling were forced to take the corporal's hint, and keep their breath for other purposes than conversation.

When they had got over the worst, however, the boat got jammed on a rock, and the work of getting her off devolved on the crew on board of her, unless she were so fast as to require the aid of the others, who for the present got a much-required rest.

"A set of duffers, those chaps," said the sergeant in charge of the party, a young fellow named Barton, of good parentage, and Kavanagh's particular friend off duty. "A regular Nile reis, with his crew of four natives, would never have stuck the nuggar *there*."

"I wish we had them Canadian vogajaws, sergeant," said Corporal Adams.

"Ay, they are first-rate," replied the sergeant.

"A good many boats have them, haven't they?"

"Oh, yes! most I suppose, or we should not get on at all. But we have not had the luck to get them for our craft. There are only a few of these who know how to work a boat up rapids at all, and I fancy they are only apprentices at it. As for the others, one of them owned to me that he had never been on any river before the Nile but the Thames at Putney, and his idea of a rapid was the tide rushing under the bridge."

"But sure, sergeant, he can sing 'Row, brothers, row,' iligantly, he can," said Grady.

"Ay, but he can't do it," replied the sergeant. "He ought to be in the water now. There's Captain Reece overboard and shoving; I must try and get to him. Stand by the rope, men, and haul away like blazes when she shifts."

What with poling, and shoving, and pulling at the rope, the nuggar was floated once more at last, and on they went again, and by-and-by the river widened, and the current was not so strong, and so long as they kept the rope pretty taut the boat came along without any very great exertion.

"Have a pipe out of my baccy-box, just to show there's no malice?" said Grady to Tarrant.

"Thankee, I will," replied Tarrant, "for mine is so wet it won't burn. I went up to my neck in shoving off the first time we stuck, before we took to towing."

"Eh, but that was a chance for the crocodiles!" cried MacIntosh. "I saw ye go souse under, Tarrant, and thought one of them had got ye by the leg. Ye might have grumbled a bit then, and folks would have said you had reason."

"It is all very fine," said Tarrant, "and if you chaps are pleased, you are welcome; but I don't call this riding on a camel. I had as soon have stopped with my own regiment, amongst sensible and pleasant lads, and taken my chance, as have volunteered to join this corps, if I had known I was to march all the same, and lug a beast of a boat after me too. I expected to have a camel to ride on."

"Thank you for putting me in mind that I'm mounted," said Grady; "I had almost forgotten it."

"Make your minds easy," said Sergeant Barton.

"You will have plenty of camel riding in a day or two, quite as much as you like perhaps."

"And I hope it will be before I have worn out my third pair of boots," said MacIntosh. "Eh, but this is a grievous waste of shoe-leather."

"I had sooner wear that out than my own skin," said Kavanagh.

"I'm not that sure," replied MacIntosh. "The skin grows again, and the shoe-leather doesn't."

The sergeant laughed.

"Well, I think I may promise you that you will have no more of this work after to-morrow," he said. "You will get your camels at Wady Halfa." Barton had been specially instructed in camel drill, and selected for his proficiency to assist in training the corps to which Kavanagh belonged.

His story was a very simple one; he was not one of the plucked, who, failing to get their commissions, join the ranks rather than not serve at all, for it was most likely that he would have succeeded in any competitive examination, being a clever and industrious youth, who was doing well at Oxford when his father lost all his money, having shares in a bank which suddenly failed, and left him responsible to the extent of every penny he possessed. The undergraduate had been accustomed to a handsome allowance, and owed bills which he was now unable to pay. This he could not help, but being an honourable man he would not incur a farthing more, but took his name off the boards at once, divided his caution money, and what was obtained by the sale of his horse, the furniture of his rooms, and whatever else he possessed, amongst his creditors, and enlisted. Having once chosen his profession, he went at it with prodigious zeal, and lost no opportunity of attending any school of instruction which was open to him. When he had once acquired his drill, he was soon made corporal, then sergeant. He distinguished himself at Hythe; he learnt signalling both with flags and flashes. And when useful men were wanted for the formation of Camel Corps, and the battalions in Egypt searched for them, he was one of the first pitched upon to learn and then to instruct. For, when people talk of the super-human intelligence of German officers and soldiers, and speak of ours as a set of dunder-headed idiots, you need not quite take all they say for absolute fact. I think if you took the adjutants, sergeant-majors, and musketry instructors of the British army, you would find it hard to pick out an equal number of men in any country, even Germany itself, to beat them for intelligence, common sense, and promptitude.

"There will be a new drill to learn!" growled Tarrant.

"Oh, that won't be much," said Kavanagh. "Lots of old words of command would do over again, I should say. For instance, 'Shouldare—oop!' only it would be the camel's shoulder which has to be mounted."

"Now, that's mighty clever," said Grady. "Will you tell me something, Kavanagh, you that's a real scholar now—can a man be two things at the same time?"

"Of course he can; he can be an Irishman and a barge horse, you see."

"Ah, then a Mounted Infantry man can be a trooper and a foot soldier all at once. And a camel rider, would you call him a horse soldier, now?"

"No, Pat, I could not afford it. I'm an Irishman as well as yourself, and dull people would think it was a blunder."

"That's a true word," said Grady. "And have you not noticed now, when folks laugh at an Irishman, he is mostly quite right if they had the understanding? Now you have observed, and heard, what a bad country Egypt is for the eyes. Sure they give us green goggles, or we should get the—what do you call it, Mr. Corporal, sir, if you plaze?"

"The hop-fallimy," replied Corporal Adams, proud of being appealed to.

"Thank you; the hop-family, what with the sun, and the sand, and the flies. And if you get the hop-family you are likely to go blind, and that is a bad thing. Is it not curious that the great river of a country that is so bad for the eyes should have cataracts itself in it? Now that would sound foolish to many people, but you, who are an Irishman, see the bearings of it, don't you now?"

"But," observed MacIntosh, "a cataract in the eye is a skin, or something growing over it, and a cataract in the river is a kind of waterfall. They are not the same sort of thing at all."

"And is that so? To be sure, now, what a stupid mistake then I made. And did you ever undergo the operation, now, MacIntosh?"

"Well, beyond vaccination and the lugging out of a broken tooth, I don't call to mind that I have been in the surgeon's hands; and if ye want to know the truth, I don't care if I never am. Eh, but that tooth now, it took a tug!"

"I thought you had never had it done," said Grady. "It's a pity, sure. And what do you say makes a cataract in the Nile?"

"Surely you have seen enough of them for yersel'. It's a rapid where the water comes down a steep part with great vehemence. But what operation are ye talking of? I expect ye mean some sauce or other."

"Sure, no; it's only that which they say a Scotchman must have done before a joke can be got into his head. But I don't belave it at all; folks are such liars!" said Grady.

"I would have ye to know," said MacIntosh, when the others had stopped laughing, "that a Scotchman is not deficient in wut, but he can't see it in mere nonsense."

All this talk was not spoken right off the reel, as it reads, but at intervals, during pauses in the harder part of the work, and rests. And it was lucky they could keep their spirits up; there is health and vigour in that:

> "The merry heart goes all the day;
> The heavy tires in a mile—a!"

Shakespeare is always right.

But the sergeant was better than his word, and that was their last afternoon of rowing or towing, for they reached the place where the camels were collected that evening before sun-down. On the very next day the new drill commenced, for there was not an hour to be lost.

The last days of 1884 had arrived, and Khartoum still held out. The chances of reaching that place and rescuing Gordon were always present to every mind; that was the one goal to which all efforts were tending. But there was no good in for ever talking about it; on the contrary, it was more healthy to divert the thoughts, if possible, in other directions.

A fall from a horse is unpleasant, and risky to the bones, but a tumble off a camel is worse, because it is more dangerous to fall ten feet than five. The first step was a difficulty—to mount the creature at all, that is. It looks easy enough, for it lies down for you. Apparently all you have to do is to throw one leg over and settle yourself in the saddle. But the camel has a habit of springing up like a Jack-in-the-box just as your ankle is on a level with his back, and away you go flying. Experienced travellers, who have camel drivers and attendants, make one of them stand on the creature's fore legs to keep them down while they settle themselves; but troopers had no such luxuries provided for them, and had to look after their animals themselves, and it took several trials and severe rolls on the sand before some of them managed to mount at all. There the camel lay, quiet and tame and lazy, to all appearance as a cat dozing before the fire. But the moment the foot was over his back he resembled the same cat when she sees a mouse, and away you went. Taught by experience, you spring into the saddle with a vault. Up goes the camel on the first two joints of his fore-legs with a jerk which sends the small of your back against the hinder pommel so violently that you think the spine broken. Before you have time to decide this important question in your mind, the hind legs go up with an equally spasmodic movement, and you hit the front pommel hard with your stomach.

Surely now you are settled; not a bit of it. The beast jumps from his knees to his feet with a third spring, and your back gets another severe blow from the hind pommel. After these three pommellings you are mounted. But when you want to get off, and your camel lies down for you, you get it all over again; only your stomach gets the hits one and three, and your back the middle one. Opinions differ as to which is the most pleasant, but after several repetitions of it you feel as if you had been down in the middle of a scrimmage at football, and both sides had taken you for the object to be kicked at. The ordinary traveller, when once on his camel, would stop there some hours; and again, when he got off, would remain off till it was time to renew his journey, and so he would not get so much of it. But a soldier learning camel drill must go on till he is perfect.

After mounting, dismounting, and re-mounting a certain number of times, the troopers learned to anticipate the camel jerks, and avoid the high pommels which rose in front and rear of the saddles, or rather to use them as aids instead of encumbrances. But it took a good deal of practice, and some were longer about falling into it than others. But they were not always at drill, though they had so much of it.

Some went in for fishing, and hooks and lines had been provided by the authorities for that purpose. But the sport was very poor, little being caught, and after trying it once or twice Kavanagh preferred to sit under the tree or in an arbour and smoke his pipe either alone or with a companion—Sergeant Barton for choice, but he was not always available. When that was the case the honest Grady would sometimes join him, and though he would rather have been left to his own thoughts, it was not in his nature to show a want of cordiality towards a good fellow who made advances to him. From the day of his enlistment Reginald Kavanagh had frankly accepted the situation, and had been careful above all things to avoid giving himself any airs of superiority.

"This is a mighty pretty spot you have fixed on, any way," said Grady, stretching himself under the grateful shade of a palm tree, "and reminds me of Oireland entirely!"

"It is rather like Merrion Square," said Kavanagh, gravely; "or that perhaps combined with the Phœnix Park, with a touch of the Lakes of Killarney."

"Sure, now, you are making fun of a poor boy! Look at that bird now! Isn't he an illigant bird that? There's a many of them about, and they are the best looking I have seen at all in Egypt."

"Do they remind you of Ireland, too?" asked Kavanagh.

"Well, now, you are too hard on me."

"Not a bit of it, it is only natural that they should, for they are called Paddy birds."

"And is that a fact now?"

"Certainly it is. Sergeant Barton told me, and he has been some time in Egypt, and knows most of the birds and animals," replied Kavanagh.

"Well, now, it is only natural that the loveliest bird in the country should be called Paddy. Are not the finest men and the prettiest girls at all Irishmen? They call us every bad name there is, but they can't do without us. Why, the general is an Irishman, and the Goughs and Napiers are Irishmen, and the Duke of Wellington was an Irishman."

"And Grady and Kavanagh, the best men that ever rode on camels—or who will be when they can sit them—are Irishmen," cried Kavanagh, laughing, and Grady chuckled too.

"But, now, there's a thing I want to ask you, since you are larned about animals. You may not have thought it, for I am no scholar, but when I was a gossoon I went to school," said Grady presently, "and they had pictures of bastes hung about the walls, and the queerest baste of all to my fancy, barring the elephant, was the camel. I remember purty well what they told me from the mouth, though I was bad at the reading and the sums and that; and the master he said that a camel with one hump was meant for carrying things, water and potatoes and other necessities, and that was why he had only one, to make more room, and have something to tie them on by. And he said there was another camel with two humps, and he was created for riding, and was called a dromedary, and when ye rode him, ye sat at your ease between the two humps, which made a soft saddle, just like an arm-chair ye straddled on, only without arms. And ye could go fast and easy for a week, with provisions all round ye, and the dromedary he only wanted to eat and drink once a week. Now, have the dromedaries died out, do ye think? or are they more expensive, and is the War Office that mane it won't afford them, but trates Christians like baggage?"

"They were out of it altogether at your school, Grady," said Kavanagh. "A dromedary is only a better bred camel; it is like a hack or hunter, and a cart-horse, you know; the dromedary answering to the former. But both are camels, just the same as both the others are horses, and one hump unluckily is all either of them possess."

"But I saw the pictures of them," said Grady, with a puzzled look.

"I wish that the pictures had been painted from real animals, and not from the artist's fancy," repeated Kavanagh. "It was a general idea, I know—I had it myself—that there were two-humped camels, mighty pleasant to ride. But I believe it is all a mistake."

"The one-humped beggar is not easy to ride, any how!" said Grady.

"No, that I vow he isn't!" cried Kavanagh. "Some of the camels trained to trot, and called hygeens, are a bit easier, I believe. The Arabs say that they can drink a cup of coffee on their backs without spilling it while they are going at speed."

"We have not got any of them in our troop," said Grady. "Well, we will get a bit of a holiday, plaze the pigs, the day after to-morrow, and not before I want it, for one. For what with them saddle peaks, and the rolls on the sand I have got, I don't know whether my inwards or my outwards are the sorest. But the show is beginning; and, faith, it's worth coming all the way to Egypt to see the sun set."

This was one of the things which made Kavanagh like Grady's company; he had a real innate love of the beauties of Nature, which you would rarely find in an Englishman of the same class. Together they watched the glories of the transformation scene shifting before them. Low on the horizon the deepest crimson changing and blending as it rose into violet; higher up the blue of the sapphire and the green of the emerald; and when these colours were the most intense, the two rose, and turned back to camp slowly and reluctantly, still gazing in silence. For now the after-glow succeeded; first the sky was a most brilliant orange, such a tint as would cause the painter who could at all approach it to be accused of the most absurd exaggeration by those who had not seen the real colour, while those who had would esteem it far too faint. This changed to an equally brilliant rose colour; and then, in a few seconds, suddenly, as if "Lights out" had been sounded in the zenith, darkness!

"It is like going to church," said Grady.

"Yes," replied Kavanagh; "that makes one feel God great and man little, doesn't it?"

"Aye!"

They were barely a quarter of an hour from camp, and the fires guided them; for hot as it was in the daytime the nights were chilly, and a bonfire in the open acceptable. They found their mates gathered round the largest in great excitement.

"Here, you chaps," was the cry which assailed them when they made their appearance, "can either of you make a plum-pudding?"

"Of course," replied Kavanagh. "There's nothing easier if you only have the materials."

"Well, the materials have just come; how do you work them up?"

"Why, make them into a pudding and boil it, of course."

"Any idiot knows that; but how do you make them into a pudding? If we spoil one, you know, we shan't have any opportunity of trying a second time, so none of your experiments."

"That's serious!"

"I should think it was!"

"Well, you take the flour and put it in a basin, and moisten it with water; and you put in your plums and raisins and citron, and beat up half a dozen eggs and put them in too, and three glasses of brandy, and anything else that's good you have got, and you knead it all up for a good bit, and put it in a cloth, and tie it up tight with a piece of string, and boil it as long as you can; all to-night and to-morrow and to-morrow night, and so right up to dinner-time."

"It sounds pretty right," said the first speaker, doubtfully; "but how do you know? did you ever make one?"

"Why, I cannot say that exactly, but I have seen many made, and helped to stir them."

"Lately?"

"Not so very, when I was a boy."

"It would be a sinful waste to put sperrits into a pudding," observed MacIntosh. "It would all boil away, and no one be a bit the better."

"No fear! Good liquor's too scarce for that," cried another.

"Brandy is a great improvement, when you have it, for all that," maintained Kavanagh.

But though this part of his recipe sounded to all like the dissolving of Cleopatra's pearls in her drink for wilful waste, the other items of it confirmed the previous opinion of the chief cook of the troop, and the precious ingredients were entrusted to his care. When they were well mixed, an unforeseen difficulty arose about a bag to boil it in; but that was met by the sacrifice of a haversack, and at last it was consigned to the gipsy kettle which was to bring it to perfection. If it were literally true that a watched pot never boils, this would have had a poor chance, for when off drill or duty next day every man ran to have a look at it; but the proverb happily fell through, and it bubbled away famously. Christmas-day dawned, and would have been hot in England for July.

It is a curious experience the first Christmas spent away from home in a warm climate, such a contrast to all early associations. There were decorations of palm-branches, and instead of holly cactus, which represented it well for prickliness. And there was church parade; and afterwards came dinner of tinned roast beef, fish which some of the persevering had caught in the Nile, and an ostrich egg, which a friendly native had brought in, and which proved fresh. And the pudding!

It was an anxious moment when the string was cut, and the remains of the ancient haversack were opened, and every one was relieved when the object of interest did *not* fall to crumbs as some feared, but remained firm and intact till cut. Was it good? Well, the proof of the pudding is in the eating, and there was not a crumb or a plum left when the party rose. Then a delightful afternoon of idleness and complete rest, which took the ache out of many a poor fellow's bones, and talk of friends in England, and reminiscences of home. And some lucky ones got letters which succeeded in reaching them the right day, and got away alone to read them; while others kept the link by writing. Rather melancholy, but pleasant all the same, for the element of hope kept all sweet. And at night a huge bonfire was lit; it was cold of nights, and officers and men gathered round it for a sing-song. And there was a platform of barrels and planks on which various performances, fiddling, a hornpipe, recitations, nigger melodies, took place, the highest in command enjoying themselves as heartily as the humblest. And there was a tot of rum, not enough to hurt the weakest head indeed, but still a taste, for every one to drink to absent friends, and a rousing chorus or two, and sound sleep closing a day of thorough enjoyment. For to *taste* a holiday you must have a long spell of real hard work.

By this time the men were more at home with their queer steeds, and mounting and dismounting was no longer a painful and even perilous performance. The camels also had become accustomed to the drill, and learned to know what was expected of them. All animals work better and pick up ideas quicker in company. Sometimes, indeed, one would drop suddenly on his knees without rhyme or reason that any one could guess at, and send his rider flying over his head if he were not looking out sharply; but such instances of eccentric conduct were rare, and grew still less frequent as the bipeds and quadrupeds got to know one another better.

A move was now made to Korti, higher up the Nile, a good deal nearer the fourth cataract than the third in fact. But this journey was made on camel back instead of by boat. Now, travelling by boat is not unpleasant when the boat takes you, but when you have to take the boat it is quite a different matter, and riding, even on a camel, is far preferable. And those long days on camel back, near the Nile all the way, and consequently with no stint of water, were about the most pleasant experiences Kavanagh and his companions had.

"Well, Tarrant, I hope you are happy now," said a trooper one day, as the column was on the march.

"Happy! With tinned meat and no beer, and more flies in the open in the middle of winter than you get over a stable at home in August! I know I wish I was back in Windsor barracks."

"Never mind, old boy; if you were there you would wish you were here."

"And a jolly idiot I should be."

"Don't fret about that same," interposed Grady, who was riding near. "It's your misfortune, not your fault. Faith, we wud all be clever if we could; but sure, I thought ye would be aisy in your mind now that you had got your camel."

CHAPTER XIX.

ACROSS THE LOOP.

KORTI was the pleasantest place Kavanagh had been to yet. It was healthy, there were plenty of trees to give shade, forage was easily got for the camels, and fresh provisions for the men, for the villages about seemed more prosperous than usual, and the inhabitants more friendly. Here the camel drill was polished up and brought to perfection. They worked in this way. You must know that though the soldiers rode camels on the march, they were not intended to fight on their backs, except perhaps incidentally when they were out scouting.

So their object when in immediate contact with the enemy was to get rid of their camels for the time being, but so that they might find them again and remount at the shortest possible notice. The battalion being in column—that is, suppose a double row of men on camels, forming a front and rear rank, and some way behind them another double row, and then a third, and then a fourth; that forms what is meant by a column—well, then, the battalion, as I say, being in column, the word of command, signifying what formation the men are to take after they have dismounted, is given, followed by the words, "Close order!" Upon this the rear rank of the leading line jambs up to the front rank, which halts at the word. All the rear rows break into a trot and jamb up to the front in turn.

When all are close and compact, the camels are

told to lie down; the men dismount, and tie up their animals' legs, so that they cannot rise, with the head rope. The men who have to run out and mark the places where the others are to form when ready, get their camels knee-lashed for them by the two men whose duty it is to remain with the animals of their company.

By the time the beasts are in a square, helpless mass, the markers are "covered" (or got into their proper places according to the order accurately) by an officer, and the men form on them at once. After a good deal of drill this was done very quickly, as such things are when each man knows exactly what to do and how to do it, since it is confusion and uncertainty which cause delay. When the battalion had to move away and manœuvre at some little distance from the camels, one company was always to be left to defend them.

The pleasant time at Korti was soon over, and they started across the desert for Shendy. If you will look at the map you will see that from Korti (which you will find in the neighbourhood of Old Dongola, Ambukoi, Merawi, places written large) the Nile stretches to the north for a hundred miles and more as far as Abû Hamed, when it makes a bend completely round, and goes south all the rest of its course. So that by cutting across the desert from Korti to Shendy, or rather Matammeh, which is on the nearer bank of the river, an enormous distance is cut off.

And since time was of the utmost importance, if Khartoum and Gordon were to be rescued, a force under General Stewart was to take the short cut, while the rest followed the tedious windings of the

Nile, actually turning their backs for a precious hundred miles on the way they wanted to go. It was provoking, but it could not be helped; water carriage was absolutely necessary for the existence of the expedition.

Those who were to go with General Stewart's force were in high spirits, and the others envied them exceedingly, for they were going straight at the throat of the enemy, and would probably relieve Khartoum, disperse the Arab hordes, finish the campaign; who knew? They might even bring the Mahdi back in a cage, perhaps, before those following the river would have a chance of distinguishing themselves. They need not have distressed themselves; there would be plenty of hard fighting for all.

You might as well know how our friend Reginald Kavanagh was dressed when he mounted his camel for the desert ride. Picture him then in a loose red flannel tunic, corduroy knee-breeches, serge leggings, white pith helmet with a puggaree round it. Over his shoulder he wore a bandolier belt with sockets for fifty cartridges, and a rifle pocket, in which the butt of the rifle was secured. The bandolier made him look something like a mediæval musketeer; or might have reminded an admirer of Dumas' wonderful story —and who is not?—of Artagnan, Athos, Porthos, and Aramis.

The Naval Brigade was also mounted on camels, and it was great fun to see them start. The camel has been called the ship of the desert, but that was by a poet, who thought rightly enough that he said a pretty thing, but who did not mean it literally. Jack did.

"How this craft does roll!" cried one,

"Hard a port, Bill, or you'll foul me."

"What d'ye come across my bows for, then?"

"Can't help it; this here won't answer the helm. Port, will you!"

"Port it is."

"Mind, messmate, your camel's going to founder, I think."

But the warning came too late; the beast dropped on its knees, and Jack went flying over his hideous head.

Love of adventure and excitement is one thing, patient endurance is another. You want to combine the two to get good soldiers, and Englishmen hitherto have done pretty well. So did these, only after a certain number of hours' march they were less jocular and more vicious. When they got to the first wells, where they expected to have a rest, being by that time pretty well baked, the supply of water was found to be so scarce that they had to push on at once; but they did it for the most part in silence.

"Well, Tarrant," said Kavanagh, when they had been plodding on for some two hours in dead silence, "have you not got a growl for us?"

"No, I haven't," replied the champion grumbler. "I did get a drink at Hasheen, but this poor brute I am riding didn't, so I leave the growling to him."

"Sure it ought to be put in the *Gazette*," cried Grady, waking up. "First grumbler, Tarrant's camel, *vice* Tarrant, contented."

"I never said I was contented," replied Tarrant. "Only it is a consolation to know there's some one worse off than yourself."

"Meaning the camels?"

"Aye, and not only them. Don't you remember

that 19th Hussar chap who came up the last halt? There was a go!"

"What do you mean?"

"Didn't you hear? Why, he belonged to Captain Fanshawe's troop, who went skirmishing about, and caught a sheikh, called Abu Zoolah. Well, he said that a while ago the Mudir of Dongola had offered a thousand dollars for his head, and now it isn't worth the price of a pint. Just think what a chance to nearly get, and miss! There's a lot of beer in a thousand dollars."

"Sure, yes, that's hard lines," observed Grady. "What fun it would be to go out shooting, and get a thousand dollars for every man you bagged."

"Aye, that would make a man hold straight, if anything would," said MacIntosh. And there were a few spurts of talk like that, but mostly they plodded on in silence.

It took close upon three days to reach Gakdul Wells, and during all that time the camels were not watered, the supply at intermediate wells being barely sufficient for the men. But when they got to Gakdul there was abundance of the life-restoring element for all, beasts and men, thanks to the Royal Engineers and their pumps. For the place was as wild and romantic as you can imagine, the wells being hidden away in deep caverns with precipitous sides, in the midst of frowning and rugged rocks. The sailors, with their contempt of heights, and entire freedom from giddiness, swung themselves down into the most horrible abysses, if only they had a rope made fast at top, without a moment's hesitation, fixing pipes by which the precious fluid was pumped up and conveyed to the troops.

It was a treat to see the camels drink when at last they got the chance; they sucked the water up with a loud noise, and you could trace it flowing down their necks in waves. Four days is the longest period they can go without a supply. There are people in India and elsewhere who believe that when they die their souls go into the bodies of animals, and Kavanagh's acquaintance with his camel enabled him to understand this odd notion, for when he looked in its eyes for some time he almost expected it to speak. It was an unsatisfactory beast in some respects, for it would not be petted in any way, and it was impossible to make friends with it. Try to pet it, and it growled; persist, and it tried to bite him. I have known a dog of much the same disposition, but then he made one or two exceptions, and showed as much exaggerated fondness for them as made up for his general want of amiability.

But the camel was consistent, and steadily refused to form the slightest attachment to anything human. You remember the genii in the "Arabian Nights Entertainments" who were forced to serve powerful magicians, but who hated them and longed to tear them in pieces all the time, and did so, too, if the omission of some necessary incantation gave them the power. Well, the camel seemed like one of these subjugated spirits, an excellent servant, but a most unwilling one, and resenting the power to which, forced by inevitable destiny, he yielded implicit obedience. Evidently he was a fatalist, like the people he lived amongst.

When he was being loaded for the journey he moaned and howled as if he were being beaten to death, and whenever a start was made, the outcry of hundreds of the creatures remonstrating at once was something perfectly unparalleled in the way of horrid and dismal noises.

"Sure," said Grady on the first occasion, "I have often heard spake of a howling wilderness, but I never knew what it meant before at all. But I see now; it's the camel that does the howling."

But once started he seemed to make up his mind to the inevitable. While he was uncertain what Fate had in store for him he groaned and lamented, but once he knew the worst he thought it was no use bothering, and proceeded on his way in apparent content.

Indeed, that seemed to be his one aim and object, to be always going straight on to some place a long way off and never arriving, like the Wandering Jew. As for his appearance, you have probably often seen a camel in the Zoological Gardens or a wild beast show, and know his weird, shapeless, uncanny look, with the beard on his upper lip, and the hard natural pads on all parts of him which touch the ground when he subsides for loading or unloading; his chest, knees, and so on. An experienced man has described his motion when he trots in this way:—"Put a horse into a cart without springs, in the cart put a rickety table; on the table place a music-stool screwed up as high as it will go. Now seat yourself on the music-stool and gallop over a ploughed field, and you will have a very correct notion of the sensation of riding a trotting camel." But with practice the motion is much easier, and with so many hours in the day in the saddle the troops had plenty of practice.

The position at Gakdul was naturally strong, and with the aid of art was made perfectly impregnable, forming a place to fall back upon in case of need.

The camels, it has been explained, utterly declined all friendly advances, but the affections of the company Kavanagh belonged to were not on that account destined to grow utterly rusty for want of use, since a dog had attached himself in every sense of the word to it. Where the dog came from and to whom he belonged originally were matters as mysterious as his breed, which seemed to partake of several varieties, amongst which the native sheep dog was the most perceptible.

But his virtues were manifold. He joined on that day of the march when the towing commenced, and posted himself, as no one did it for him, and he was enlisted under the name of *Hump*, not because of any personal deformity, but after the distinguishing characteristic of the camel. When the battalion took to riding, and, though still following the course of the Nile, often lost sight of it for some hours, either because the track was better or to cut off a corner, Hump carried his own water-bottle, ingeniously constructed for him by a man named Thomas Dobbs, out of an old preserved meat tin covered with a bit of felt, to prevent its becoming too hot ; and this was fastened round his neck. When a halt was called, and he wanted a drink, he went up to one of the men, who would take off the cover and pour a little out for him. This was all very well while the river was near, but when they were about to strike across the desert, where water would be scarce, and he would hardly be able to carry enough for his own wants, it was determined to leave him behind, and he was made over to a man who promised to take charge of him, and who was to remain on the Nile.

But in the bivouac at Gakdul, Dobbs awoke with

a start under the impression that a snake was gliding over his face, and sitting up found that it was Hump licking him, the empty water-bottle still round his neck.

It now seemed hopeless to get rid of him, so they let him take his chance; to live if he could manage to supply himself, and to be shot should his sufferings from thirst prove too great. Poor Hump! the most thoughtful feared that he had a poor chance of reaching a good old age. And yet he developed a wonderful talent for finding water in unexpected places, which was useful to himself and others. Sometimes when men would turn away in disappointment from a mud-hole which was indicated by a native guide as a well, but which proved to be dry, Hump would sniff out some place near, and scratch, and six inches or so below the surface water would begin to ooze and trickle.

On January 16th, 1885, at noon, the column on the march was roused from the lethargy induced by monotonous riding hour after hour under a warm sun by distant firing.

"By Jabers!" cried Grady. "There's an inimy somewheres after all. I began to think Mr. Mahdi had packed up his things—it's a mighty small portmanteau most of them require—and gone out of the country entirely, with all his people."

"Make your mind quite easy, Grady," said Sergeant Barton, who was riding near. "The Arabs won't baulk you, if you want something to remind you of Donnybrook."

"It isn't for myself, Mr. Sergeant, sir, that I care. I am a peaceable man, and would sooner get what I want quietly. It's my friend Tarrant here who is spoiling for a fight, and to see him pining away before me very eyes, just for want of a little divarshion with his rifle, makes me feel quite low."

"Here come the scouts back!" cried Kavanagh, and sure enough the Hussars were seen riding in. For some time all was suspense and conjecture amongst our friends; but after awhile the news circulated from the staff to the regimental officers, from the officers to the sergeants, from the sergeants to the men, that the enemy were in position at the Wells of Abu Klea, twenty-three miles from Matammeh, the place on the Nile they were working for. Where was Abu Klea? Straight to their front was a ridge of fantastically-shaped rocks, and there the enemy was in position.

A little nearer square was formed, and in that formation the force advanced to the foot of the ridge, and was there halted. Then, after awhile, orders were issued to form a zereba for the night, and it was soon made, the materials being plentiful and close at hand, and the camels and stores were placed within it.

"Men for picket!" cried a sergeant, and Kavanagh, who had been warned for the duty, stepped forward and fell in with the others, and presently they were marched off and posted on one of the hills commanding the zereba.

The officer in command took careful note of the position and posted his sentries, taking care to be in communication with the pickets on his right and left, and the zereba in his rear. The sentries were double, that is, there were two men on each post, and were changed every hour.

An hour's sentry-go may seem to you but a short spell, but if you had a swarm of agile sharp-sighted savages prowling about you all the time, and knew that your own life and those of others who depended on you would be sacrificed if your vigilance flagged, perhaps you would find it long enough.

It was ten o'clock when Kavanagh was roused to go on; Dobbs was his companion, and Corporal Adams posted them.

"You are to challenge any one approximating this post," he said; "and if they say 'friend' or 'rounds' you must stop them and make them give the countersign. If they can't you must run them in, and if they won't be run in you must run them through with your bayonet; if they won't be run through you must wait and see if there's many of them, and if there is you must shoot. But you musn't alarm the camp without reason, mind you."

And with these somewhat conflicting "must's" and "must not's" he left them in the gloom. The position was as uncomfortable a one as Kavanagh had ever been in. His imagination peopled the night around him with supple forms ready to leap upon him from behind every time he turned in walking his beat. I won't say that either he or Thomas Dobbs was frightened, for that would be a slur on a soldier, and one or the other might have me up for it; but they did not half like it. They had been on about twenty minutes when Kavanagh thought he saw something move by a rock a little in front of him, and the next time he met Dobbs, as they both patrolled to the same spot and turned, he whispered his suspicions to him, and he went with him a few paces back along his beat and gazed in the direction, but could distinguish nothing. Kavanagh did not know whether to challenge or not, but thought it best to wait and watch; perhaps he might have been mistaken.

Presently he heard Dobbs cry, "Who goes there?" in a decidedly startled voice, and he brought his own rifle down to the charge. But immediately afterwards Dobbs said—

"What! is it you, Hump, old boy, come to do a bit of sentry-go? By jingo, you made me jump!"

And no wonder; in such a ticklish situation, to have something jump upon you in the dark, when all your nerves are on the stretch, must be very startling.

Five minutes passed, and there again by the rock Kavanagh was certain he saw a figure move this time, and he, in his turn, called—

"Who goes there?" again bringing down his bayonet.

There was no reply, and he waited, uncertain what to do next, when Hump suddenly dashed forward with a low, angry growl; and presently exclamations were heard in an unknown tongue indeed, but which, from the accent, did not appear to be blessings.

"Good dog, Hump; shake him, boy!" cried Dobbs; but the animal was evidently doing his best in that direction without encouragement.

But the man, who could not have been a dozen yards off, shook himself free somehow, and Hump retired growling, from which Kavanagh felt convinced there were more than one or two Arabs near. Presently he made out three objects against the sky-line, and thought he ought to delay no longer, so he fired at them.

Whether he hit anything he could not, of course, tell; but in reply to his shot there were at least twenty flashes of fire in his front, and the bullets came buzzing about the ears of Kavanagh and Dobbs like a swarm of hornets, though neither was touched.

The picket turned out, and, as the Arabs were some of them quite close to them, the sentries retired upon it. The enemy kept on firing for about five minutes, then ceased ; and the sentries were advanced again, but somewhat closer in than before, since, but for the dog, these two would have been cut off.

They were relieved presently ; but there were two other alarms in the night, and the troops in the zereba did not get a very sound rest, having thus to stand to their arms three times.

The morning at length dawned, and a sharp fire was maintained for some time from the hills, the pickets being withdrawn into the zereba. Then the enemy advanced in two long lines, with banners flying, five thousand of them, an imposing spectacle, and the English soldiers grasped their weapons, thinking that the struggle had come at last. But not yet was it to be. The enemy declined to push the attack home, but halted at a distance, keeping up a galling fire. So, as men began to drop, and the day was slipping on, General Stewart determined at ten o'clock to take the initiative.

The camels and other encumbrances were left in the zereba with a guard, and the square advanced, working round the left of the enemy's position. The Arabs retreated, and some of our young soldiers began to anticipate an easy victory. But the enemy showed that they too could manœuvre ; suddenly wheeling to the left, they came down like an avalanche on the rear of the square, bearing back the men composing it, and breaking in at one of the corners.

Why detail the scene? It was very much the same as that which occurred the year before at Tamai, on the Red Sea side, to the Second Brigade, and which was described while we were following the fortunes of Tom Strachan. The hand-to-hand fighting was desperate, the slaughter terrible, and the enemy was finally beaten back. No matter; a step was taken, though deep in blood, towards the great object—the relief of Khartoum, and the rescue of Gordon, and hope beat high in every breast.

Next day, January the nineteenth, General Stewart left his wounded at the wells of Abu Klea, which had been won, and pushed forward for Matammeh at three in the afternoon. No resistance was met with, no sign of the enemy perceived all night, and when the day dawned a thread of silver shone in the southeast, and a hundred voices broke out simultaneously in a chorus of—

"The Nile!"

Yes, there was the river, and as the light grew stronger the town of Matammeh could be distinguished. At the same time the tam-tams were heard beating, and the enemy appeared swarming over the hills which intervened between the British army and the river.

Another zereba was constructed, for the men were exhausted with fatigue and want of food, and it was not thought wise to give battle until they were refreshed, for it is ill fighting on an empty stomach. So breakfast was got ready, the troops of the Mahdi gathering round the while, like the masses of a thunder-cloud.

Presently it burst forth, with rifle flashes for lightning, and a deadly leaden hail. Vainly the men piled up camel furniture, barrels, sacks, sand-bags, for protection; the bullets came amongst them in a storm, and they fell in all directions. And then a rumour ran through all the ranks which spread, not dismay, indeed, nor consternation, but a stern tightening of the heart-strings and bracing of the muscles, with a desire to shoot straight and strike home. The general was hit! Yes, the noble Stewart was down!

Sir Charles Wilson now took command. A redoubt was constructed by the Royal Engineers on the right of the zereba, and manned by fifty-five Life Guardsmen and Scots Greys under Lord Cochrane, and by this means the enemy's fire was somewhat held in check.

At length the longed-for opportunity for vengeance came; the square left the zereba and advanced upon the foe. Straight it went for the sandy ridge held by the enemy, who came charging down with their accustomed reckless courage.

But this time they did not get up to the square. The ground was too open, the zone of fire too unimpeded, the shooting too steady. Down they went in hecatombs. At one hundred yards their pace was checked, those behind embarrassed by the heaps of dead and dying blocking their path. Still they struggled on to get to close quarters with the English, but at thirty yards the withering volleys were too deadly even for their supernatural bravery, and they broke and fled. Steadily advanced the English troops over the ridge of sand, firing carefully while the fugitives were within range; then down to the

Nile at Gubat, near Matammeh, victorious indeed, but having paid a high price for victory.

"If them Arabs takes to shooting straight, and won't come on any more, it strikes me we shall be in a hole," said Thomas Dobbs to Grady.

"True for you, me boy," replied the Irishman.

"Or at any rate we shall not be able to go about in square for them to get all round and blaze away into the brown of us." And there were some of higher rank who began to entertain the same misgivings.

To resist a rush, the square was excellent, but for a long-continued fire without coming to close quarters it was impossible. Many of the more sanguine, however, hoped that the tremendous losses the Arabs had sustained would dishearten them — that they would awake to the fact that the Mahdi was by no means invincible, and had deceived them.

As for Gordon, had they not had a message from him? "All right; could hold out for years."

Their chivalrous dash across the desert, and the hard fighting against enormous odds, the loss of valuable men, and the fall of their general, were not fruitless then, since the object of the expedition would be attained.

"Sure we will all get a bar with *Khartoum* on it under a medal!" said Grady.

"Medals! Bars! Yah!" cried Tarrant.

"I'd sooner have tuppence a day extra for beer."

"We've got naither the medal nor the bar nor Khartoum yet, d'ye ken?" said MacIntosh.

CHAPTER XX.

BIR-HUMP.

"And when will we be after attacking Matammeh?" asked Grady, as he sat over the bivouac fire.

"Precious soon, I should think; we can't get on to Khartoum till it's taken," said Kavanagh.

"And for why not?" asked Grady again.

"Eh, man!" exclaimed MacIntosh, "ye would na go past it and leave all these thousands of heathens in our rear, would ye? With an army at Khartoum in front, and the army here in our rear, we should be between two fires, don't ye see? Never a mouthful of grub or a cartridge could get to us, and we should be peppered on all sides at once."

"We might as well risk it and get it over," said Tarrant.

"We get nothing fit to eat as it is."

"I call that stupid, talking like that!" cried Dobbs. "I know the rations are a deal better than ever I expected; capital, I call them."

"So they are," said MacIntosh; "but if Tarrant had sheep's-head, haggis, and whusky itsel' for dinner, he would na be contented."

"Every man to his taste," growled Tarrant; "and if a chap likes tinned meat he's welcome. I prefer good beef and mutton, fresh killed, with plenty of potatoes and white bread."

"And a little tripe and onions, or a swatebread after it, with pudding and lashings of sherry wine, I'll be bound," said Grady.

"Get along wid ye, it's Lord Mayor of London ye ought to be. Why, man, it's fighting and not ating ye've come out here for."

"Well, I got plenty of that between Abu Klea and this, anyway," replied Tarrant. "A bullet went through my water-bottle early on the eighteenth, and I was without a drop for hours. I believe I have worse luck than anybody."

"Worse luck than anybody, you ungrateful beggar!" cried Smith.

"And how about Richardson, your rear rank man, who got the same bullet which spoilt your bottle into his body, and died in pain that evening? I suppose you would rather *his* water-bottle had been hit and *your* inwards!"

Tarrant busied himself in stuffing and lighting his pipe, and made no reply.

"Well, for my part, I hope we shall have a cut in at Matammeh to-morrow," said Kavanagh, "so as to get on up the river at once."

"Aye, I hope we may," echoed half a dozen voices in chorus.

"Gordon and the poor chaps with him must be pretty well sick of waiting to be relieved, hemmed in all the time by those blood-thirsty savages."

"Eh, but it must have been bad last March, when our people won the victory at Tamai, and they thought at Khartoum that they were coming across to them," said MacIntosh.

"And then to hear they had gone awa again, and left them without a bit of help but themselves."

"Sure, won't they be glad when they hear our guns!" cried Grady. "And won't they come out and tackle the naygurs that have been bothering them on the one side, while we pitch into them on the other! We'll double them up and destroy them entoirely."

"I doubt if we go at Matammeh before we get reinforcements," said MacIntosh.

"And what will we want with reinforcements?" asked Grady; "haven't we bate the inimy into fiddle-strings already?"

"Yes, if they only knew it," said Kavanagh. "But they seem to take a lot of persuading before they own themselves beaten."

"They do, the poor ignorant creatures," said Grady, reflectively. "And we can't kill the lot of 'em, which is what they seem to want; they are too many."

"If there *is* a big fight in a day or two we shan't be in it," said Corporal Adams, who had come up in time to hear the end of the conversation.

"The orders are out, and our company has got to go ten miles off to-morrow."

"Only our company, corporal?"

"That's all detailed in orders."

"And does it say what for?"

"It does not; rikkernottering most like. But you will hear them read presently."

That was done, and Corporal Adams was quite correct. This particular company was ordered to take a certain amount of ammunition both for mouth and rifle, and march out in a certain specified direction. If they found water they were to make a zereba, or otherwise entrench themselves and remain until further orders; if not, they were to return at once. There was a little disappointment amongst both officers and men of the company.

"We will be out of all the fun entirely," said Grady. "They will catch the Mahdi, relieve Khartoum, rescue Gordon, and have all their names in the newspapers—and we will have nothing to say to it at all, at all."

"Don't you believe it," said Kavanagh. "The general would not send a rifle away if he were going to attack. He has heard something, or knows something we can't guess at, and means waiting for more troops to come up, you may depend. And our expedition has something to do, I should not wonder, with covering the flank of the reinforcements. We shall be called in, no fear, before the big battle is fought."

But even with those who thought differently the matter did not weigh very heavily. They had already fallen into the true campaigning frame of mind which takes things as they come—good quarters and bad; fighting and resting; outpost duty or guarding stores, even wounds and death—very philosophically.

As the company was to start some time before daybreak, the men wisely left off discussing matters, and went to sleep. Then came their rising while it was still night, and the raking together of the embers of the bivouac fire, and breakfasting; then the saddling and lading of camels, amid the dismal lamentations of those grievance-mongering animals; then the start in darkness, and the mind adapting itself to the lethargic monotony of the tramp. Every one was chilly; every one was a trifle sullen at not being in bed; no one was inclined to talk.

The silence was only broken by the *swish, swish, swish* of the camels' feet through the sand, the most ghostlike and uncanny of sounds; so slight, so continuous, so wide-spread. To meet a train of camels in the dark would be enough to convert any unbeliever in supernatural phenomena, I mean if he did not know anything about it.

When the sun rose every man seemed to wake up and feel new life in him, and they began to talk, just as the dicky birds tune up for a song on the like occasion. Yet the scene was desolate and dreary enough for Dante or Gustave Doré.

After some hours' march they passed this barren land and approached the foot of a hill where the mimosa was plentiful again, and other shrubs were seen, with herbage, scant indeed, but good for camels, who will browse upon what would hardly tempt a donkey. Here a halt was called, and while the men dismounted and lay down, the three officers who were with the company explored the spot. There were two mud holes which supplied water, and had a couple of palms near them, pretty well in the open, and a third spring a hundred yards from the others, larger and deeper, and apparently yielding a better supply than both the others put together, but so near a patch of rocks and thick mimosas which would afford dangerous cover to an enemy, should any be in the neighbourhood, that it would never do to camp close by it.

So when the colour-sergeant was called out presently, he learned that it had been determined to form the zereba so as to include the two smaller water holes and the palm-trees, and the ground was marked out accordingly. Then all set to work to cut down mimosa bushes, and make a hedge of them all round, a gap, just admitting of one camel to pass at a time, being left on the side nearest the outside well, but not at the corner, and this gap was marked by a short hedge inside facing it. It was determined to use this outside well while they had the place to themselves, and reserve those within the zereba in case of an attack.

The space enclosed was as limited as was consistent with convenience to render it more capable of defence, and the hedge was breast high, so that the men could fire over it without their aim being in any way impeded. Shrubs beyond those required to form the zereba were cut down and stored for firewood, so as to remove all cover where Arabs might conceal themselves as far as possible.

Most of this work was done before dinner, and the men had two hours' rest. After that tapes were brought out and the lines of a trench marked off, six feet from the hedge all round, and when that was done the men began to dig it out, five feet wide, one foot and a foot and a half deep, throwing the soil out on the hedge side, flattening it down and making it as firm as they could, so that if exposed to heavy fire the men might find protection, since the prickly walls, though difficult for men to struggle through, would not stop bullets. And so a good day's work ended, and the night sentries were posted between the trench and the hedge.

There was no alarm that night. The next morning the camels were taken outside the zereba and watered at the large well, from which also a supply was drawn for the company; and it sufficed for all, evidently a valuable spring. That day the trench was completed, deepened a little, but not much, as it would not do for the defenders to be too low behind the hedge, and a small watch-tower commenced in the centre of the square. Some quaint, distorted trees were found at a little distance, and from one of these enough timber was got for the erection contemplated. There was a flat rock which formed a foundation for it, and a rustic-looking affair, something like a summer-house, was raised some twelve feet from the rock it stood on, which was already six feet from the level plain. From this elevation an extensive view could be obtained.

On the third day a balcony was made round the top of the watch-tower, the sides of which were composed of logs, which it was reckoned would be bullet-proof. A few good marksmen might, without being exposed, do considerable execution from this. It also had a roof fixed over it, and the look-out man had thus a protection from the sun. The saddles, with all cases and packages, were arranged to form an inner court of the zereba, within which were the camels, and when they were lying down they were very well protected. Hump, who of course had followed his company, took great interest in all these proceedings, and when the men were at work he stood with his head on one side watching them critically, and from the expression of his face, and the vibration of his tail, it was gathered that on the whole he approved. Captain Reece, who commanded the company, did not, as a matter of fact, much expect an attack, but he thought it only right to be prepared in case one were made, and being a man of an ingenious turn of mind, who, when a boy at Harton, was known as the "Dodger," he felt a special delight in constructing devices. On being ordered off on his present duty, he had gone to a friend in the Royal Engineers and begged a good bit of gun-cotton, carried for blasting purposes, and with this he proposed to make a mine, an electric battery and a coil of wire forming part of his baggage.

There was a group of boulders two hundred yards off, which was certain to be taken advantage of by an enemy, since it formed a perfectly safe redoubt from which to fire on the zereba, or to shelter a group forming the forlorn hope of an attack. This Reece fixed upon as the most favourable spot for his mine, and here the gun-cotton was placed in the position he deemed most adapted for a favourable explosion, and connected by a wire, which there was no great delay or difficulty in concealing in the sandy soil with the zereba, and so with the electric battery.

"It's a sight of trouble we have taken to resave the inimy, and it will be mighty onpolite of him if he doesn't come at all," said Grady.

"I don't believe there's any Arabs about these parts," said MacIntosh; "they air all together at Matammeh, or else before Khartoum."

"You think yourself very clever, no doubt," said Corporal Adams, indignantly. "But do you suppose that the captain would have taken all this trouble without good information?"

"Nay, but with all due respect to the captain, and the colonel, and the general, and yersel', too, corporal," said MacIntosh, "the reports they have acted upon are native reports, and they may be good, and they may be bad, they may be honest, and they *may* want to get detachments sent aboot to weaken the force at Gubat."

"Well, I think you are very presumpterous," said the corporal, "very presumpterous indeed, to suppose your superior officers can be took in by a lot of Johnnies that you can see through. They may attack us or they may not, seeing how ready we are for them; but they are somewhere's, you may take a haveadavy."

As everybody is generally somewhere, it was difficult to contradict this statement. Besides it is imprudent for a private to contradict a corporal, who has many ways of making himself disagreeable or the reverse. So the prudent Scot acquiesced.

"Well, I am a paceable boy meself, and hate fighting," said Grady.

"But still it seems a pity to make such iligant fortifications and not to thry them. Is there not sinse in that, now, Kavanagh?"

"I don't know about sense, but there's a lot of human nature in it," replied Kavanagh. "I know I learned to box when I was a lad, and was never happy until I had a turn up to try my skill without the gloves. And a jolly good licking I got for my pains."

"To be sure!" cried Grady. "And if ye get a new knife ye want to cut something with it, or a new gun ye must be after shooting with it; and so on with anything at all. And now we have got the fortifications one is a thrifle curious to know if the Johnnies could get into them."

I don't know whether many of the company wanted to be attacked, or, indeed, if any did, but certainly there was a restlessness about them. They listened all day for firing in the direction of Matammeh, some lying down with their ears to the ground to hear the farther. But all was still as the desert only can be, and the great battle which was expected had certainly not yet begun. But expectation of a fight excites men, and if at a distance they itch to be in it, this feeling even actuating men who fail to show any particular heroism when the pinch comes.

However, wishing or not wishing to be attacked

could make no difference; the Arabs were not likely to consult their feelings on the subject. There was no alarm that night, and all but the men on duty slept soundly by the bivouac fires. In the course of the next morning the camels were to be taken to the outside well to be watered, and a few impediments which blocked the gap being removed they began to move out. The leader had gone twenty paces, and three others were following, when Grant, one of the lieutenants who was in the gallery of the look-out with a field-glass, shouted, "Halt! Come back!"

The man with the leading camel looked round to see if the order applied to him, and saw the lieutenant beckoning to him. "Come back at once!" he repeated. The four camels went to the right-about not a bit too soon; for a puff of smoke spurted up from a mimosa bush beyond, and the vicious whiz of a bullet hinted to the leader of the camel nearest to it that it would be better for him not to stop to wind up his watch or pare his nails before he got under shelter.

Pop, pop, pop, pop! a camel is a big mark, and it was clever to miss the lot. One indeed had a lock of hair chipped off him, as if the marksman were an artist who wanted a painting brush; but that was the nearest approach to a casualty.

The other bullets went high over everything, save one or two, which struck the sand and sent little stones flying about in a dangerous manner. But they came in contact with nothing vulnerable, and the four were back in the enclosure presently.

MacIntosh, Cleary, and two other men, the crack shots of the company, were ordered up into the balcony to try if they could show the attacking party that they could make a better use of their weapons than they could. Captain Reece was now up there, and the bullets were whizzing about and thudding into the logs in a nerve-shaking manner.

"Crouch down, men, till they are a bit tired of wasting their cartridges," said the captain, standing erect himself, however; "you could not get a fair shot yet for the smoke."

When they had done so, he sat on a block of wood himself, and was then protected by the balcony. The two lieutenants and the non-commissioned officers were below cautioning the men, who were now in position all round the zereba, against firing until ordered.

It was a picked corps, and they were perfectly in hand, so that not one single shot was fired during this first storm. And a storm it was; the air seemed perfectly alive with the rush of bullets, all aimed high. Whether it did not occur to the Arabs that the bushes of the enclosure were not impervious, or the watch-tower offered a more tempting mark, or the Remington rifle stocks did not suit their arms and shoulders, and came up high I don't know, but certainly all the bullets which hit anything struck the wooden erection and the rock it stood upon. Splinters of wood and chips of stone were flying in all directions, but nothing was wounded which minded it, not a man or a camel or Hump, who thought the whole affair got up for his amusement, and barked with delight at the noise.

The leaden shower raged for about five minutes, died down to a sputtering, and ceased. Every man grasped his weapon and peered over the hedge, expecting a rush. But the enemy seemed to want to know whether they had annihilated everything with their fusillade, and kept close in cover. Slowly the smoke lifted, and rolled above their positions.

"Now there is a chance for you, MacIntosh," said the captain; "above that bush, do you see? About three hundred yards."

MacIntosh took a steady aim and pulled.

The man he aimed at staggered, and came down in a sitting position, seizing his right leg, which was broken, with both hands.

"An outer!" cried Captain Reece, who had his field-glass directed on the spot.

"A miss," he said presently, as another man fired at an Arab darting from a distant to a nearer bit of cover.

"Don't shoot at them running."

An Arab was taking careful note of the zereba from the rocks two hundred yards off, his head and shoulders only being exposed. Cleary rested his rifle on the top of the balcony, pulled the stock firmly to his shoulder, got a fine sight on his mark, and pressed the trigger. A flash! a crack!

"A bull for you, Cleary!" exclaimed the captain. "You have nailed him through the head."

The enemy were now more cautious, and not more than half a dozen shots were got in the next hour, but most of them told. During that time the Arabs indulged in no more continued storms of fire; only Captain Reece drew occasional volleys, mostly from a considerable distance, as he stood fully exposed, reconnoitring the position.

He did not do this recklessly or out of bravado, but simply because it was of the utmost importance to gain some idea of their numbers, which he put at about five or six hundred; not more in the immediate neighbourhood. It was an uncomfortable position, being cramped up there, imprisoned in so small a space, but not a dangerous one. The enemy kept up a dropping fire, which had no effect beyond wasting their cartridges, though after nightfall it was annoying in two ways; the English had to bivouac in the cold, for they could not light fires, and their sleep was disturbed by constant alerts. In the morning there was a lull, not a shot being fired for some hours. The marksmen went up to the balcony, but, seeing no chance of a shot, were withdrawn, and only the look-out man left there. There was some idea that the enemy might have gone away, and no one would have been sorry; for the wells inside the zereba were very inefficient, the water being soon exhausted, and a tedious waiting entailed before the wells filled again. Already the men had to be put on an allowance, and in that country, where the throat is always parched, any stint of water is the greatest possible privation.

But just as it was in contemplation to send out an exploring party, numbers of them were sighted again amongst the more distant bushes, and it did not go out. Dinner time arrived, and the meal was served out. Before the men had quite finished two sentries fired shots, and all sprang to their arms, which were handy; for every man ate, drank, slept with his rifle close to him, as it was impossible to tell at what moment he might require it.

In half a minute every man was at the hedge with a cartridge in his rifle, and that was not too soon, for the Arabs came at a fast run on two sides simultaneously, and even lapped round and threatened a third.

"Steady, now! don't shoot till you have your man

covered. There's no hurry. The nearer they are the better!" cried the officers, and sergeants and corporals seconded them well. Yet the commands were not necessary, so cool and steady were the men. It was as if they had been waiting so long for a chance, that they were afraid of wasting it now they had got it. Nothing could be more deliberate than the way they aimed.

"Why did you not fire then, MacIntosh?" Sergeant Barton happened to ask; "you had a fair chance," the Arab being about forty yards off, and the Scotsman "drawing a bead" on him.

"I was trying to get two in a line," said the economist; and presently he succeeded. Being protected by the hedge naturally made the men cooler, and able to afford to reserve their fire.

If any Arabs were shot so far off as a hundred yards it was as much as it was, and then only because the marksman felt he was "on." Indeed, with far inferior defenders the position would have been impregnable; held by such men as these, to attack it was suicide. It is hardly an exaggeration to say that every shot told; and if several hit one man, on the other hand some single bolts struck two men, and that helped to bring up the average. For a good ten minutes the plucky fanatics persevered, thirsting like tigers for the blood of their foes; and the carnage was fearful. They had no artillery to shake the defence with before attacking, and the fire was uniform as well as deadly.

"Give it 'em hot, boys!" "That's your sort!" "Bravo, old Waterproof!" this last cheer being for MacIntosh, who shot a chief who was leading on his tribes-men, brandishing a huge two-handed sword.

"Camels for ever!" "Faugh-a-ballah!" "Ha! ha!" "Hurrah! hurrah! hurra-a-ah!" and the cheers were heard for miles across the barren waste, disturbing the beasts and birds of prey on the sites of neighbouring battle-fields from their unholy repast, as the Arabs drew off to their cover in confusion, leaving the whole ground between it and the zereba strewed with their dead and dying. As they pressed back more fell, the soldiers firing at longer distances now the prospect of many more immediate chances was small. The champion marksmen ran for the balcony again, and the last victims dropped to their rifles. And soon was apparent the astonishing vitality of the Arab race. The wounded, who were not mortally stricken, were seen crawling and dragging themselves to cover in all directions. Had they but got the order, how delighted would the soldiers have been to quit the zereba, and dash upon the disordered foe; and that Captain Reece burned to give that order you may be perfectly certain. But that would have been contrary to the tenor of his instructions; and, besides, might, after all, have turned victory into disaster, for the Arabs probably had received reinforcements before the attack, and the little band of Englishmen might find themselves smothered with numbers in the bush.

There was no more sign of the enemy that day; they lay close in cover, watching. During the night they stole out and removed many of their dead, which those in the zereba were glad of, for the numbers threatened presently to poison the air. The next day water began to grow very scarce indeed, and two men with a corporal were permitted to leave the zereba and approach the well, to try if they could get a supply without molestation, so quiet and hidden were the enemy. But they had hardly got half-way before a storm of fire was poured upon them, and they had to run back as hard as they could go, one dropping—the first casualty. The corporal and the other man, who was no other than Grady, stopped, picked him up, and carried him in, the bullets cutting the ground up in puffs of dust all around. But they were not hit, and got their comrade inside amidst cheers from all who were watching them.

Poor Hump seemed likely to come off badly, for however great a pet you may make of an animal, when it comes to a question whether you or he are to go thirsty, the animal is apt to come off second best. And the camels, who reverse the recipe of " little and often," and require " much and seldom," must fill the reservoirs, as they call their stomachs, at certain intervals, or die. And if they died the company would probably die too. Poor Hump! every consideration was against his getting a drink. He whined, and looked very plaintive, with his tongue hanging out. He scratched and scratched, but the water was exhausted, and only trickled into the legitimate holes by dribblets. Everybody was very sorry for him, but still more sorry for himself.

So Hump took the matter into his own hands—I was going to say, but he had not got any. I mean that he fell back on his own resources, and he simply ran across to the outside well, drank his fill, and ran back again. It never occurred to the Arabs to take the trouble to shoot at a dog, so he was quite unmolested. After he had made two journeys a bright idea came into the head of Thomas Dobbs. The next time Hump prepared to start on a watering expedition, he took off the lid of his water-bottle, which was suspended round his neck, so when the dog plunged his nose to lap, the tin went into the water and got filled; and though some of it got spilled as he trotted back, enough remained to wet the ingenious Dobbs's whistle. And he improved upon this; he cut a round piece of wood, filling the can so loosely as to lie at the bottom when it was empty, and floating to the surface when full, but prevented from tumbling out by the edges of the top of the tin being bent in a bit. This prevented most of the spilling, and every excursion Hump made he brought back the best part of a pint. And a pint of water, look you, was worth a good deal more than a pint of champagne in England.

Two more days passed; the Arabs burst out now and then into a spurt of volley firing, but would not attempt another attack. They probably knew the nature of the wells, and trusted to thirst to fight for them.

The little party in the zereba kept a sharp lookout for rescue, you may depend, for their position was growing more and more critical every hour. To the south was the spring, with a few trees, and the thick mimosa bush beyond. On the east were more mimosas and rocky ground in which the enemy could find cover to within five hundred yards at the furthest part; up to two hundred at one point. But on the northern and western sides the country was quite open, and the view was only bounded by sand-hills a good mile off. And it was from one of these directions that they expected help would come.

So when dust was noticed, amidst which an occasional glitter flashed, on the western horizon, eyes began to sparkle and hearts to beat high, as those of shipwrecked men in an open boat when a sail comes in sight. No doubt it was a party sent to relieve them—cavalry, by the pace they came, for the cloud of dust rolled rapidly nearer. In five minutes it was within a thousand yards, and then out of it burst a single horseman, riding straight for the zereba, and the enemy, running from their cover on the southern side, strove to intercept him with their fire as he passed, while presently some twenty Arab horsemen became visible, racing after the fugitive, the foremost about twenty yards from his heels. *Bang! bang! bang!* from the Arabs, who had run out, and were somewhat too far for the zereba fire. But the hunted man came on untouched.

It is not easy, even for good shots, to hit flying with ball, and the Arabs were not good shots, but the exact reverse. Nearer now, with his horse well in hand, not seeking to increase his distance, glancing back to judge how far off his pursuers were. The footmen of the enemy, provoked at not being able to stop him, ran out in his course too close to the English, and two of them were presently down on the sand. Others not heeding sought to cut him off, and the English could not fire without risk to him also, as they were straight in his direction.

Whipping out his sword, which had hitherto been sheathed, he flourished it in salutation of his friends, and rode straight at a couple of Arabs in his path, loosening his rein, and digging with his spurs as he did so. He knocked one down with his horse's shoulder, and put aside the spear of the other, as he passed, and without waiting to cut at him, went straight at the zereba hedge. The horse, though covered with foam, had a good bit left in him yet, and rose at it nobly, without an attempt to refuse, and landed safely on the inside. His pursuers came within ten yards. There was a spurt of fire, and four saddles were empty.

The Arab horsemen wheeled round, and the broadsides of the horses presented too fair a mark. Half a dozen of the poor animals were brought down by the bullets, and before they could get away the riders too were slain. Neither did those who in the excitement of the moment had run out from their cover entirely escape; several deliberate shots were aimed at them, and several fresh corpses dotted the plain.

"The curse of Cromwell on them!" cried Grady; "the more you shoot the more there are!"

And it really looked like it. It was a similar phenomenon to that of the wasps in August, when, if you kill one, three come to his funeral. The man who had occasioned this commotion was carried by his horse safely over the zereba hedge, as has been said. Directly he landed he found himself on the edge of the trench, and this, too, the animal cleverly got over.

The rider at once dismounted, and saw Captain Reece before him.

"Rather an unceremonious way of coming into a gentleman's parlour," he said; "but I don't think I have done any damage."

"Not a bit; and no matter if you had," said Reece. "We cannot show you much hospitality, I fear, for we are short of everything."

"By Jove!" exclaimed the new comer, "I beg your pardon if I am wrong, but is not your name Reece?"

"Yes."

"You do not remember me?"

"Well, I am sure you will pardon me; I cannot call to mind exactly where I have had the pleasure of meeting you. Was it at the Rag? No, no; surely at Simla, was it not?"

"Not exactly," said the new arrival.

"Don't you remember a little idiot who was your fag at Harton, and used to boil your eggs hard and burn your toast, for which you very properly corrected him?"

"What, Strachan!" cried Captain Reece. "Impossible! You can't be Tom Strachan!"

"As sure as you are Dodger Reece. I should not have dared to call you that to your face then, though."

"Well, but, you know, I should never have recognised you."

"I daresay not; I was twelve years old when you left Harton, and I have altered a bit since, no doubt. You were seventeen, and have not changed so much."

"I am very glad to see you, anyhow," said Reece, "and we will have a good chat presently. Just now I must not lose my opportunity; the rocks seem pretty crowded. The beggars are blazing away from every crevice about them."

Strachan wisely asked no questions, but watched and followed. The Arabs had evidently gathered in considerable numbers about the pile of boulders among which the gun-cotton mine was buried. Reece had forbidden any one to molest them from the balcony, not wishing to drive them away. He now went to his battery, attached the wires, brought two ends together, and the ground shook. There was a roar and a rattle; blocks of stone, arms, heads, legs went flying into the air, and a whole posse of Arabs were seen scuttling away into the mimosa bushes.

"What is bred in the bone," said Strachan to himself.

"He is a Dodger still!"

The men got some more shots at their enemies in the confusion caused by the explosion. It was a useful measure, this, however; for six men with water-cans, and six with rifles, who were waiting close to the gap, rushed out to the well the moment they heard the explosion, and in the confusion into which the enemy were thrown by an event which seemed to them supernatural, in the dust and in the smoke they accomplished their task of filling the cans and retiring without being observed, much less attacked.

It was not until they were safely back in the zereba that the Arabs began firing harmless volleys, in evident anger at having been out-manœuvred. The water gained was not so much in quantity, but was a great boon nevertheless, for it had been absolutely necessary to water the camels, and that had absorbed every drop of their own springs for the last twelve hours, and was very insufficient for the poor animals then. Strachan loosened his horse's girths and rubbed him down with a palm-leaf or two, doing what he could for him after his gallant efforts. It was pitiful to hear him whinny as he smelt the water in the distance, and not to be able to get him any. But perhaps a little could be spared from what trickled out by-and-by.

Presently Captain Reece came back to his visitor,

"Well, now I have time to ask, how on earth did you come to choose this desert for a steeple-chase course, and our little zereba for a goal?" he asked.

"I am acting on the staff," said Strachan; "only galloping, you know. And I was sent out to find you if I could, and tell you to make for Shebacat, and, if you could, to get on to Abu Klea at once. If I found any of the enemy out in this direction, and could not get on, I was to return at once, and a force was to be sent to relieve you; but it was important to avoid this if possible, I was given to understand. However, I had no chance of returning, for the first glimpse I got of the enemy consisted of a small body of mounted Arabs, who cut off my retreat, and chased me all the way here."

"We are not to make back to Gubat, then?" asked Reece in surprise.

"No," said Strachan.

"Matammeh has not been carried?"

"Not yet; I suppose it may be soon; everybody seems to expect it. But I don't see the use now."

"Why not?"

"Well," said Strachan, "one hates to be the bearer of bad news, but it must come. The expedition has been too late: Khartoum has fallen."

The two other officers had come up and heard this, and their faces showed the blank dismay which had fallen upon their hearts, as the words fell upon their ears.

Khartoum fallen! Why, then, what were they fighting for? What was to happen next? All seemed chaos.

"And Gordon?" was the first question which rose to all lips.

"There is no certain news, yet," said Strachan; "but the rumours of his death are only too probable.

He was not the sort of man to be taken alive, I think, was he?"

"No, no!"

"But when did you hear this?" asked Reece.

"Only last night," replied Strachan. "Gordon's four steamers arrived while you were at Abu Kru, the camp at Gubat, I think?"

"Yes, and two of them, the *Bordein* and *Telhhoweiya*, had started with Sir Charles Wilson up the river. That was on the 24th of January."

"Exactly. Well, it seems when they got to Khartoum they found it in the hands of the Mahdi, and it was with the greatest difficulty they got away, having to run the gauntlet of several batteries and a tremendous fusillade. Both steamers were wrecked coming down, and Sir Charles Wilson, with the crews and the Royal Sussex men who went with him, is on an island watched by the enemy, who have got guns posted, waiting to be brought off. Stuart Wortley came down in a small boat with the news last night."

"I could go straight to Shebacat; but for Abu Klea I am not so certain," said Reece.

"I can guide you as straight as a die," replied Strachan.

"Indeed, from Shebacat you cannot miss the track."

Captain Reece then said he had some immediate business to look to, and retired to the watch-tower, partly to have another look round, but principally to get away alone for a bit to think. It was clear to him that he must get away as soon as possible, but yet leaving would cause him to incur responsibility, which he hated. He was a brave man enough where personal danger was concerned, but to have to decide upon a matter where grave interests were at stake threw him into a cold sweat. Let a superior officer be in command, and he was as jolly as possible under any circumstances; supposing he got killed, and all got killed, it had nothing to do with him—that was the commanding officer's look out; and he obeyed him cheerfully, reserving the right to criticise him freely afterwards, supposing he were alive to do so.

But here he himself had to take a decided step; he was commanding officer, and Strachan had brought him no definite orders. Suppose they were intercepted, and cut to pieces. The blame would fall on him. Why did he quit the zereba? Suppose he delayed, and a force had to be sent to his rescue, and it were proved afterwards that he could have saved the small main body all that risk and trouble, and very likely loss, if he had shown a little more enterprise. Or suppose that the enemy, now a small body, assembled in force, cut off his retreat, now open, prevented all rescue, and cut them to pieces. In any case he would be blamed. He dreaded the second alternative most, because then he would be alive and ashamed. Still it made his ears burn to think what would be said of him, even after he could not hear or know, if he failed.

The more he thought about it, however, the more he saw that the first risk was the best to incur, and he finally determined to march that night and stand the racket. He examined the enemy's position once more carefully through his field-glass, and could only make out a few camels and a couple of horses. Indeed, they could not have watered any large number, especially as they had to do so entirely by night, the well being under the fire of the zereba all the daytime. And from men on foot they had nothing to fear, let them get the shortest of starts. There was the cavalry which had hunted Strachan, but they were but a handful. And the route to Shebacat was open desert, so far as the eye could reach from the balcony, with but few mimosas or black rocks.

When he had quite settled his plans he felt easier, and returned to the others. The two juniors had shown Strachan what little hospitality was in their power, including an iron tea-cupful of muddy water for himself and a pint for his horse, who asked for more, poor fellow! with all the earnestness of Oliver Twist in the workhouse.

"Are you Strachan of the Blankshire?" asked Grant.

"Yes," said Strachan.

"Were you not wounded at Tamai last spring?"

"Yes, I was; but I soon got all right."

"Is not Edwards in your battalion?"

"Yes, he is; do you know him?"

"Very well; we were at Sandhurst together."

And this discovery of a common friend made these two feel like comrades at once.

"Well, Strachan," said Reece, coming up, "are you ready to pilot us to-night?"

"Perfectly ready, sir," replied Strachan.

"Well, then, we will be off directly after sundown. Since Khartoum has fallen, the troops before it will be set free, and the country perhaps will be flooded with them. This may be our best chance."

"Certainly."

The three officers of camelry had to prepare their men for the start, and see that they got the saddles and other packages, which had been piled together to make an inner defence, separated and placed in proper position for instant adjustment.

Tom Strachan, left alone, wandered off to the watch-tower, to have a look at it and mount to the balcony. On his way across he met a soldier, who advanced his rifle and brought his right hand smartly across in salute, whom he recognised.

"Kavanagh!" he cried.

"Yes, sir, here I am," replied Kavanagh. "No, please don't shake hands now or here," he added, hurriedly. "I do not want to be recognised at all. My captain has not remembered being with me at Harton, I am glad to say."

"I have your sword still," said Strachan.

"Yes, and did good work with it at Tamai," replied Kavanagh.

"I am glad of that."

"It is a good one, indeed," said Strachan; "but I don't know that I have done anything wonderful with it!"

"Oh, yes, I read about it in the papers. You were mentioned in despatches."

"They were very kind, because I was wounded. Have you heard anything of the missing will, or Harry Forsyth?"

"Not a word; but I hope for better times still," he replied.

"So do I, Reginald, with all my heart. You have found life as a private soldier a severe trial, I fear."

"Not out here, campaigning," replied Kavanagh. "At home it was certainly trying at first. But the sergeant is waiting for me."

And he saluted again and passed on, leaving his

old chum very serious and meditative, which was not by any means his accustomed state of mind.

Presently Hump came up to make friends, and, when Strachan met Grant again he learned the story of the dog and his excursions to the well, and how Thomas Dobbs had made him fetch water.

"You were saying you did not know the name of this place," cried Strachan, laughing; "you should call it after him. *Bir* is the Arabic I believe for a well; you should name it *Bir-Hump.*"

The suggestion was repeated, adopted, and spread, and the entire company always alluded to the place as *Bir-Hump* from that hour forward.

The day waned; the camels were saddled and loaded as quietly as might be, Strachan tightened the girths of his horse, and when the sun had set and the after-glow faded into darkness, all mounted, and the camels, led by Strachan, defiled out of the zereba like a string of ghosts.

Every man had his rifle in his hand, ready to sell his life as dearly as he could; but the Arabs did not issue from their cover, and they sped on at a sharp trot unmolested, Strachan keeping a correct course by a compass he had, with an ingenious phosphorescent contrivance, by which he could distinguish the north point. When an hour had elapsed they all began to breathe more freely, for it is uncanny work expecting to be attacked every minute in the dark. But still strict silence was maintained.

During the long night tramp, with no jingling of accoutrements, beat of hoofs, light laugh, or homely talk to break the stillness, nothing but the light *brushing* sound, more like the whisper of sound than sound itself, caused by the movement of the camels' feet over the sand, the minds of the most thoughtless could not avoid reflection, and probably there was not one of all that company who did not think of Gordon. And of him there was not a little to think. The long waiting, month after month; never disheartened or beaten; trying every device, every stratagem, to keep the foes which environed him at bay; maintaining well even *his* reputation; anxious not for himself but for others, ready to sacrifice self indeed at any moment, cheerfully, for the sake of those whom he had undertaken to rescue; struggling on against fanatic courage without, and weakness, frailty, half-heartedness within; seeing the hearts of those in whom he was forced to trust grow fainter and fainter by degrees, in spite of his constant struggles against the effects of hope deferred upon them.

And then, when the reward was just within his reach—not personal honours, for which he cared so little, but what to him was the dearest object, the rescue of those whom he had undertaken to save if possible—to lose all by treachery, the treason of those he had trusted and forgiven.

"Trust makes troth," says the proverb, and Gordon had proved the truth of it again and again.

But it failed him; the endurance of some who had long wavered was now quite worn out, and so he was killed, and all his heroic work nullified, all those who had depended on his efforts for safety being destroyed with him. It was a perfectly maddening thought that the ship should founder thus in the entrance of the harbour; that after so many tedious marches, thirst-sufferings, struggles against the forces of nature, desperate battles, and wide-spread misery and wretchedness, they should be just a couple of days too late.

So little would have done it. A week's earlier start, a little more energy in some clerk, tailor, bootmaker, shipwright—who knows?

The mind seems forced in such a case to try and fix blame upon somebody. There was no redeeming feature for the most persevering maker of the best of things to turn to. Experience gained? There was no use in it, for Gordons do not crop up every century.

His example? The lesson of it was spoiled, since his devotion resulted in failure, and he died in the bitterness of feeling that his efforts had not been appreciated, and that he had been but lukewarmly supported.

We do not mean to imply that this was so. History must judge of that. We know only partial facts, and our judgment must also necessarily be affected by our feelings. But it is to be feared that it seemed so to him.

The moon rose, and gloomy thoughts were lightened. There was no enemy in sight, and talk began to circulate amongst the men. Captain Reece, for his part, was inclined to forget everything else in his delight at having given the enemy the slip. To have carried out his orders, and sustained such an attack with the loss of but one man wounded, and he doing well, was a legitimate source of satisfaction. It is true that he was not out of the wood yet; the Arabs who had chased Strachan might belong to a large body that had seized Shebacat.

This proved not to be the case, however, and a halt was called at the wells there. First the men were supplied, and Strachan's horse had a good satisfactory drink, and then the camels got an instalment of water. Then they mounted again, and pushed on to Abu Klea, where they arrived at sunrise, and Reece reported himself to the officer in command with a feeling of intense relief. He had got well out of it, at any rate, and Tom Strachan also had accomplished his mission satisfactorily; and next day he returned to head-quarters, not, however, without having seized the opportunity of a short unnoticed interview with his old chum Kavanagh before he started.

CHAPTER XXI.

THE CONVOY.

KAVANAGH and his friends had no long rest at Abu Klea; they were soon off again across the Desert, making for the Nile. It was not a cheerful duty they were performing, for they were convoying a body of sick and wounded to Korti, and that was rather too close a connection with the wrong side of the theatre of war. I expect that hospital nurses take quite a different view of a campaign from that entertained by high-spirited subalterns. And this present business was worse than the scenes in a hospital. Do what you will to lighten his sufferings, the transport of a wounded man must always be a painful operation.

These were being conveyed on camels. You have seen the seats in which little children often ride on ponies, one on each side, with a board for the feet to rest on. There were similar affairs on camels' backs, with two wounded men sitting back to back. Others, whose hurts were more serious, or of a nature which prevented their sitting up, were slung in a species of litter.

But, in despite of depressing influences, the escort were lightening the journey with chat and jest, when they were called to seriousness by the word—

"Attention!"

Silence fell upon the escort, and every man was in his proper place in a second. Arabs had been seen in the mimosa bushes to the right of the convoy, and it was impossible to keep quite clear of them, though, of course, the object of such a party is to avoid collision with the enemy as much as possible.

Half a dozen puffs of smoke spurted out of the cover, and as many bullets came singing overhead. The convoy did not halt, but moved steadily on, some of the escort dismounting, while the others led their camels. When the men on foot got a chance they halted and fired, and then doubled on again, and as they shot a very great deal better than their enemies, they made them chary of exposing themselves, and so held their fire in check. As the convoy came abreast of the position, however, the vollies broke out afresh, and the skirmishers spread, some in front, others in rear of it, to draw the fire on themselves, and away from the sick and wounded men. But not with entire success, for it seemed to be the object of the ambushed Arabs to annoy these with their fire rather than to fight the escort. There was a poor fellow named Binks, whose right hand had been shattered and amputated, riding sideways on a camel, balanced by another invalid whose head had come in contact with a fragment of a shell, and was bandaged up. Binks had been despondent about himself from the first, not caring very much whether he lived or died, now that he was so mutilated, for how was he to get his living without a right hand? he asked. It was in vain that Kavanagh assured him that he could do very well in the Corps of Commissionaires; he had not been very steady in the early part of his soldiering career, and his name had several entries against it in the Regimental Defaulters' Book, which he was convinced would tell fatally against his chances.

Suddenly he flung up his left arm, the right being in a sling, and gave a deep gasp, collapsing in his seat, and falling up against his companion. All his doubts and difficulties about the future were solved, poor fellow! for he was shot through the heart. Presently a camel was wounded, and sank down, groaning pitifully, if pity could have been spared for it, but most of that was absorbed by the soldier, suffering grievously from dysentery, whom he carried, and who was now thrown violently to the ground. A halt was necessary while he was otherwise accommodated, and the covering party pushed close up to the shrubby ground, taking advantage of the mimosas in their turn, and inflicting some loss on the enemy, who seemed now to have quite altered their former tactics, and to prefer distant to close quarters. When the convoy moved on again they closed upon it once more, ready to run up to it at the first signs of a rush upon it. The Soudanese, however, made none; on the contrary, they seemed to find the marksmanship of the escort too accurate for their taste, for they drew off to a distance where the bush was thicker, but so far that the fire they maintained was a mere waste of ammunition.

"Where's Grady?" cried a man. "Why don't he come and take his camel?"

"Grady!" called the corporal.

"Grady!" called the sergeant; but even *his* superior authority evoked no answer.

The officer in command again halted the convoy.

"He may be only wounded; we must not leave him," he said.

"Who saw him last?"

"I can find the place exactly, sir," said Kavanagh, "because of a bit of rock among the scrub which marked the place, and he was making towards it."

"Is it far?"

"No, not five hundred yards; it was just before we ran in."

"Then double out and look for him. Go with him, another of you, and Corporal Adams."

But just as this start was being made Grady appeared, shoving before him a man dressed in bernouse and cap, bearing the Mahdi's colours of blue and white, whom he grasped by the scruff of the neck, and, when he showed unwillingness to advance, expedited his movements with a bump from his knee. What had happened was this. While skirmishing he had caught sight of a pair of human heels protruding from a bush which grew on the side of a rock, and he came to the conclusion that there probably were legs attached to those heels, and a body in continuation. So he made a detour, and crept up very softly from behind till he was within reach of those heels, which he promptly seized—or rather the ankles above them—and drew out a wriggling Arab with a rifle in his hand, which he could not get a chance of using against the person who was drawing him.

Flattering himself that he was entirely concealed, he thought he had got a beautiful place for a pot-shot when the skirmishers had passed, and the convoy came abreast of him. And so indeed he had, and with the barrel of his Remington in the natural rest formed by a fork in the boughs of a tree, he had a first-rate chance of bagging something. But he reckoned without his extremities; had he been a foot shorter, or the scrub a foot deeper, he would have remained unnoticed.

"Come out, you spalpeen, and drop that gun, will ye?" cried Grady, and both directions were obeyed, involuntarily enough; for, as he spoke, the butt of the rifle was brought with such a jerk against the stem of a mimosa, that the owner lost his grip of it, and the same jerk landed him clear of the bush.

"Be quiet, my jewel, till I pick up your shooting-iron," said Grady, who wanted to take back the rifle as a prize and a trophy, but feared that his nimble captive would escape him while he reached for it.

So he knelt on the Arab's back, he lying on his face, and taking a piece of twine out of his pocket, he tied his elbows together. Then he reached out and got the rifle, and slung it over his shoulder.

"And will ye plaze to get up?" he said. "You must excuse me if I am a thrifle rough, but it's owing to the resistance ye make;" and as Grady, a very powerful man, was the stronger, his captive found himself on his feet and emerging into the open, without any volition of his own.

"Sure, and it's in mighty good luck ye should estame yourself, to fall into the hands of a tender-hearted boy like meself, who lets the dirty life stop in your haythen carcase. By all the laws of your warfare, I am bound to put my bayonet into your stomach instead of making ye a prisoner, just as if ye were a respectable sodger, who gave and took quarter like a Christian. Get along wid ye! Ye are as bad to drive as a pig, and not a hundredth part the value of him, nor such good company either. Get on, I say, or they'll be thinking you've took me, and not that I've took you. Ye've got to go before the captain, and tell him what he chooses to ask you, so where's the use of struggling, making us both so uncomfortable this warm day? It's proud ye should be to have spache with a real gentleman and a British officer, ye poor haythen vagabond!"

It may be observed that the last sentence was uttered in the possible, though not the certain and obvious hearing of the officer alluded to.

"Why, Grady, what have you been up to?" was the question which greeted him.

"Sure and I've made an important capture; look at the clothes of him! How do you know that it is not the Mahdi himself?"

Here the officer commanding the detachment rode up.

"Well done, Grady," he said; "we were wanting a prisoner, and may get some valuable information out of this one. A very neat thing indeed; I shall remember it."

Grady saluted, and went to his camel.

The prisoner had his arms freed, and was given another camel, as he seemed quiet and philosophical, and had a couple of friendly natives for companions to pump him. And the convoy went on its slow and painful journey.

Assured by the other Arabs that no harm would be done him, the captured man became cheerful and communicative. Of course there are different sorts of Arabs, as there are of English or Frenchmen, and this one was a philosopher who saw no particular merit in struggling against the inevitable, and was inclined to make himself as comfortable as circumstances permitted. Indeed, he and his captor would have found much in common if they had passed a social evening together, and been able to hold converse; though for that it would have been necessary either for Grady to learn Arabic, or for the native to learn English, and neither might have thought it worth the trouble.

He belonged to a tribe which had not been very keen about espousing the Mahdi's cause. They were old-fashioned in their ideas, and did not like new-fangled notions. Besides, this might be an impostor. Mahomet was good enough for them, and they wanted no other prophet. Then they had profitable business relations with the Egyptians, and had no desire to break off communication with them. And they also saw that something was to be made out of the English, especially if they established themselves at Khartoum and opened up a trade with the black tribes towards the Equator. So they were inclined to join us, and throw in their lot with ours. But one day a proclamation was issued which filled them with dismay. The English, to reconcile the inhabitants of the Soudan to their presence, announced that they only desired to rescue General Gordon and his garrison at Khartoum, and then they would retire from the Soudan.

But that meant that this particular tribe, and any others who supported the English, would presently be left alone to stand the brunt of the Mahdi's power; and the Mahdi's motto was not "Rescue and retire," but "Annihilate and stop!" If they had been strong enough to stand alone it would have been different, but without the English alliance they were powerless to resist the False Prophet.

Therefore the only course for them seemed to be to join him, and so escape the vengeance which would otherwise overtake them. And since they had hesitated and therefore incurred suspicion, it was advisable, they thought, to show the greater zeal, and they in many instances adopted the Mahdi's uniform, as the present prisoner had done. But they did not thoroughly believe in him; they were not at any rate fanatical in his cause, and were not likely to impale themselves on bayonets to encourage the others, as his more earnest adherents thought it a privilege to do. At the same time they were Mohammedans, and to kill an unbeliever must be always a meritorious action in their eyes. So it was a pleasure to them to pepper the Christians a bit, when occasion offered, not to mention that any sort of a fight was attractive to such a warlike race. But still there was no venom in their hostility; we were enemies, of course, but enemies who might any day become friends; and Grady's prisoner did not think it necessarily behoved him to sulk, refuse food, commit suicide, or, which was much the same thing, attempt to escape. So he was soon chatting freely with the natives, of whom there were a good many, for the camels conveying the invalids were led and tended by them. It stands to reason that all he said about his own tribe and others, and the number of the Mahdi's followers, and the distribution of his forces, could not be accepted as implicitly correct. For, in the first place, he most likely had no accurate knowledge on many of these and similar points; and in the next place, if he had, he might more than possibly wish to mislead, rather than afford useful information.

But after a certain amount of practice an officer with a head on his shoulders learns how to sift the reports gathered from spies, deserters, prisoners, and peasants, and to get a few grains of valuable fact out of bushels of chaff. So the chief interpreter went to work, and translated much useless and some practical talk.

The most interesting account he had to give could not be called useful, however, because it referred to past events, and these were already fully reported; but the present party had not heard them. It was concerning the death of Colonel Stewart, the only English companion Gordon had for so long, and of which the man professed to have been a witness in the October of 1884. The following was the Arab's account, transcribed from the note-book of Sergeant Barton, who could take things down in shorthand, when men spoke slowly and deliberately, or with the delay, as in the present instance, of an interpreter :—

"When Gordon Pasha knew that there was no hope, and that Khartoum must fall, because, though he could hold his own against the enemy without, treason in the heart of the place was a thing against which he was powerless, and he knew, though no one else may have done so, that he was betrayed, he sent off Colonel Stewart in a steamer for a pretended purpose which imposed upon him, his real object being to save his friend by getting him out of the way when the attack, which he expected from day to day, came.

"Nothing would have made Colonel Stewart leave Khartoum if he had suspected this, but he did not, and he set out in the firm conviction that his going would really be useful. So say those that should know. What is certain is that he went, and that his steamer struck on a rock in the Wad Gamr country, for I myself have seen it. I was with the Sheikh Omar at Berti at the time. Sheikh Omar had a nephew Sulieman Wad Gamr, a very bitter enemy of the Turk, and of any one who supported the Turk, but a man with a double face, who promised most and smiled the sweetest, when he had the dagger concealed in his sleeve.

"Colonel Stewart did not like the look of him when he came to offer his services, but Hassan Bey, who was with the Englishman, thought that Sulieman was to be trusted, and so a conference was held, and Sulieman undertook to find camels to take all the shipwrecked travellers on to Merawi if he could. Afterwards he came and said that he knew of camels, but the people who owned them were afraid that they would be taken from them by force, and if those who came to conclude the bargain had arms in their hands, there was no chance of any camels being brought forward, but if those who were to bargain for them were unarmed, it was very certain that as many as were necessary might be got. And when, seeing no other way than to trust Sulieman, Colonel Stewart agreed to this, he was directed to go at a certain hour to the house of one Fakreitman, who was blind, but to be sure to take no weapons, neither he nor any of the party. They went to Fakreitman, the blind man's house, accordingly, and Sulieman met them there with the men that he had instructed to carry out his secret, and others who were not entrusted. I was in the courtyard with others serving under the Sheikh Omar, and we wondered where the camels were, for we saw none in the neighbourhood, and yet the bargaining was going on. Then suddenly, at a signal from Sulieman Wad Gamr, the appointed men attacked Colonel Stewart and his companions, and there was such a scuffle as is possible when there are sharp swords and daggers on one side and no weapons at all on the other.

"Colonel Stewart and others were soon put to death. Hassan Bey seized the owner of the house, the blind man, Fakreitman, and held him before him as a shield, and so got clear of the house with only a slight wound. We outside might have dispatched him, but we had no orders, and did not interfere. And so he got clear, and letting the blind man go, escaped."

Such was the prisoner's account, and there was no reason to doubt the general tenor of it, though of course the details were not to be implicitly relied upon.

The man was asked why, since he seemed to bear no particular grudge against the English, he took such pains to establish himself in a good position for a sure shot at the convoy. It was not a wise question. The Arab laughed, and asked if the English had any particular enmity to the Soudanese.

"No," was the reply. "On the contrary, we wish to be friends with them."

"And yet," said the prisoner, "you have killed twenty thousand of us in the last few moons. When we fight we mean to kill; and when we hunt we mean to kill. Are you not the same?"

There was no denying this; war is of necessity a game for two to play at, or else it would be sheer murder.

He was questioned about Gordon's death, but, though he was willing enough to talk on the subject, his information was at third or fourth hand, and did not profess to be personal, like the other account.

"Ah! that was a man, Gordon Pasha!" he said. "If HE had declared himself a prophet, or the great sheikh of the Soudan, the Mahdi would have lost all his followers but a few slave hunters, and all would have gathered under Gordon's standard. He was just, and when he said a thing every one knew that it was true. The Turks were never just; they took bribes, and they sought by word and deed to deceive. But Gordon Pasha was the wisest and the most just ruler that ever came into the country, and he feared nothing except to offend Allah. The highest and the lowest were the same to him, and it was a pity to kill him. There will never be such another."

"Why, then, was he murdered?"

"The Mahdi knew that he was a rival, and must overthrow him if he could, or else lose his power himself. And he was betrayed by those who had sinned against him, and been forgiven, but did not believe in the forgiveness. And besides that, the Mahdi offered them money from the first, and when you got so near Khartoum he increased this to a large sum. But all this would not have availed if men had known that Gordon was going to remain as their sheikh; but where was the use of joining a sheikh who was leaving to-morrow against another who was sure to stop?"

He was a shrewd fellow, this prisoner of Grady's, and knew how to trim his sails to the prevailing wind. The marches of the convoy were slow, as the patients could not bear the jolt of a camel's trot; and the old medical direction, "When taken to be well shaken," would have been death to most of them, so the halts were fixed at various intermediate wells, where zerebas had been formed and held till the last load had passed, when the detachment performing that duty likewise retired. The body of

Binks was carried on to the bivouac for that night, and decently buried there.

On the following morning the captured Arab was nowhere to be seen, and it was at first feared that he had escaped in the night. But he was soon discovered, the cause of his disappearance being that he had discarded his Mahdi uniform, which was now a little bundle about the size of a cocoa-nut, hanging from a projection of a camel's harness. Such clothing as he wore fitted well, nature herself having measured him for it; and since he was still a young man, there were no wrinkles in it. You know how difficult it is to recognise a fellow if you come upon him down a back-water bathing, and will understand why the prisoner was missed at first. He came up presently and offered to take service, and tend a camel. It appeared to him that he had to go along with the party anyhow, and might as well improve the shining hour and earn a little money.

Earlier in the march one of the natives in charge of camels had been killed by one of the scattered volleys which every now and then harassed them on their journey, and two others had taken the opportunity of deserting, so that the new volunteer's services were gladly accepted. And there was the little bundle, ready to be shaken out and put on again should the fortune of war land him to-morrow amongst the adherents of the Mahdi. Quite a man of the world, this Arab.

In the course of his long talk with the interpreter the day before, Kavanagh, who was riding at his side, rifle in hand, having been made responsible for his safe custody, heard a name repeated several times which struck him as familiar, and which he yet could not associate with anything in particular. *Burrachee!* where on earth had he ever heard the word Burrachee? He had dreamt it, or fancied it, or was thinking of that word which expresses the taste given to wine by the skin in which it is stored in some places. And he tried to drive it from his head. But that night he was for guard, and while doing his tour of sentry it flashed upon him in a second.

Burrachee, the Sheikh Burrachee; that was the name of the Mohammedan uncle of Harry Forsyth, who lived amongst the Arabs of the Soudan, and to whom Harry meant to have recourse in finding the portentous will, the absence of which was the cause that he, Reginald Kavanagh, was tramping up and down a narrow path under the stars, with a chance of being shot or sprung upon every minute, instead of being snugly tucked up between the sheets, snoring to the nightingales.

His mind was easier for having remembered the association with the name, but his curiosity was excited to know whether there was any connection between that and the same word used by the Arab, and he took an early opportunity on the march next day to ask Sergeant Barton to get him the loan of the interpreter for a bit. For the interpreter was a person of consequence, in his own estimation at least, and not to be lightly appropriated by privates.

But tact can do a great deal, and by approaching the question in a judicious manner, his services were secured, and he blandly expressed his readiness to put any questions to the ex-prisoner which Kavanagh might desire, and to translate the answers.

This was the result in one language. To give the Arabic and then the English would involve mere repetition, so I am sure that you will excuse that. Besides I could not do it.

Q. " Do you know the Sheikh Burrachee ? "

A. " Yes, everybody knows the Sheikh Burrachee."

Q. " Is he not a foreigner to the Soudan ? "

A. " It is said so. He is rich, wise, learned, and he is a True Believer. But his features are not those of the Turk or of the Arab."

Q. " Do you know whether a man of his race, much younger, has joined him lately ? "

A. "Truly, yes, I have heard something of such an event. Some say his son, others a man made by magic by the sheikh, who is a great magician, and can make ghosts come and go as he commands."

Q. "Did you ever hear of any—(Kavanagh was regularly bothered to know how to ask after a legal document like a will, and the interpreter could not help him; at last he hit on the word Firman) of any Firman the young man was seeking for ? "

A. " No, I have never seen either of them; I speak from hearsay, and know nothing more than I have told you."

There was nothing more to be got out of Grady's captive.

But still, to know that Forsyth had reached his uncle was something. And the probability was that he was living, for if he had been dead the news would very likely have reached this gossiping Arab.

" I told you about the missing will in which I have an interest," Kavanagh said to Sergeant Barton, when all that could had been got out of the Arab.

" Yes; and Daireh the Egyptian led your friend, who undertook to trace it, a pretty dance out here, and all over the Soudan."

"Yes; well I expect that he has traced him, for it seems he is living with this Sheikh Burrachee, as he calls himself, who is as mad as a hatter, and he would not do that without a very strong reason."

"Then the man who may be the Irish shiekh's son, or may be merely a magical illusion, and vanish or turn into a cat some fine morning, is your friend, I suppose?" said Barton.

"Sure to be," replied Kavanagh; "though whether he has found Daireh yet is another question, and if, having found him, he has also got the will is still more problematical."

"It would be hard lines if, after all that risk and trouble and running his man to earth, he should find the will destroyed or lost after all," said Barton. "I cannot believe in such ill luck!"

"No more should I three months ago," said Kavanagh; "but after getting to Khartoum just three days too late I am prepared for anything. What is the journey undertaken by Forsyth compared to the expedition fitted out, the persevering struggle against the forces of Nature, and the opposition of hosts of desperate foes for the purpose of rescuing Gordon? And that all that should fail seemed too bad to be possible. Yet so it was. I shall always be prepared for the worst for the rest of my life."

CHAPTER XXII.

SWORD *VERSUS* BAYONET.

AFTER the skirmish which was fatal to poor Binks, and in which Grady effected his clever capture, the convoy had not been annoyed, save now and then by a distant shot which fell short; but in the afternoon of the day that Kavanagh got his information about Harry Forsyth, such as it was, out of the man Grady had taken prisoner, bullets fell closer again.

They had entered a wide valley, and there was water on the south side of it, near the black rocks. No zereba was formed here, possibly because troops could not be spared to guard it, or the spot was considered too near the next wells, or there was good reason to know that there was no force of the enemy of any consequence in the neighbourhood. Whether it was the cause or not, this latter fact was probably the case, but there were individual sharp-shooters about who were inclined to make themselves a nuisance.

Perched high up among fantastic blocks of stone, which would have tempted an artist to draw out his sketch-book, they got excellent shots at the party below them, and as there was no chance of a return, they being entirely concealed, and their presence merely indicated by the little puffs of white smoke which spurted out here and there, there was nothing to disturb their aim. For nothing spoils a rifleman's shooting like being exposed to accurate fire himself; which was probably the reason why duellists, who could perform wonders in the shooting gallery, used so often to miss each other at twelve paces in the days of single combat, when George the Fourth was Regent.

The range, however, was a long one, and the fire *plunging*, or perpendicular. Now horizontal fire has this characteristic, that if a bullet misses one object it goes straight on and may strike another; or it may pass through a fleshy substance which does not offer too great resistance, and strike another beyond. But a plunging fire, if it misses the object aimed at, goes into the ground and is harmless.

And so it happened that no mischief was done for some time, though several bullets came thudding down in the midst of men and camels. At length, with the fatality which seemed throughout this campaign to attend upon non-combatants, a shot struck a poor Egyptian camel driver on the neck, passing through his spine, and shortly afterwards a surgeon was wounded in the foot.

There did not seem to be more than two or three riflemen firing at them, but they were far above the average in marksmanship, and more dangerous, at a distance, than a score of ordinary soldiers of the Mahdi. Six men, of whom Kavanagh was one, were told off to dislodge them; not more, because they would certainly retire before a strong body, and return, when they withdrew from the pursuit, to their former positions and practice. Indeed, the officer who went with the six thought that number too numerous to show, and advanced in front with a file only, while the others had orders to creep up on the flanks, concealing themselves entirely, if possible.

Those in front got fired at several times as they scaled the rocks, but to hit a small object shifting behind cover was far beyond the Arabs' skill yet, though they *had* made a vast improvement, and the risk of advancing upon them in this way was not great. And when the two men had got within a couple of hundred yards of the nearest Arab's lurking-place, the officer called to them to halt, keep under cover, and fire if they got a chance, or even if they didn't, his object being to keep them amused while the flankers gained higher ground, and obtained fair shots at them.

But one of those in front was MacIntosh, for whom the wilful waste of a bullet was almost an impossibility, frugality and marksmanship combining to render the task painful to his feelings. He prided himself on his shooting, and did not like even to appear to make a miss. Not able to catch a glimpse of a foe where he was, he crept thirty yards higher, to a nice flat stone just breast high, which commanded a much wider view. But still he could see nothing to shoot at; so he exposed himself, standing fairly up. *Pat!* came a ball against a rock five yards on his right; it would not do for Wimbledon that.

"Eh! they must practise a wee bit afore they challenge the Scottish team!" murmured MacIntosh, as he dropped on one knee behind the stone over which he held his Martini-Henry at the ready, his eye being fixed on the spot the shot came from.

The Arab probably thought that he had dropped his man, for he raised his head and shoulders above the cover to look. That was the opportunity MacIntosh was waiting for. He had him covered in a moment, his rifle was as steady and motionless as if it grew out of the rock itself. His finger pressed the trigger, and the Arab he aimed at fell forwards, his arms hanging over the rocky parapet, the Remington falling from his hands.

When they examined his body afterwards, it was found that the bullet had struck him in the exact centre of the forehead.

"I am sorry for the puir mon, but it was an unco' good shot!" was the complacent remark of MacIntosh, as he contemplated his handiwork. But that was later on. At the time he fired he remained still, as ordered, looking out for another chance.

The other man had taken what he was told more literally, and fired once or twice at spots from which flashes had issued, without a hope of hitting anything but stones, and uncertain, indeed, whether the Arab who had last fired was still there or had shifted his quarters. And shots were fired back, principally at the officer, who showed his head as he peered about, trying to see how his men were getting on.

Meantime, the files on the flanks were climbing cunningly, Kavanagh being one of the two men on the right, until they got rather above the level of the Arabs in ambush, and a man on the left got the first shot. The Arab was lying down, peering to his front, and afforded a steady aim, not fifty yards off. It was almost impossible to miss him, unless the marksman were flurried, and the soldier was as cool as if on parade, and hit him in the back, between the shoulder-blades: that made two.

The last report showing they were enfiladed, three other Arabs bolted from their hiding-places, and made for the higher ground. Bang! bang! bang! went the rifles from below and each side: there they were still, active as monkeys, darting between and over the fantastic boulders; bang! bang! as they re-appeared, without effect. Then five rifles exploding together, like a volley, as a retreating Arab paused, and turned to fire a shot back; and this time the bullets found a billet, for he sank down in a heap. The other two got away, in spite of the leaden invitations to stop sent after them.

Directly the first flanking shot was heard, the officer in front cried "Forward!" to the two men with him, MacIntosh and the other, and all three pushed up amongst the rocks. As they worked up higher, the surface of the mountain side became so rugged that they could not keep sight of each other, and hunt about in a satisfactory manner at the same time. While firing was going on, indeed, they had a guide as to the direction of their friends, but when that ceased, they were somewhat more scattered and isolated than prudence dictated. But prudence is apt to be forgotten in the excitement of a hunt, and a man-hunt is the most thrilling of all chases. They searched about, with bayonets fixed, and fingers on trigger-guards, expecting an antagonist behind each new rock.

Kavanagh, making for a point where he last saw the end of a bernouse vanishing, wandered further than the others, perhaps, and came suddenly on a hole in the side of the rock. Not a natural fissure, but evidently a man-made doorway; oval, with carved pillars at the sides, and an inscription over the door. Kavanagh's first impulse was to go in, his second one not to. Why, there might be an army inside! But by the time the risk occurred to him he was through the portals, and he was afraid of turning, not knowing what was behind him. So he took a pace to his rear, still looking into the interior, and holding his rifle at the ready.

It was by no means dark inside, though coming out of the intense glare it seemed so at the first moment. But light came in from openings high up, showing a chamber which would *not* contain an army, but was of handsome dimensions for all that, and empty. Empty to all appearance, so far as human beings were concerned that is, but inhabited by stone heroes of the past. There they sat, solemn and gigantic, heedless of the lapse of ages, staring into the future with blind eyes.

The walls and the bases of the statues were covered with hieroglyphics, which would no doubt have told all about them to officials of the British Museum not present.

What a long time it must have taken to write a letter when you had to draw a dog to express a dog, a man when you meant a man, and so forth. It would be rather amusing reading, though, so far as some of my friends, who are not good artists, are concerned. And yours? If a fellow could draw a little bit, however, one might spend nine or ten hours after breakfast very pleasantly in deciphering his correspondence; though it must have been annoying, if one wanted some such matter as a pyramid in a hurry, to have to draw a stag and a knight for "Dear Sir," an eye for "I," and so forth throughout the piece. And when ingenious innovators took prominent curves and angles of these drawings to express the things, and so invented hieroglyphics, no doubt busy men with a large correspondence found advantage in it!

Kavanagh had little time for these reflections, for he had hardly made a rapid inspection of this curious old temple, burying-place, or whatever it was, before he heard a shot in the distance outside, and running to the entrance he saw an Arab, who had doubtless been unearthed on another side and bolted here, pausing a hundred yards off to have a return shot at the man probably who had fired at him, and the report of whose rifle had disturbed Kavanagh's day-dream. Of course he did not know that an enemy was up there, or he would not have stopped for his shot.

As he was getting his sight to bear on some one below, Kavanagh was doing the same for him, and just as he was going to pull he got a violent shock on the hip, which disconcerted his aim; and perhaps that was lucky for MacIntosh, whom he had got nicely at the end of his foresight. Kavanagh had hardly fired, however, and had not time to open the breach and put another cartridge into his rifle, before he heard a noise in the cavern-temple behind him, and, turning sharply, saw a figure with a sword in the right hand and a shield on the left arm, literally bounding towards him.

The Arab must have been concealed behind one of the figures, or in a recess which had escaped the explorer's notice, and, not possessing fire-arms himself, had not chosen to attack while his enemy's rifle was certain to be loaded; but directly he heard him fire he seized his opportunity with the promptitude of a really good soldier, and went for him before he could re-load.

Kavanagh brought his weapon down to the charge and waited for him, and now a really interesting set-to began, and it was a pity there was no one to witness it. The Arab, a fanatic fakir, approached with his shield well advanced, and his sword, which a man might have shaved with, in his strong right hand, watching for an opening. He made a cut; Kavanagh turned it with his bayonet and re-posted. The thrust was parried by the shield, but the force of it made the Arab stagger back.

Kavanagh followed, feinted low, and when the shield went down delivered the point over the top of it, just touching his opponent's chest, who saved his life by jumping back with a slight wound. Kavanagh followed further into the cavern. Each now knew that the other was not to be trifled with, and they circled round, eyes glaring into eyes, trying to draw on an attack, the statues around looking straight before them, heedless witnesses of the conflict. Kavanagh feinted again, but the Arab was not to be caught by the same trick a second time, and instead of warding the thrust seized that moment to make a dash and a cut, and his sword bit deeply into the other's side, cutting through bandolier and karkee into the flesh.

Kavanagh, wounded, but not disabled, at the same moment dashed his rifle, held across, into his opponent's face, and as he staggered back darted his bayonet at him over the shield, piercing his shoulder. Yet he could still swing his right arm, still wield his razor-edged weapon.

And still they faced each other, bleeding freely. Kavanagh had this in his mind fixedly, that if he thrust the point of his bayonet through the shield, and so got it entangled, he was done, for his active opponent would step within distance, and cut him down in a moment. As if to force him to risk this, the Arab suddenly crouched down, and covering himself well with his shield, made a spring at him, cutting at his left arm. Kavanagh jumped back and saved his wrist, but it was so near a thing that the edge of the sword touched his hand, severing the little finger, which fell on the ground, and making a deep cut in the rifle stock. Unaware of the mutilation, Kavanagh re-posted, darting out his weapon over the shield with his right hand, and piercing his enemy through the neck.

But even for such a wound as that the brave Soudanese would not be denied, but forced his way to close quarters, and cut his enemy over the side of the head; a blow which would have been instantly fatal had it been delivered with his accustomed force, but the wound through the shoulder took the strength out of it, and loss of blood and the shock of the throat wound helped to weaken him; indeed, his sword dropped from his hand with the effort. Kavanagh, almost blind with the blood which deluged his face, shortened arms and sought to transfix his assailant, who, however, managed to seize the muzzle of the rifle and close, and a species of rough-and-tumble conflict ensued for about half a minute, each striving to throw the other, and both as weak as babies.

Kavanagh, however, had most strength left, for though both were losing much blood, that which ebbed from the Arab drained more important veins, and the wound in his throat especially was terrible. His grasp relaxed, his eyes lost the light of fanaticism and the joy of combat, and grew filmy and expressionless, and he fell heavily at the foot of a gigantic, blubber-lipped statue.

Kavanagh caught up his rifle and turned the bayonet downwards, but there was no fight left in his foe, and in spite of the customs of this barbarous war he could not thrust. So he left the Arab lying there, and staggered to the portal, where he was forced to lean against a pillar, so giddy and faint was he. He had enough strength and wits left, however, to slip a cartridge into his rifle and fire it off, as a guide to his friends where to find him; and it was as well he did so, as they were searching for him close by, and might not have hit upon the entrance to the cave-temple for some time, so curiously was it masked by the rocks The report, however, directed them right, and just as Kavanagh was slipping from the pillar to the ground, he heard a voice say—

"Here he is, sir!" and saw comrades close, though their voices sounded somehow a long way off.

"My eye, you have had a good bout, mate;" one said to him, "but where is the other fellow?"

"In there," replied Kavanagh, faintly; "don't kill him, he's a good 'un."

"Dinna kill him, indeed!" said MacIntosh, presently, as he bent over the body of the Arab and took his scarf for bandages. "There's nae much need for any one to do that!"

Kavanagh's wounds were rudely bound up, just to check the bleeding for the present, and the officer having some spirits in a flask gave him a drain, and asked him if he thought he could walk down to camp. Being somewhat revived, he said he could, and set out, supported by a couple of men, one on each side. It was a slow progress, but the distance was not great, and he managed to get down all right, and then a surgeon dressed his wounds for him.

"The bandolier and a tobacco-pipe in the pocket of your karkee jacket have done you a good turn, my lad," he said; "for the body cut has gone right through them, and might have been fatal but for that resistance. It is pretty deep as it is, but you will be all right; and your other hurts are not serious, only sword cuts. But your little finger will not grow again, you know."

The wounds might not be serious in a surgeon's estimation, but they were very painful, and to feel so weak and helpless was depressing to the spirits. The attack, however, had been successful, and the handful of sharp-shooters killed or effectually dispersed, for no more shots were fired at the convoy either that evening, during the night, or on the following morning, when it got under weigh again. So he had the pleasure of reflecting that his discomforts were not altogether incurred in vain. The most provoking thing he found was to be told that he was so very lucky only to be slashed all over with sword cuts, and not to have any bullet wounds. What he had got ached and smarted and throbbed to an extent calculated to try the patience of Job, and what was the use of endeavouring to persuade him that he was one of the favourites of fortune? He succeeded to the seat on a camel vacated by the ill-fated Binks, and every jolt hurt his side; the head and hand wounds were not much affected by the motion, but every violent jerk caused the other to gape and bleed, and the dressing had to be renewed at every halt where water was obtainable. But the comrade who rode alongside and congratulated him on not having any gun-shot wounds meant well, and he restrained his impatience. Only when Grady, whom he credited with more sense, went on the same tack, he said, "Thank you, Paddy; did you ever see a codfish crimped?"

"No, sure, but I have seen a salmon."

"Alive?"

"In course; it's no use doing it after he's dead."

"And did you congratulate him?"

"Indeed, I did not, and it was a cruel thing I thought it," said Grady. "Ah, and sure I see what you are after! And it is like a crimped fish ye are with the deep slashes, and only those would think light of them who have not got them. But you will soon be all right again after the clane cuts, while a poke or a bullet-hole is a long time haling if it does not kill ye entirely. That is what the boys mane."

It was after a couple of days that Kavanagh was able to hold this conversation. Before that he was incapacitated for talking not only by weakness, but also because the cut on the side of his head had reached his cheek, and slicing through it nicked the tongue.

Taking food and drink was therefore quite painful enough just at first without talking. But it was surprising how quickly this part began to heal. He could not smoke yet, however, and that resource for whiling away some of the long hours failed him.

"It was a regular duel ye had with the haythen in his temple, and ye won it fair and square, anyhow, without shooting," said Grady. "The other was as dead as Julius Sayser when the boys saw him, for I was not to the fore myself, having had my little tour the day before."

"I remember," said Kavanagh. "And how is your prisoner getting on? He has not slipped away yet, has he?"

"Sorra a bit of it, he seems quite plazed to be living with dacent people for a change. He tould the interpreter that it was a mighty great friend of the Mahdi's ye killed; a man some people reckoned very holy—a *faker* he called him. At least, a man like that lived up by that cavern ye discovered."

"I don't know who he was," said Kavanagh, "but I wish he had recovered. He was a game one that, to fight as he did after he got his death-wound."

Sergeant Barton, who came up just then, heard this last remark, and said, smiling—

"That is true enough, but his opponent must have a good bit of pluck, too, it seems to me."

"Not so much as you think," replied Kavanagh, meditatively. "I do not say it out of mock modesty, but it is a simple fact that fear of that sharp edge made me strain all my faculties to keep it at a distance. But I was horribly afraid of it all the same."

"Well, I suppose that the other was afraid of your bayonet point, if you come to that."

"I don't believe it; he did not mind it more than a pin, if he could only kill me at the same time."

Here an officer came up and asked Kavanagh how he was; adding, "I have good news for you. We shall reach Korti to-day, and then you will be more comfortable."

CHAPTER XXIII.

IN THE RANKS OF THE ENEMY.

HARRY FORSYTH had put off the evil day as long as he could, but at length he found himself forced to turn an apparent traitor to his Queen and country, or else to give up the object of his journey when his trials, dangers, and sufferings had been crowned with success, and probably to lose his life into the bargain.

The detachment in which the Sheikh Burrachee held a command came to a precipitous rocky mountain overlooking the Nile, and here they were to stop the English advance. No position could have been more judiciously chosen: the rocks looked down on a narrow gorge of the river still more straightened by an island named Dulka, which it was determined to garrison strongly with riflemen, and there was debate as to who should undertake this duty. Harry hoped that it would be the tribe with which his uncle had become associated, and of which he himself was now supposed to be a member, because he thought it would be hardly difficult to slip away down the stream somehow, by swimming if no other means were to be had, and so join the English before they attacked, and avoid even the appearance of being a partaker of his uncle's crimes. But this chance was denied to him, and others went to the island, while the Sheikh Burrachee and his men were posted in the steepest part, the very citadel of this natural fortress.

To escape from there before the assault was obviously impossible. Up to that time Harry had taken it for granted in his own mind that his countrymen would carry any position they chose, with more or less loss, and pass on, but he now began to fear that this one was really impregnable. Parts of it were difficult to climb if unopposed, but with an enemy with a rifle in his hand behind every crag and boulder, it looked simply impossible for any living thing to make the ascent. Now for the first time Harry Forsyth became an active hypocrite, for he had only been a passive one up to this. He busied himself about to select a good commanding spot in which to ensconce himself with his rifle with an energy which delighted his uncle extremely. And so much was thought of his shooting that he was sure not to be interfered with.

"Not a man of them can ever pass the Rackabit el Gamel by water, and they can as soon take these rocks as scale the heavens. Here the freedom of the Soudan will be worked out; the authority of the Mahdi established!" exclaimed the sheikh. Rackabit el Gamel, or the Camel's Neck, is the name of the gorge by Dulka Island.

When the sun rose on the tenth of February, eighteen hundred and eighty-five, Harry Forsyth, from his lofty position on the heights of Kirbekan, strained his eyes in the direction from which the British force was expected to come. Nothing yet; yes, those red ants, as they seem in the far distance, what are they? And there were larger black ants in rear of them.

And now in the clearer light grey ants aligned with the red. The red ants, had he known it, were the Black Watch, going into action in their red coats and kilts; the grey were the men of the South

Staffordshire Regiment; the large black ants in rear were the guns. He did not know these details, but he recognised English troops, not seen now for a long time by him, and his heart beat high with excitement and hope. Now was his chance of escape. Unless he were killed during the assault, or taken prisoner and shot before he had time to explain himself, he would surely be able to get away in the confusion of fight. Even if the English were repulsed, he could feign pursuit and so come up with them.

Suddenly he saw both red and grey masses scatter out from their centres, as they broke into extended order, and at the same time what he could now distinguish as cavalry swept round to the right. It was a beautiful sight. While he was gazing at it his uncle passed him in a state of great enthusiasm.

He waved a rifle with his right hand, and a banner, with texts from the Koran inscribed upon it, with his left, and cried, "They come! they come! The Lord hath delivered them into our hands at last!" And it was with difficulty that he could restrain himself from forfeiting the advantages of the strong position, and rushing down to meet the advancing troops at once.

He had not long to restrain his impatience; the red and the grey lines swept into the base, and were among the boulders in a trice. Then the whole mountain side seemed to burst forth into flame and smoke, and from his commanding position Harry could see that here and there an advancing figure stopped, and came on no more, but dotted the ground with a scarlet or brown patch.

The scene would have resembled a holiday sham fight but for those figures which lay motionless, taking no further part, so orderly and regular was the advance. Presently the combat entered on a new phase. Unchecked by the storm of fire which had broken out upon them, the Highlanders and South Staffordshire pressed steadily on amongst the rocks; when there was room they squeezed between them; when this could not be done they swarmed over them; still they pressed steadily on. Steadily, indeed, but slowly. Behind each rock there was an Arab, and when a soldier wriggled round it or swarmed over it, he found himself engaged in a hand-to-hand conflict, in which, however, the bayonet generally proved victorious over sword or spear. It was most magnificent fighting; each individual man had to force his independent way in the face of a deadly fire from hidden foes, at whose covers he went straight. If he were hit there was an end of his course; but, if he stood up, into the hiding-place where his foe lay concealed, he was bound to go; and then, if he killed his man, as he mostly did, forwards and upwards at another. There was no sense of support afforded by the touch of comrades, and the being an item of a serried mass, as in the case of the majority of the battles of the Soudan, fought in square formation. Then there might be unsteady or pusillanimous soldiers, whose faults were hidden by their firmer comrades, from whose presence and example they gained confidence; but at Kirbekan every soldier fought on his own account, as it were, and failure in courage or dash in any individual would have been at once perceptible. But there was no such failure, and the Black Watch and South Staffordshire fought as British soldiers fought in the Peninsula, at Waterloo, at Alma, and at Inkerman.

Higher and higher they came, and the Arabs

began to grow uncontrollably excited. The Sheikh Burrachee came to the post occupied by Harry, who immediately let loose his rifle at a fine rock near which there was nobody. But he might have spared himself the trouble; his uncle never noticed him; he only came there because the spot afforded the best view of a portion of the English advance.

"It is impossible!" he cried; "and yet there they are. Has Sheytan given them charmed lives?" and he charged down, waving his banner, and calling on his tribesmen to follow him and extirpate the infidels.

Harry saw him falter on the brow of a crag, stretch his arms wide, drop weapon and banner, and fall backwards. Forgetting everything else at the sight, he ran down to him and raised his head.

He was quite dead.

"Poor Uncle Ralph! you were kind to me, and you loved my dear mother. Would that you had met with a better fate!" he said, as he turned away, and looked about for the means of escape.

There was no reason for further delay; the Arabs had too much to do to look after themselves to notice him; and his uncle was dead!

Round the side of the rock he crept, keeping well under shelter, till he found a side where no fight was raging, and here he clambered cautiously down into the plain, and made for that part of the Nile where he had seen the English pontoons and boats.

After about an hour's cautious approach, he came near enough to hail the nearest sentry.

"I am an English prisoner, released by your attack!" he cried; and after his report of himself had been carefully heard by an officer, he was received with welcome and eagerly questioned as to what he knew about the progress of the fight.

"Most of the points had been carried when I made my escape," Harry said; "but I fear the loss has been very heavy."

Heavy indeed it proved when the full news came in! Colonel Eyre, commanding the South Staffordshire, fell at the head of his regiment at the first onset; Colonel Green was killed at the hottest moment of the struggle; and shortly afterwards General Earle, the commander of the expedition himself, was shot dead from a stubbornly-defended building.

Harry told his story, was examined, cross-examined, re-examined; for all he had to say was most interesting, and very different from the meagre and often contradictory reports to be gleaned from natives. He told them of the force in Dulka Island. But they knew of that, and heeded it not, finding no difficulty in shelling the Arabs there out of it without an attack.

The only thing he was reticent about was the story of his uncle. Poor, crack-brained visionary, he had gone to his account now, and what need was there to recount his treasonable vagaries?

An old Harton boy is almost sure to find some mutual acquaintance in any group of English officers he may fall in with in any part of the world, and when at the evening meal he was chatting with his hospitable entertainers, Strachan's name happened to be mentioned.

"What, Tom Strachan, of the Blankshire?" he cried.

"That's the man!"

"Is his regiment in the Soudan?"

"No, but *he* is. He is an active card, and volunteered to act on the staff, and has done a good bit of galloping business. I think he is working in the Transport now, at least he was when we heard last from Korti."

From this and all else he could gather Korti was the place Harry now had to try and make for, and he was soon once more on his travels down the river.

We will not follow his footsteps, since he met with no adventures to be compared at all with those he had gone through. And very glad he was of it, for the one thing he now dreaded most was delay.

He had not long been at Korti before he saw the very old friend he had been asking after, and soon got an opportunity of speaking to him, busy as he seemed to be.

"Don't you know me?" he asked.

"Know you! Of course I do, just as if you were my brother; but just now I forget whether it is tinned meats or bullocks. By Jove! Is it possible! Harry Forsyth! And how are you, old fellow? One would think Korti was the centre of the world, for every fellow comes here. I say, who was to know you dressed up like that? Well, and what are you up to? Have you found that will yet?"

"Yes."

"Nonsense! And *got* it?"

"Yes."

"You must tell me all about that. I was just going to get something to eat; come along and share it. You have fallen upon the right boy for grub, I can tell you; I am in the provisioning department just for the moment, and there is no order against looking after number one."

"And you found your uncle who had turned wild man?" observed Tom Strachan, as the two filled and lit their pipes after a capital repast.

"Yes, poor fellow!" answered Harry. "Without him I don't suppose I should have got the will."

"And where did you run your Egyptian clerk to earth?"

"At El Obeid, and we got it out of him with the kourbash."

"Of course; you know the cynical saying here. As Nature provides an antidote growing in the same district with every poison, all we have to do is to learn how to seek it. So when the Egyptian was placed on the Nile the hippopotamus was created to provide whips to rule him with. But you must tell your story at greater length to-morrow morning to a friend of mine who is lying wounded here, waiting for a chance to be transported to Cairo. For I have a lot of things to see to; reports to make out—you would never believe; and must run away presently."

Next morning Harry Forsyth called on Strachan at the time and place appointed, and was taken by him to the hospital which had been established near the banks of the river. They found the friend of Strachan's they proposed to visit lying on a bamboo couch under an awning, over which again spread a palm-tree. There was a pleasant view of the river and the country, and altogether it was as cheery a spot as could have been selected.

There was a visitor already with the invalid: a soldier who was standing near, his head leaning on his rifle.

"I tell ye what it is," he was saying; "I'll say nothing about flesh wounds and bullet wounds since it worries ye, but ye have the best luck of it to be wounded at all, in my thinking. Won't ye be getting out of this baste of a country at once, and shan't we poor beggars what's whole and sound have to stop here and stew, and be ate up with the flies entirely? I tell ye so long as ye aint crippled it's the best chance to be a bit hurt, and get away, now there's no more fighting to be done. And they say there will perhaps be some real fun going on in India, out Afghanistan way, against the Rooshians; and we will be left here with the flies and crocodiles. But here's the officer coming. I'll come and see you again, when I'm off duty."

And Grady stepped briskly away, making the sling of his rifle *tell* with a smart salute, as he passed Strachan. And then Harry Forsyth stepped up to the couch, and found himself looking on the drawn and pain-worn features of Reginald Kavanagh.

"I flatter myself that I have managed that with considerable dramatic talent," said Tom Strachan, as he stood looking at the two, holding each other's hands in silence, and looking into each other's eyes.

"Yes," said Harry Forsyth, answering the question in the other's look; "I have found it, and it is here in my breast, all perfectly right."

"Yes, he has found it," echoed Strachan. "Where there's a will there's a way, and the way in this instance was the kourbash. I hope the fellow got it hot, Harry."

"Pretty fairly; I think Kavanagh would have been satisfied, though he has been disappointed in his desire to wield the lash himself. Don't you remember?"

"Well, all you have got to do now," said Strachan to Kavanagh, "is to get back to England as quick as they will take you, purchase your discharge, and enjoy your *otium cum dignitate*."

"Thank you, sir; if you will kindly say a word for me it will help," replied Kavanagh.

The little word *sir* struck with strange harshness on Harry Forsyth's ears. But, of course, Kavanagh was but a full private, and Strachan was an officer, if he came to think and realise it. He had been about to say:

"Here we three chums have met at last, ever so many miles up the Nile, and I shall believe in presentiments as long as I live;" but he did not like, after that word *sir*, to class his two old friends in the same category; it might make an awkwardness, he felt.

"I do not like the idea of quitting the service altogether," said Kavanagh.

"If we have this war with Russia they talk about, and I get well in time, and can qualify, I wonder if I shall have a chance of getting a commission. Surely it will not be so difficult as it was when I tried before, and I nearly qualified. I wonder whether my service in the ranks would be allowed to count in any way."

"It very well might," said Strachan; "for there are all sorts of chances going when good men are really wanted. If not, you must go back into the old Militia Battalion of the Blankshire, as I mean to do when I am shelved; and then we shall get a chance of airing our medals, if they give us any, for one month in the year at any rate."

"And what are your wounds, Kavanagh?" asked Harry presently.

"Sword cuts; one in the body is troublesome, but is getting better since I got away from camel back, though sometimes I feel down-hearted, progress is so slow."

"Oh, you must not give way to that sort of feeling," said Forsyth. "Why, I lay senseless for months and months from a cut on the head; how long I have no idea yet; I shall have to puzzle it out some day, but at present it is logarithms over again to think of it. I should certainly have died if it had not been for my dear old black nurse, Fatima, the loss of whom is the only thing I shall regret in leaving this part of the world. And if ever I come back, it will be to hunt her out and buy her."

"Fatima! Come, now for a touch of romance, Harry!" cried Strachan, laughing.

"Black as your Sunday hat in London; blubber lips, hair like coarse wool; feet like canoes, and the best heart in the world, and—there she is!"

It was true enough; Fatima was searching about, looking for Harry Forsyth, just like a dear, faithful old dog. Ever since the episode of the letter she had thought he wanted to go to his own people, and sought how to aid him; after the fight at Kirbekan she lost him, and made her way down to Korti, as the best place, so far as she could learn, to gain tidings of any Englishman. The delight she expressed on thus unexpectedly seeing him again was touching to a degree.

"You will have some one else to nurse now, Fatima," said Harry in Arabic, pointing to Kavanagh.

"Your brother is my master; I will cure him!" she said, nodding cheerfully to Kavanagh, and showing her white teeth.

"I am afraid Fatima would want to be nurse and doctor all in one, as she was with me," said Harry, "and that would hardly agree with discipline. But you might do worse than that, I can tell you. Meantime, what am I to do with her, I wonder? part from her willingly I never will. I tell you, Kavanagh, you would never have had a chance of your money, if I had not fallen into her hands, after I fell for dead in the wilderness; for I should never have pulled through but for her. How astonished my dear old mother and sister will be when I bring them a black servant! But she will soon learn their ways."

"You are my good genius, Forsyth," said Kavanagh; "and if you will call on the Principal Medical Officer, and other great authorities, I have no doubt you will be able to help me to get away the quicker."

"I should like to go home with you," said Forsyth, "and will if I can. Let us once get to Cairo, and I can raise any necessary money on the strength of this," and he tapped the will on his chest.

"Would it be too great a presumption to ask to see this portentous document?" asked Strachan. "I own to feeling some curiosity about it."

"Not at all." And he unwound it from its wrappings and produced it.

"And because a rascal clerk ran away with that bit of parchment, Kavanagh had to enlist as a private, and you had to go wandering over the world for years, leaving your mother and sister in poverty and anxiety!" said Tom Strachan, meditatively. "People are always talking about red tape in the army; surely there is still more of it in the law."

"Oh, yes, naturally one would expect that."

"Ah, well, I hope he got it hot; I *do* hope he got it hot! I will introduce you to all the people who can help you, Harry, but I must be off just now."

Forsyth got every assistance from the authorities to take his wounded friend away. And his old connection with Mr. Williams and the English firm at Cairo stood him in good stead; so that he reached Cairo, and embarked for England with Fatima and her patient sooner than he had expected.

CHAPTER XXIV.

AT SHEEN.

THE severity of the May of 1885 had at last abated, and the arrows on the vanes proved that they had not got fixed by rust, as many suspected, in a north-easterly direction, by turning to the south and west, so that those inhabitants of Great Britain who had not succumbed to pneumonia were able to let their fires out, open their windows, and enjoy out-of-door games with impunity.

Mrs. Forsyth and Beatrice now reaped the benefit of their work in the garden, for the tulips, the various *arias* and *otises* made the borders resplendent, while the delicious scent of the wallflowers was almost oppressive. The May blossom was full out on the hedge which bounded the little domain, and the apple-trees in that part devoted to fruit and vegetables were one mass of pink and white.

Though still at Sheen, the Forsyths were not in their original cottage. When their fortunes changed for the better, Mrs. Forsyth had moved into a larger villa, with a verandah round it, and modest stabling, and a nice lawn. And on this lawn white chalk lines were drawn, and a net fixed, on one side of which Beatrice Forsyth, racquet in hand, was employed in affording exercise for her brother Harry, who was on the other. He took the large court to her small court, and as she had a special talent for placing the balls, she made him run about rarely. The original layer out of that garden, who flourished before lawn tennis was invented, had perpetrated a prophetic pun by planting a service tree on one side of the ground, and under this sat Mrs. Forsyth before a garden table which had wools and work-box on it, for she could not bear to sit idle. Not far from her, and still under the shade of the service tree, was a lounging chair or couch of cane and wicker-work of the most comfortable description, with arms so broad and flat that you could lodge books and papers upon them, and the right arm had a circular hollow to hold a tumbler.

In this chair reclined a good-looking young man, whose pale and delicate features and thin hands told of recent illness, and together with a crimson scar across his face gave him that appearance which ladies call interesting, the effect being heightened by the shawls and rugs which were strewn about him. Rice paper and a packet of Egyptian tobacco lay on one of the arms of his couch, but it was only between the games that he occasionally twiddled up a cigarette, so conscientiously did he attend to his duties as umpire.

"Vantage out," said Harry, who was serving. Beatrice returned the ball high, and very far back indeed, and immediately cried—

"I think it was just in!"

"I think *not*," said Harry, grinning. "How was it, umpire?"

"Line ball!" said Kavanagh, who from his position could not possibly have seen.

"Game and set!" cried Trix, delighted, though as a matter of fact the ball had fallen a foot beyond the base line, and they both came to the tree for a rest.

"I hope you will be able to play yourself soon," said Harry Forsyth.

"I could play now," replied Kavanagh; "my side

does not hurt me a bit whatever I do. It is only weakness that stops me, and I feel stronger every morning."

"Then we shall have a four set without recourse to neighbours when Mary Strachan arrives," said Beatrice.

"Mary Strachan! Is she coming?" cried Kavanagh.

"Yes; mamma asked her, and she is to arrive early next week."

"That *will* be jolly! We only want Tom too."

"I don't despair of seeing *him* before the autumn," said Harry. "I heard from him yesterday, and he thought he should come home when the Guards did. And if we kiss and make it up with the various folks we are at loggerheads with, I don't think there will be much more fighting for you military parties to do."

"Who do you mean?" asked Kavanagh. "I am not a military person. I have got my discharge, sir, and might pass the commander-in-chief himself without saluting. Not that I would though, God bless him."

"Is it not time that you had your jelly and glass of port wine?" observed Mrs. Forsyth.

"Not quite," said Harry; "Fatima would not let him miss it by a minute. I believe she sits watching the clock, now she has learned what the figures mean, and why the hands go round."

"That is right; speak up for your slave," said Beatrice. "Any imputation upon her punctuality might depreciate her market value."

"I would not sell her for her weight in gold, and that must be something towards settling the National Debt," said Harry. "She nursed me back into life, I know."

"I can never repay her," murmured Mrs. Forsyth.

At that moment the object of conversation appeared with a tray in her hand, and a broad smile on her honest black face. She was robed in white, with a red shawl and a yellow handkerchief round her head. They had tried to put her into a print gown and a mob cap, but she looked so queer and was so uncomfortable that they let her choose her own costume. Nursing was certainly her strong point, and she tended Kavanagh as carefully as if he had been a baby. Only she always thought it cold, and wanted to smother him with wraps.

It was no use resisting, so he had to put them away quietly when her back was turned.

"I shall have apoplexy if I am convalescent long," said Kavanagh, swallowing the last spoonful of his jelly. "I am eating and drinking good things the whole day long."

"But think of the privations you have to make up for," said Mrs. Forsyth.

"Oh, mother, what a dear you are!" cried Harry. "Now I know why we have asparagus every day for dinner! *Apropos* of dinner, who do you think is coming to feed with us this evening, Kavanagh?"

"Invalids are excused guessing," said Kavanagh.

"Your old militia captain, Royce. He has got his majority now, by-the-by, and he is set upon having you back into the regiment."

Royce was punctual; and I propose to you a novelty in story endings. Let the curtain fall upon our friends as they are going in to dinner.

www.ingramcontent.com/pod-product-compliance
Lightning Source LLC
Chambersburg PA
CBHW031414230426
43668CB00007B/306